LITERATURE AND THE LEFT IN FRANCE

The Humanities Research Centre/Macmillan series

General editor: Professor Ian Donaldson, Director of HRC

This series is designed for publications deriving from the Humanities Research Centre of the Australian National University, Canberra. The series, which is an occasional one, includes monographs by the academic staff and Visiting Fellows of the Humanities Research Centre, and collections of essays from the Centre's conferences and seminars.

Ian Donaldson (*editor*): JONSON AND SHAKESPEARE

Ian Donaldson (*editor*): TRANSFORMATIONS IN MODERN EUROPEAN DRAMA

J. E. Flower: LITERATURE AND THE LEFT IN FRANCE

Oliver MacDonagh, W. F. Mandle and Pauric Travers (*editors*): IRISH CULTURE AND NATIONALISM, 1750–1950

LITERATURE AND THE LEFT IN FRANCE

Society, Politics and the Novel since the Late Nineteenth Century

J. E. Flower

BARNES & NOBLE BOOKS
TOTOWA, NEW JERSEY

First published in the USA 1983 by
BARNES & NOBLE BOOKS
81 Adams Drive, Totowa,
New Jersey, 07512

Library of Congress Catalog Card Number 76–2895
ISBN 0–389–20285–1

Printed in Hong Kong

For C. who came out of Sondalo

Contents

Acknowledgement

The original concept of this book was an ambitious one which, had it been realized, would have resulted in a study embracing not only the novel, but poetry and the theatre as well. However modest by comparison, the present volume none the less still owes a great deal to a number of people and institutions whose advice and help have been invaluable. In particular I wish to record my thanks to the following: John Cruickshank whose comments on a near final draft helped to give some shape to much that threatened to be rather formless; Tony Greaves whose eye for detail and whose pertinent queries were much appreciated at an earlier stage; the British Academy whose generosity allowed me to collect material and to make a number of brief visits to various libraries both in France and in the United Kingdom; the Humanities Research Centre at the National University of Australia which provided ideal (if unlikely) surroundings in which I was able to find my way through much of the vast amount of primary material; the University of Exeter which generously granted me study leave for two terms in 1980/81 when most of the final draft was written; my colleagues who took on my teaching and other duties during my absence; the staff of the university libraries (and in particular of the Inter-Library Loans Departments) at Exeter, Reading and East Anglia who cheerfully pursued material which was not only obscure but often untraceable; the Librarians at the Institut des Recherches Marxiste in Paris; Reg Carr for a number of helpful suggestions; Andrew Best for his encouragement; Julia Steward for her editorial advice; and Janet Chambers, Lorraine Oliver and Elaine Youngs for their efficient and speedy typing.

Exeter   JOHN FLOWER

Foreword

The essay 'Literature and the Left' which George Orwell wrote for *Tribune* and from which the title of this book is borrowed was published on 4 June 1943.[1] In it Orwell debates two of his favourite themes: the relationship between literature or art and politics, and the distorting effect which left-wing political sympathy frequently has on literary criticism and evaluation. Or to put it in his own words, the essay is about 'making what are ostensibly literary judgements for political ends'. In so doing and despite allusions to Shakespeare and to one of his most admired writers, Jonathan Swift, Orwell reflects specifically on the previous twenty years of English literature and on the case of T. S. Eliot in particular. But he is not only concerned with the general historical reception of literary works. In the second half of his essay he also touches on the question of writers' potential political efficacy, concluding that in the face of their being contemptuously dismissed by the Left as 'bourgeois intellectuals' when they fail or refuse 'to turn themselves into gramophone records', most of them retreat 'into individualism'.

Although there was a time in Britain in the 1930s when writers and intellectuals like Auden or Spender did become closely involved with politics and with the Communist Party in particular – the period of the Fellow Travellers[2] – the issues to which Orwell here refers have not been as central to British cultural history as they have elsewhere in Europe and especially in France. The reasons for this are various and well-known. Traditionally politics or political debate have always been nearer to the surface of French life than British, and it has always been generally accepted that writers and intellectuals in France have had more central and influential roles to play than their counterparts across the Channel. There are also several other reasons. First, the Left in France, especially with the emergence in the 1920s of an active

ix

and substantial national Communist Party (the PCF), has been more prominent. Second, the coincidence in the late-nineteenth century of rapid industrial growth with free, compulsory primary education up to the age of 13 (from 1882) resulted (indeed as in England as well) in a new literate and increasingly articulate working class. Third, newspapers and journals benefitting from an expanding readership grew both in quantity and influence. And finally a number of imaginative writers also aware of this expansion and often with strong social consciences themselves, not only wrote for but turned to working-class people for the subjects of their works. No less crucial to the development of a body of socially and politically conscious literature in France were the two world wars in which French experience was on both occasions unique.

For a variety of inter-connected historical, economic, social and political reasons a certain context has therefore been created in France, since about the middle of the nineteenth century, in which a literature dealing almost exclusively with the working class has evolved. In this context as well writing has increasingly come to be regarded by many as a weapon in a struggle on behalf of that class. This is not to suggest of course that such developments are uniquely French or that something similar has not occurred in Britain or elsewhere. In this country and roughly during the same period Dickens, Morris, Bennett, Gissing, Galsworthy, Shaw and Orwell himself, to name but a few, have contributed, each in his own manner, to the search for a new realism, for ways of giving as full a picture of English society as possible and of drawing attention to the lot of the underprivileged. But as John Morris has amply demonstrated,[3] writers within the British tradition have, whatever their sympathies, regularly fought shy of allowing their literary works to become mere extensions of political programmes or expressions of political ideology. Indeed it would not be unreasonable to claim that on any graph which attempted to chart the relationship between a country's writers and intellectuals and its political preoccupations and developments, Britain might well appear at one extreme point. At the other we could just as reasonably expect to find the Soviet Union. What in particular separates the two countries in this way – and what is also directly relevant to the case of France which on the same graph would appear somewhere around the middle and perhaps slightly nearer to the Soviet Union – is the 1917 Revolution.

In its repercussions on cultural and literary matters this is so for two reasons in particular. The first quite simply is that the society which most modern Soviet writing 'realistically' describes is a post-revolution one; what Bloch, making the point, described in 1934 as '(un) pays révolutionnaire ou révolutionné'.[4] The second is that since literature comes to be seen as a contributory factor to the revolution (regarded by Marxists as a permanent feature of socio-economic progress) it may be modified by extra-literary factors which in turn may take the form of politically inspired controls and directives. While the echoes of these two factors may not have been very pronounced in British literature, in France they have had a considerable influence on a whole body of writing and especially on that which during the 1930s and 1950s was overtly militant. In this we repeatedly find not only hints and even visions of a *post*-revolution society or the portrait of the exemplary worker or intellectual, but also extensive debates about the qualities demanded of successful revolutionary writing and about the role of the writer himself. In most cases such matters as these have been the concerns of politically active writers – people like Aragon, Nizan, Stil or Courtade, most of them proponents of socialist realism and without exception members of the PCF. Following the examples of Soviet writers and theorists like Mayakovsky, Fadeyev, Plekanhov and above all Zdhanov, they have attempted to produce a literature inspired by a belief in the historical inevitability of the revolution and full of examples of enlightened behaviour, of moral and political fortitude and of a new society. At the same time there has also developed since the late nineteenth century a more socially conscious literature in the conventional sense (more akin to the British tradition) which is usually descriptive in method and sometimes sentimental in tone, but, in stated intention at least, apolitical. It is within this tradition that during the late 1920s we observe the emergence of populism championed by Lemonnier and Thérive with its post-naturalist emphasis on the observation of working-class mores, and of the proletarian literature for which Poulaille was the leading spokesman. As we shall see, Poulaille differed from the populists in his belief that only if it were written by working-class people themselves could proletarian literature be truly accurate in its presentation and dignified in tone.

Despite considerable differences in their stated aims and ambitions, writers from all of these groups or movements shared a preference for the novel as the most suitable form for the expression of their ideas, a fact which very largely reflects their concern for the accessibility of their works. Indeed this awareness of audience appears to have grown in importance, prompting from the early years of the twentieth century a series of literary *enquêtes* in which the question 'Pour *qui* écrivez-vous?' is regularly asked.

While there is no doubt that the rhetoric of the tract can be more easily disguised in or transposed to the novel than poetry, neither poetry nor indeed drama was entirely eclipsed, though they do present problems of a rather different nature. Poetry, except perhaps that of the most naïve and elementary kind, is by definition more dense and inaccessible than prose and therefore attracts a more restricted audience. Sartre distinguished in *Qu'est-ce que la littérature?* between the concentrated nature of the poetic image defying a single interpretation and what he claims are the less ambiguous signals emitted by prose which lead the reader forward through certain kinds of experience.[5] Such a distinction may be limited, but it is useful and clearly had validity for many. There have of course been notable exceptions. During the occupation, for example, the density of a poem by, say, Aragon or Eluard or Cassou which demanded close attention and effort before its meaning could be absorbed, became in its own way a symbol of the spirit of the very resistance which it was attempting to strengthen.[6] And in a different way again, we have the earlier work of the Surrealists whose experiments with language were only part of their preoccupation with total revolution. (Whatever their aims, however, their writing remained a highly self-conscious and intellectual activity dismissed by a number of apolitical writers as narcissistic and ultimately by the militants as anarchic and irresponsible.)[7]

And just as poetry presents its own special problems, so too do plays. In 1903 Romain Rolland wrote in the preface of the first edition of his *Théâtre du Peuple*: 'Il s'agit d'élever *le Théâtre par et pour le Peuple*. Il s'agit de fonder un art nouveau pour un monde nouveau'.[8] Such a statement closely reflected much contemporary thinking, and Rolland may well have had in mind a small but significant and increasing number of plays written between 1880 and 1914 (including his own *Danton* (1900) or *Le 14 juillet* (1902) for instance) which illustrated a variety of socialist ideas.[9] But just as poems are built around inner tensions which when released in the form of images allow for a variety of interpretations and responses, so too are plays more than texts. A full study of the theatre in the light of Rolland's words would need to concern itself just as much with productions as with the bare script. For more recent years it would clearly necessitate a survey of the roles of organizations like the Théâtre National Populaire or the Centres Dramatiques with directors like Roger Planchon, Jean Vilar or Jean-Louis Barrault, quite as much as a study of the ambitions and experimentation of a self-declared revolutionary writer like Artaud (in, say, his play about the Commune, *Le Printemps 71*) or of the enthusiastic reception given especially by left-wing critics to the plays of Brecht.

Such considerations as these take us far away from the issues raised by Orwell. They also suggest the potentially vast and amorphous nature of the subject implied by the all-embracing title of 'Literature and the Left' even within the relatively narrow national limits of France. Before attempting to indicate and justify the much more restricted range of this study, a word should be added about the bibliography. Just as the subject itself is potentially limitless, so too is the amount of secondary literature, and I include only those books and articles which I have found to be of particular interest or value. Much of this material is of a theoretical nature and has been written by critics of marked political persuasion themselves. It should therefore be considered accordingly. However, within this selected body of work two well-established books in particular deserve mention. The first, chronologically, is David Caute's *Communism and the French Intellectuals, 1914–1960* (1964), a detailed account of this complex relationship as it affected a variety of different fields, cultural, political and scientific alike. The second is Jean-Pierre Bernard's *Le Parti Communiste Français et la Question littéraire, 1921–1939* (1972), a non-theoretical and largely historical account of the relationship between a number of imaginative writers and the party which also raises such important issues as those of interference, allegiance and betrayal.[10]

However, unlike most of the work which exists within the general area of investigation and which has tended to concentrate either on ideas or on literature as a sociological phenomenon, this book attempts something rather different. It sets out to explore the effects which the aims, intentions and preoccupations of a number of writers have had upon the imaginative works in and through which they have been expressed. I try to avoid the kind of

a priori assumptions or *parti pris politique* to which Orwell objects.
In so doing of course – and this is one of the paradoxes of such a
study – I lay myself open to the charge, especially from those
fundamentally opposed to Orwell's liberal attitude, either of
attempting to work from an unstructured and therefore untenable
position, or of opting for a reactionary *belle-lettriste* tradition. A less
committed criticism would query its arbitrarily selective nature.
Few would dispute the claim already made that because of certain
socio-economic factors in particular, a literature dealing essentially with the working class had a vigorous development in
France from about the beginning of the last third of the nineteenth
century. (Such a claim does not imply that a similar literature had
not existed earlier, albeit on a smaller scale, nor that an
unrecorded oral tradition should be discounted.[11]) The selection
of works by Zola, the Goncourt brothers and Philippe rather than
by Vallès (especially) or by Huysmans or Mirbeau as particular
illustrative examples of this early period is clearly open to
debate;[12] so too is that made from the many dozens of novels
published during the 1920s and 1930s which attracted the
description of populist or proletarian or sometimes both. And the
omission of any discussion of Aragon's *Les Communistes* in its two
versions may equally surprise some. On the whole choice has
been dictated by the simple matters of availability and space, but
essentially I have tried to use books which are particularly
representative of their kind. In this respect Stil, Courtade and
Vailland seem to me to be more interesting than Aragon whose
earlier work, in any case, has been discussed at length elswhere. I
hope as well to have drawn attention to certain writers like
Charles-Louis Philippe or Pierre Courtade who for some time
have been in danger of becoming eclipsed. Indeed in this respect
it is also interesting to consider the case of Nizan. Fifteen years
ago he was a neglected, almost forgotten figure: now he is the
centre of much critical attention, and is the subject of at least eight
full-length studies in French and in English.

   Given this selection and the general intention outlined above
this study concentrates on a number of issues. In broad terms it
examines ways in which the novel has been used to explore and
expose certain aspects of working-class existence and in some
cases to serve as a positive call for action. It further considers the
novel's emergence, especially in the 1930s and 1950s as a vehicle
for left-wing socio-political ideas. These two areas of investigation

in turn suggest a number of rather more specific topics: the changes in attitude about the legitimate concerns of literature; the role and status of the writer and intellectual; the debates surrounding the question of artistic freedom and the readiness with which some writers have attempted to produce their work in accordance with certain politically inspired directives; the questions of readership and of shifting critical reception; and the issue, dear to Marxist writers and critics in particular of *fond* or *contenu* and *forme*. Once again it should be stressed that the principal concern is as much for literature and in particular the novel as for ideas. While quite detailed analyses of novels – in part or in whole – predominate, considerable attention is paid as well to essays – particularly those of a discursive nature – and to journals like *Clarté*, *Commune*, *Europe*, *Pensée* or *La Nouvelle Critique*, in which much relevant debate has been conducted.

In general the structure follows a chronological pattern. Part I examines the emergence of a socially and politically aware literature during the late-nineteenth and early-twentieth centuries. Part II considers the interwar period paying special attention both to populist and proletarian writing and to the growing call for a militant literature with the first French examples of socialist realism. Part III concentrates on the post-Second World War years, on the strictly controlled writing of the New Left in the 1950s and on the eventual *détente* of the following decade. And were there adequate space for a fourth part, it would focus in particular on the critical responses to literature developed by left-wing intellectuals since the conference on art and culture, organized by the Central Committee of the PCF at Argenteuil in March 1966. This, as the Conclusion much more briefly indicates, would necessitate not only an analysis of the transactions of the two 'colloques de Cluny' in 1968 and 1970, but of a vast number of articles and books in which Marxism and new criticism have been brought together with increasingly complex results.

A final word should be added about the use of 'working class' either as noun or adjective. First the characters who people most of the novels (as well as the readers for whom some are intended) are almost all from urban environments in a post-industrial revolution society. Novels about rural working-class people – beekeepers, shepherds, tree cutters – certainly exist, but they tend to belong to a rather different tradition and to present different problems. Second, I have tried where possible to avoid the politically significant and emotive words proletariat and proletarian. It may be true that these are essential if the political (Marxist) point is to be made that economic and social divisions continue to exist in a society which has, during the last 30 years in particular, apparently become much more classless. To use them in a study such as this, however, seems to me to court the danger of encouraging a political interpretation where none is necessarily intended.

Part I

Introduction

Anything other than the most brief and superficial indication of how, between the Middle Ages and the late-nineteenth century, writers turned to the lower classes of French society for the subjects of their work, is clearly beyond the scope of this introduction. The fullest survey of this kind is to be found in the various books by Michel Ragon, especially in his *Histoire de la littérature prolétarienne en France* (1974),[1] and can be supplemented by anthologies like *Les Ecrivains témoins du peuple* (1964) by Françoise and Jean Fourastié.[2] This latter volume, less well researched than Ragon's book and composed almost entirely of prose extracts, opens with one from Raoul or Rodolphe Glaber's Chroniques (1047) written originally in Latin and describing the great famines of the early eleventh century, and closes with another from Georges Douart's *Opération Amitié* (1958), an account of voluntary service in India.

While the Fourastiés' choice of texts is guided, they claim, by a concern for 'la sincérité, l'émotion (et) la réalité du récit',[3] Ragon's ambitions are rather wider. He distinguishes between *écrivains ouvriers* ('les prolétaires qui écrivent') and *écrivains prolétariens* ('les autodidactes anciens prolétaires devenus des intellectuels prolétariens').[4] He also acknowledges the difficulty of giving precise limits to the concept of 'popular literature' in general, largely because of its origins (its authors frequently came from aristocratic or bourgeois backgrounds) and its readership. Ragon does not, however, distinguish carefully enough between literature of this kind which essentially records, and that which positively protests. And even though he would no doubt argue that the overtly politically motivated literature of the mid-twentieth century stands outside his terms of reference, it is surprising, for example, to find no mention in his work of a writer like André Stil. Nor does he attempt, even in a fairly general way,

3

to assess the shared or common stylistic devices and characteristics of popular writing.

Whatever their shortcomings, however, these works do present evidence of a long tradition to which many of the novels discussed in this book owe a great deal. From the eleventh and twelfth centuries in poems like Rutebeuf's 'Ci encoumence li diz des ribaux de Greive'[5] or Chrétien de Troyes' description of the virgins spinning in the tower in *Yvain*, the plight or exploitation of working-class people have, it is claimed, regularly been the subject of imaginative literature. To reproduce here much of the material which these critics use would clearly be a waste of space, but we might note in passing that from the evidence they offer, it is nearly all descriptive. What protest there is, is generally either implied or muted, and it is tempting to speculate on that undoubtedly considerable body of work – poems and 'chansons' in particular – passed on orally from one generation to another and possibly more militant or aggressive in tone which has unfortunately been lost.

Where a shift of emphasis does begin to appear of course is during the eighteenth century when we find an increasing awareness on the part of the writer that literature can and indeed should serve a moral, social and even political purpose. And in many ways reflecting substantial changes in economic and social patterns, a body of imaginative literature (by Marivaux, Prévost or Restif de la Bretonne for example) seeks its subject matter in the lower classes of society. But it is not until the post-revolutionary years of the early nineteenth century that 'le peuple' becomes such a fruitful source of inspiration for novelists and poets in particular: Hugo, Balzac, Lamartine, George Sand, even Vigny (in a novel like *Stello*), as well as a large number of minor writers, produce works in which the worker or peasant is romanticized, idealized and dignified. Much of this writing, which took the form of direct witness, was published in reviews and papers, many of them new, like *La Ruche populaire, Le Globe, La Foi nouvelle* or *L'Atelier*. And the whole development of this trend was in large part encouraged by such peuple as Michelet, Fourier, Proudhon in his *Principes de l'Art*, or Nodier, whose speech on his being received into the French Academy called for a socially motivated art. Nor should we forget Mme de Staël's important essay *De la littérature considérée dans ses rapports avec les institutions sociales* (1800) in which she writes: 'Mais l'art d'écrire serait aussi une arme, la parole serait aussi une action.'[6]

The tradition of popular writing as essentially a descriptive account of different aspects of working-class life continued, and later manifested itself in the works of writers like Charles-Louis Philippe, Pierre Hamp or Henri Poulaille. But it was the fast-growing awareness of the potential social and political role and function of art which became the subject of much, often bitter debate and, in literary terms, resulted in something rather different. Indeed by the last quarter of the nineteenth century positions were already firmly engaged in a debate in which Naturalism and Zola were central.

Jules Vallès, whose own indignation at injustice and inequality were expressed not only in a series of newspaper articles (in *Le Cri du Peuple*), but in the semi-autobiographical trilogy *L'Enfant* (1879), *Le Bachelier* (1881) and *L'Insurgé* (1886), accused the Naturalists of being politically unaware. Paul Alexis, replying through the columns of the same paper wrote: 'ils (les naturalistes) dégagent des fragments de vérité, matériaux au moyen desquels sera facilitée l'organisation d'une société future plus équitable, moins imparfaite, rebâtie de fond en comble' (9 November 1883). The political implications of these words, written two years before the publication of *Germinal*, were considerable. Nearly a decade later E. Museux writing in *La Plume* (1 May 1891) called for a revitalization of the arts in terms which were even more pointed and anticipated the kind of attitude to be adopted within a few years by Henri Barbusse. Museux directly attacked the notion of art's being the prerogative of a social élite which, he said, was 'vermoulue et craquant de toutes parts'; for revitalization to take place required first the establishment of 'une Société nouvelle, assise sur des bases véritables de Liberté et de Justice'. And Mirbeau in a letter to Jule Huret wrote: 'l'art doit être socialiste, s'il veut être grand'.[7]

Against this there was considerable opposition from those who firmly believed in the inviolable nature of art. Léon Bloy for example (again in *La Plume*, 15 May 1891) expressed his belief that it was essential to preserve at all costs 'l'indépendance esthétique de notre littérature', and dismissed Zola in his celebrated phrases as 'un iconographe de la décadence' and 'ce Napoléon de la fange'. But this 'new' position gained increasing support. In periodicals and newspapers like those already quoted and in essays and longer studies like Lazare's *L'Ecrivain et l'art social* (1896) or Sorel's *La Valeur de l'art social* (1901), the idea of art and of literature in particular as being a means not only of drawing attention to social injustice, but of encouraging the public generally to respond positively to it grew apace.

1 'Un roman qui aura pour cadre le monde ouvrier' (Emile Zola)

As a starting point for this study *Germinie Lacerteux* can be justified for various reasons; all are contained in the novel's 'Preface'.[1] This was not only a statement of the Goncourts' own ambitions in writing the book – and an attempt to anticipate some of the criticisms it might receive – but also a form of manifesto. From the opening lines an abrupt challenge is issued: 'Le public aime les romans faux: ce roman est un roman vrai'. Four years later in *Le Figaro* (31 January 1868) Zola was to echo these words in a provocative defence of the novel in general and of his own *Thérèse Raquin* in particular: 'Le public n'aime pas les vérités, il veut des mensonges pour son argent'.[2]

Decrying popular taste for titillating and erotic works ('les mémoires de filles, les confessions d'alcôves, les saletés érotiques') as well as for those which leave the reader's mind ultimately untroubled ('les lectures anodines et consolantes, les aventures qui finissent bien'), the Goncourt brothers promise that *Germinie Lacerteux* will shake complacency and draw attention to the everyday tragedies of working-class society. Their argument rests on the fact that in a climate of liberalism and democracy, the lower classes of society should have as much to offer the writer as any others:

> Il nous est venu la curiosité de savoir [. . .] si, dans un pays sans caste et sans aristocratie légale, les misères des petits et des pauvres parleraient à l'intérêt, à l'émotion, à la pitié, aussi haut que les misères des grands et des riches; si, en un mot, les larmes qu'on pleure en bas pourraient faire pleurer comme celles qu'on pleure en haut.

Yet so convinced do they seem to be of the value of their enter-
prise that the Goncourts unwittingly overlook some of its inherent
problems. While their assumptions about their subject matter
may indeed be justified – as Sainte-Beuve readily acknowledged
in his *Causerie du lundi* on 15 January 1865[3] – its power of appeal
rather than of shock must remain uncertain. Even more open to
question is the manner in which such material is treated.

Thirteen years later (and in spite of his frequently expressed
admiration of and praise for *Germinie Lacerteux*) Zola claimed in his
preface to *L'Assommoir*, that what made *his* novel distinctive was
not only its veracity, but its power to convey what he defined as
'l'odeur du peuple'.[4] Although Zola too, both in this novel and
later in *Germinal*, proved to be equally incapable of freeing himself
from various formative influences which shaped his presentation
of working-class society, he does in this remark point to an important difference. The success with which Germinie's life is depicted
varies according to the role and stance adopted by the narrators,
by their attitude towards their subject, and by their failure on
occasions to disguise subjective involvement and sympathy as
objective observation. To claim that the novel should become 'la
grande forme sérieuse, passionnée, vivante, de l'étude littéraire et
de l'enquête sociale' (Preface), and that it should make the public
generally aware of the misery and suffering of the working class is
one thing. To do so in a way which avoids the conventionally
selective treatment and even at times patronizing tone of the
middle-class novelist is another.

To criticise the Goncourt brothers too severely for such limitations, however, would be unreasonable. While those claims which
were made both by themselves and by sympathetic critics for the
originality of *Germinie Lacerteux* may today seem somewhat
exaggerated, its appearance was an important landmark in what
had been a growing awareness of the novel's potential in terms
both of subject matter, and of how that matter could, and indeed
should be treated. Although the advance from this position was
considerable by the time Zola published *Germinal* (1885), within
five years of the appearance of the Goncourts' novel we find Zola
outlining his own plans for a 'roman ouvrier'. Like them his
underlying aim he claims is for objectivity and truth:

Un roman qui aura pour cadre le monde ouvrier [. . .].
Peinture d'un ménage d'ouvriers à notre époque. Drame

intime et profond de la déchéance du travailleur parisien sous la déplorable influence du milieu des barrières et des cabarets. La sincérité des peintures pourra donner une grande allure à ce roman. On nous a montré jusqu'ici les ouvriers comme les soldats, sous un jour complètement faux. Ce serait faire œuvre de courage que de dire la vérité et de réclamer, par l'exposition franche des faits, de l'air, de la lumière et de l'instruction pour les basses classes.[5]

The result was *L'Assommoir*, first published in serialized form in *Le Bien public* and *La République des Lettres*.

In the 1877 preface to the novel Zola defends himself against criticism of the vulgarity of much of the language: rather more significantly he also restates his aims and alludes to some of the issues which would characterize much of his subsequent work. The intended 'roman ouvrier' is still defended: 'le premier roman sur le peuple, qui ne mente pas et qui ait l'odeur du peuple'.[6] But whereas the Goncourts had merely accepted that the plight of the working class could provide just as adequate material for a novel as the intrigues of the upper classes, Zola introduces a clear moral comment when he states that working-class people are victims, powerless to struggle against the conditions in which they live: 'ils ne sont qu'ignorants et gâtés par le milieu de rude besogne et de misère où ils vivent'.[7] These words strongly echo those he had written on 18 October 1868 in *La Tribune*: 'C'est [. . .] une simple question de milieu. Les ouvriers étouffent dans les quartiers étroits et fangeux où ils sont obligés de s'entasser'.[8]

Behind such remarks there is perhaps nothing more than a genuine indignation, barely different in degree from the plea for humanity which we find at the end of the preface to *Germinie Lacerteux*. Furthermore there is the danger that the modern reader with Zola's entire work in perspective will be tempted to give the same weight to statements made before about 1880 as to those of subsequent years – particularly of the Dreyfus Affair – when Zola emerged with *J'Accuse* as a champion for justice and individual freedom. We should not forget, however, that Zola was only too aware of the worsening situation of the working class during the Second Empire, that he was fundamentally in sympathy with the ideals which inspired the Commune, and voiced the opinion during the early 1870s that an amnesty should be reached. Furthermore friendship with people like Guesde and

Vallès could only sharpen his own sense of injustice and of the need for some action to be taken. Nevertheless Zola seemed, during the following decade, to be just as content to maintain the same basically uncommitted position concerning the use of literature as a vehicle for moral, social or political comment as he had done twenty years earlier. While in an article on Chateaubriand (*Le Figaro*, 5 September 1881) he acknowledged that literature had benefitted from political change, he also claimed that his essential task was simply to record this fact: 'C'est l'avènement de la démocratie qui renouvelle notre politique, notre littérature, nos mœurs, nos idées. Je constate un fait, rien de plus.'[9] The same year in *Les Romanciers naturalistes*, and in rather more general terms, he made the point once again:

> Je ne veux pas établir ou défendre une politique ou une religion. Mon étude est un simple coin d'analyse du monde tel qu'il est. Je constate purement. [. . .] On chercherait en vain une conclusion, une moralité, une leçon quelconque tirée des faits. Il n'y a d'étalés, de mis en lumière, uniquement que les faits, louables ou condamnables.[10]

Within four years of statements like these *Germinal* was published.

While nearly half a century later Barbusse may have regretted that Zola had not been openly partisan and militant, there is no doubt that in *L'Assommoir* and more particularly in *Germinal*, the working class was represented in a way which was new, disturbing and above all challenging. What is more, whatever their limitations and while the stylistic and structural devices used by Zola here and elsewhere are also to be found in other 'romans ouvriers' of the late-nineteenth century, there is a sense of scale and timing, together with a refusal of sentimentality and sensationalism which set Zola's works apart from the majority and make of him the most influential precursor of many whose work was to appear forty or fifty years later.

However limited *Germinie Lacerteux* may seem in retrospect, it is an important work as a bridge between the romantic portrayal of working-class people in works like *Les Misérables* or Lamartine's *Jocelyn*, and the naturalistic and frequently militant descriptions of *L'Assommoir, Germinal* or *La Terre*. It does not of course mark an irreversible and total change; the impressionistic, sentimental and often unnaturally idealized descriptions of the working class, characteristic of earlier works, continue to appear in those by Huysmans, Mirbeau and above all Charles-Louis Philippe. Indeed many such 'romantic' elements are to be found considerably later, even after about 1930 when literature was seen by many on the left to be an indispensable weapon in an ideological and political struggle.

The origins of *Germinie Lacerteux* are well known – the secret life, discovered by the Goncourts only after her death, of their maid Rose Malingre. Given the rather peculiar nature of their own lives and characters it is hardly surprising that they should admit on making the discovery to some uncertainty as to how they should respond:

> Pauvre fille! nous lui pardonnons. Et même, entrevoyant par des coins d'abîme tout ce qu'elle a dû souffrir des maquereaux du peuple, nous la plaignons. Une grande commisération nous vient pour elle; mais aussi, une grande amertume, à cette révélation accablante, nous a envahis. Notre pensée est remontée à notre mère si pure et pour laquelle nous étions tout; puis redescendant à ce cœur de Rose, que nous croyions tout à nous, nous avons eu comme une grande déception à voir qu'il y avait tout un grand côté que nous n'emplissions pas. La défiance est entrée dans l'esprit, pour toute la vie, du sexe entier de la femme. (*Journal*, 21 August 1862)

Such a mixture of sympathy for the plight of an individual and irritation at having been deceived inevitably coloured their fictional representation of the subject. And while they may have later maintained to Zola that, on reading the novel's proofs, the subject still moved them deeply, their basic uncertainty as to how to respond to a section of the population with which, for all their observations, they had no real contact was further reason for the novel's equivocal nature.[11] This possibly was one of the criticisms which they had foreseen and which led them in their preface to hint at the aristocracy's capacity for real sympathy. The paternalism of the Goncourts' attitude (as Caramaschi has observed)[12] stems, however, more from a negative one of pity than from a positive plea for justice, in spite of their impassioned outcry against the treatment of the poor inspired, in the closing pages of the novel, by the sight of the common grave in the Montmartre cemetery.

What is at once particularly noticeable in this novel which claims to treat 'ce monde sous un monde, le peuple' (Preface), is its almost exclusive concern for a single and significantly atypical representative of that class. Certainly the circumstances of working-class society as a whole are on occasions successfully evoked: Germinie's excursions through the poor districts of Paris, the descriptions of the maternity hospital or of the 'fosse commune', the interior of Germinie's own room or of the Jupillon household. And the Goncourts also attempt to convey an impression both of working-class language – by the use of a dialogue frequently charged with *non sequiturs* and exclamations, the dropping of syllables in slovenly speech, popular expressions and even, on two specific occasions, slang ('Je suis *paf*!' p. 133; 'toutes les négresses sont mortes . . .' p. 225) – and of behaviour. The description of the manner in which Jupillon and his mother plan to deceive Germinie is one particular illustration of the capacity for scheming which the authors sincerely believed working-class people possessed.[13]

As a whole, however, the evocation of working-class society remains amorphous. There is nothing of the sustained attention to the conditions of its existence or to its reactions to those conditions which we find in Zola's work. Moreover given the Goncourt's idea that 'le roman actuel se fait avec des *documents*, racontés ou relevés d'après nature, comme l'histoire se fait avec des documents écrits',[14] there is a surprising absence of the kind of detail which could have enabled the authors to claim to have been successfully realistic. As we noted earlier the real subject of the novel is not a class so much as a single and not wholly typical representative of that class.

The early information about Germinie underlines her disadvantages. Sent to work in a Paris café she is totally out of place and at the mercy of those around her:

A toute heure elle avait à subir les lâches plaisanteries, les mystifications cruelles, les méchancetés de ces hommes heureux d'avoir leur petit martyr dans cette petite fillette sauvage ne sachant rien, l'air malingre et opprimé, peureuse et ombrageuse, maigre et pitoyablement vêtue de ses mauvaises petites robes de campagne.(pp. 44, 45)

She is raped, ill-treated by her sisters, gives birth to a still-born

child and only for a few months knows peace in the service of a
retired actor. Even after she has become Mlle de Varandeuil's
maid and has apparently found some security, this early
impression of her being one of society's natural victims is stressed
once more by the first long physical description of her in which
her ugliness, somewhat incongruously coupled with a powerful
sexual attraction, is emphasized:

> De cette femme laide, s'échappait une âpre et mystérieuse
> séduction. [. . .] Tout en elle, sa bouche, ses yeux, sa laideur
> même, avait une provocation et une sollicitation. Un charme
> aphrodisiaque sortait d'elle, qui s'attaquait et s'attachait à
> l'autre sexe. Elle dégageait le désir et en donnait la commotion.
> (pp. 60, 61)

From the first chapters it becomes apparent that one of the
authors' main aims is to present Germinie as a creature whose life
ultimately depends on the whims and schemings of others or on
circumstances in general over which she has no control. Natural
preselection therefore is offered as a justification for or
explanation of her social and economic plight, a view which
persists throughout the novel in the Goncourts' constant use of
animal imagery in their descriptions of her. She follows the wife of
the first café owner for whom she works 'avec une sorte de
dévouement animal et [. . .] avec des docilités de chien' (p. 45);
raped by Joseph she is thereafter 'frappée de la peur d'une bête
éperdue qui cherche par où se sauver' (p. 47); at the Boule Noire
she experiences '(une) joie bestiale' (p. 97); when Jupillon
approaches her for a second time 'elle revint à lui comme une bête
ramenée à la main et dont on retire la corde' (p. 147) and later
feels 'cette sensation presque animale de l'approche d'un maître'
(p. 171); she adores her mistress 'avec les yeux d'un chien' (p.
163); and after she has taken to prostitution 'elle s'en allait par les
rues, battant la nuit, avec la démarche suspecte et furtive des
bêtes qui fouillent l'ombre et dont l'appétit quête' (p. 233).

Further, having reduced Germinie in this way, having shown
how her reactions are essentially conditioned reflexes, the
Goncourts also tend on occasions, like Balzac, to draw general
conclusions from particular examples. Thus in Chapter IV we are
reminded of the comfort found in religion – and especially in
confession – by working-class women in general; in Chapter L

Germinie's fear of the law is also seen as characteristic of her class as a whole. Each of these generalizations is heavily condescending. The Goncourts appear to be of the opinion that Germinie (and by implication the whole of her class) is someone essentially incapable of rising above a certain level of mediocrity, and for whom total degradation is almost unavoidable. Even though the authors may have held this view in private – and Marxist critics would argue of course that it was socially inevitable that they should have done so – it would be unfair to impute it from the evidence of the novel alone. Had they consciously depicted Germinie in this way they could hardly have made the claims for the novel which we find in its preface. And once they attempt to depict her as a creature with intelligence, sensitivity and a sense of moral values (e.g., p. 164 or p. 211) an inconsistency develops which makes it increasingly difficult for the reader to accept Germinie as a representative of her class.

In their defence it might be claimed that the Goncourts' aim, however clumsily realized, was to show that even the most subservient creature possessed individual qualities of this kind, and that only by drawing attention to them could the tragedy of her situation be seen. Such an interpretation is tempting, but there is too great a difference between the Goncourts' objective observations of Germinie as a 'test case' and their presentation of her as an independent thinking being, for it to be convincing for long. While they are sometimes successful in registering Germinie's thoughts and emotions as she does herself, they all too often allow her to become an object to be studied either by themselves or by other characters in the novel. One consequence of this is that she is discussed, again like a Balzac character, in terms of a particular group. Another is the manner in which what the authors consider to be her response to events is expressed in a language clearly not her own. Here, for example, we have her reaction to the countryside beyond the Porte de Clignancourt:

> La campagne, au loin s'étendait, étincelante et vague perdue dans le poudroiement d'or de sept heures. Tout flottant dans cette poussière de jour que le jour laisse derrière lui sur la verdure qu'il efface et les maisons qu'il fait roses. (p.84)

Or again, on the occasion when she first meets Gautruche, there is a clear distinction between what the authors offer as her reaction to the surroundings (through the use of the impersonal *on*) and her true response which is conveyed by her sudden gesture in taking Gautruche's glass: 'Germinie empoigna le verre de Gautruche, le but à moitié d'un trait et le lui tendit du côté où elle avait bu' (p. 207).

Robert Ricatte maintains that such alternating views of the central character are part of a process which makes Germinie appear a victim.[15] This indeed may be so, but it has the result of concentrating our attention on the plight of a single figure rather than on that of a whole class. An awareness of this is perhaps what prompted the authors to broaden their concern by including in the final pages their address to Paris ('Le pauvre est ton citoyen comme le riche', p. 279) so much admired by Hugo, together with the symbolic failure of Mlle de Varandeuil to find Germinie's cross in the common grave.

From our vantage point of more than a century later it is easy to look back through the mass of imaginative literature which has set out to expose the dilemmas of working-class people, extol their virtues or champion their cause, and accuse the Goncourts of a naivety and even of a basic lack of sympathy for their subject. There is, however, no reason to doubt the sincerity of the novel's Preface. Whatever their personal preference for a paternalistic society, their belief in the need for humanity and compassion and in the novel's capacity to draw the public's attention to this need appears to be beyond question. Even though as a novel *Germinie Lacerteux* may today appear somewhat timid, it is closer to the more militant works of Zola or of the early Barbusse, than to those either of Charles-Louis Philippe with their sentimental depictions of working-class society, or of Octave Mirbeau with their violent criticisms of the bourgeoisie.

By comparison with the Goncourts, Zola had a sense of impending social upheaval and of general political awareness which were considerably more acute. Furthermore not only in statements made about his own work and about *L'Assommoir* and *Germinal* in particular, but in his concern for the general state of literature and in his declared admiration for Balzac,[16] Zola showed a determination and a sense of purpose which were considerably more developed than theirs. As we have noted *L'Assommoir* was to be not only a novel about the plight of the working class, but also and more importantly a plea on behalf of that class, an attempt to 'réclamer, par l'exposition franche des faits, de l'air, de la lumière et de l'instruction pour les basses classes'; 'En un mot, un tableau très exact de la vie du peuple avec ses ordures, sa vie lachée, son langage grossier, etc. . . . Un effroyable tableau *qui portera sa morale en soi.*'[17] Such remarks do suggest that Zola's real ambitions went somewhat further than the claims for objectivity and detachment which he made especially in *Les Romanciers naturalistes.*

Unlike the Goncourts, Zola, at least ostensibly, deals with a specific issue (alcoholism)[18] of national importance, and his working-class characters have in consequence a quite different stature from Germinie. The emphasis is also somewhat different: while Germinie is shown to be by nature and temperament incapable of resisting her fate, Gervaise in *L'Assommoir* is projected in two separate ways. While, for example, she is studied for her own sake as an individual in her relationships with Lantier, Coupeau or Goujet, she is more frequently part and a representative of a collective phenomenon, a fact which is reflected in the use Zola makes of set pieces – the feast in Chapter 7, the wedding (Chapter 2) or Nana's first communion (Chapter 10). Such insistance on collective and shared experience is important. Zola believed in the need for a structured society, and saw individual attempts to rebel or aspirations to petit bourgeois values as being part of a gradual process of total disintegration and of which alcoholism was a major feature. For all its apparent dullness, therefore, the Goujet household in *L'Assommoir* does have a moral fortitude (reflected albeit naïvely in the white decor and neatness of the apartment) of which Zola clearly approves, and looks forward to what Dubois calls the Fourier inspired 'socialisme utopique' subsequently to be found in *Au Bonheur des dames* and *Quatre Evangiles.*[19] Clearly this feature of Zola's writing relates to a general theory about how society as a whole should work rather than to a specific aim to have his novels make a plea for the cause of the workers. None the less it is difficult to accept the not uncommon view that, since it contains no exposition of political or social theories, and since Zola himself remarked that 'le roman de Gervaise n'est pas le roman politique',[20] *L'Assommoir* is only political in an incidental way, especially when so many features of it suggest the contrary. No matter what he said, Zola is not concerned simply to describe objectively or scientifically 'la vie du peuple'; he does so in such a manner that even the readers of his day could have had little doubt about his intentions.

An early if obvious device is the description of the wedding party to the Louvre in Chapter 3,[21] in which it is not merely the ignorance and insensitivity of the visitors which are underlined, but their sense of being in an alien environment, and of being left, when they become lost, without sympathy or, until the very end, any guidance. Only in their own areas of Paris – characters and setting here being largely inseparable – are these people certain of their roles, accepting quite passively whatever fate befalls them. And while this may result in some stereotypes, like the opening description of the early morning scene in the boulevard de la Chapelle area or the interreflection of mood – or predicament – and weather, it does allow Zola to insert, in a variety of ways, a number of quite obvious socio-political comments. In Chapter 4 we have the description of Coupeau convalescing after his accident:

Et, quand les jambes lui revinrent, il garda une sourde rancune contre le travail. C'était un métier de malheur, de passer ses journées comme les chats, le long des gouttières. Eux pas bêtes, les bourgeois! ils vous envoyaient à la mort, bien trop poltrons pour se risquer sur une échelle, s'installant solidement au coin de leur feu et se fichant du pauvre monde. (p. 488)

Here Zola's narrative method contains three distinct stages: first, the description of Coupeau and his feeling; second, the registering of his thoughts in his own style of language; third, the voicing of a general statement about Coupeau's class and society as a whole.

In Chapter 6 Goujet reflects on the machine which can produce rivets in greater quantity and more efficiently than any worker:

En douze heures, cette sacrée mécanique en fabriquait des centaines de kilogrammes. Goujet n'avait pas de méchanceté; mais, à certains moments, il aurait volontiers pris Fifine pour taper dans toute cette ferraille, par colère de lui voir des bras plus solides que les siens. Ça lui causait un gros chagrin, même quand il se raisonnait, en se disant que la chair ne pouvait pas lutter contre le fer. Un jour, bien sûr, la machine tuerait l'ouvrier; déjà leurs journées étaient tombées de douze francs à neuf francs, et on parlait de les diminuer encore. (p. 537)

Again in this extract we find a movement from a general

description into a specific point which Zola wishes to make and which he does by projecting it in the form of or through his character's thoughts. In all examples of this kind we find a mixture of the traditional *style indirect libre* and authorial intervention with the former colouring the whole. Whereas the Goncourts frequently have Germinie express an emotional response in a language which is not her own (not unlike Flaubert and Emma Bovary), Zola, by this method and by maintaining many of the rhythms and words of popular speech, is more able to suggest that his characters are themselves responsible for the ideas and views which he wishes to draw to his reader's attention.

Elsewhere Zola has recourse to rather more obvious devices. His indignation at Marescot's greed and victimization of his tenants builds to a rhetorical climax at once deflated and given point in the final sentences by the sordid detail of reality:

> On pleurait à tous les étages, une musique de malheur ronflait le long de l'escalier et des corridors. Si chacun avait eu un mort chez lui, ça n'aurait pas produit un air d'orgues aussi abominable. Un vrai jour de jugement dernier, la fin des fins, la vie impossible, l'écrasement du pauvre monde. La femme du troisième allait faire huit jours au coin de la rue Belhomme. Un ouvrier, le maçon du cinquième, avait volé chez son patron. (p. 683)

The impersonal *on* is also sometimes used to voice a general criticism or overview in a way which only narrowly avoids direct authorial intervention. Thus Zola comments on Madame Lerat's *atelier* and on the conditions in which Nana has to work: 'On était là les unes sur les autres, on se pourrissait ensemble; juste l'histoire des paniers de pommes, quand il y a des pommes gâtées' (p. 717); or on Coupeau's brief spell at Etampes: 'On ne se doute pas combien ça désaltère les pochards, de quitter l'air de Paris, où il y a dans les rues une vraie fumée d'eau-de-vie et de vin' (p. 673).

Yet however frequent such devices are, and however much they may indeed suggest that Zola was aiming to give *L'Assommoir* a political dimension, there is something unstructured about it all. Despite his unquestionable indignation and his appeal for a radical improvement in the lot of the working class, Zola's essential position appears to be one in which pessimism and resignation are only occasionally and momentarily relieved by moments of sentimental nostalgia or permanently by death. The absence of any firmly articulated suggestion for positive social reform and of personal commitment on Zola's part to a policy of action was something which contemporary socialists and later communist critics of his work like Lukács or Barbusse regarded as a weakness. Barbusse was to write in 1932:

> Le livre reste désespérant, sans issue, purement négatif et, malgré la première apparence, de portée sociale restreinte. Il n'a de subversif contre un ordre de choses néfaste, que la vertu subversive indirecte possédée par toute œuvre de vérité – mais cette part reste trop soumise à l'appréciation de chacun lorsque la vérité qui apparaît n'est pas solidement attachée à une réalité de fond.[22]

Such criticism tends, however, to ignore both the kind of literary tradition in and against which Zola was writing (or rather, views it through a very special optic), as well as the wealth of socialist philosophy which developed during the Second Empire and early years of the Third Republic. Furthermore we know that, deeply moved by the Commune, Zola had positively envisaged writing 'un deuxième roman ouvrier . . . particulièrement politique'.[23] Although the precise date of this remark is not known, in a letter to Van Santen Kolff (6 October 1889), Zola looks back to the time of writing *L'Assommoir* as significant: 'ce n'est qu'au moment de *L'Assommoir* que, ne pouvant mettre dans ce livre l'étude du rôle politique et surtout social de l'ouvrier, je pris la résolution de réserver cette matière, pour en faire un autre roman'.[24]

Zola's increasing awareness of the revolutionary climate of the 1870s due largely to his activities as a journalist for *La Cloche, Le Bien public, Voltaire* and *Le Sémaphore de Marseille*, for example, and to his associations with people like Vallès, Guesde and Alexis is well known and has been thoroughly documented. Socialism, in a variety of forms, and in particular anarchism, which spread vigorously into Western Europe from 1878, fascinated him as much as they alarmed many of his contemporaries. According to Edmond de Goncourt, in January 1884 Zola was already projecting 'l'introduction d'une sérieuse et approfondie étude de la question sociale'[25] for a novel. In the following year *Germinal* was published.

Of all Zola's novels *Germinal* has been submitted to the most constant and painstaking scholarly analysis and scrutiny. His methods of compiling his material and of working this into the text have been the subject of a number of substantial studies of which R. H. Zakarian's *Zola's Germinal: A Critical Study of its Primary Sources* deserves particular mention.[26] Zola's preparatory work for *Germinal* was as thorough as that for any other novel, yet as he admitted in an article published in *Le Matin* (7 March 1885), the complexities of socialist philosophy and the problem of projecting them into a variety of representative characters caused him considerable difficulty: 'Quand j'ai voulu dans mon roman mettre des socialistes en scène, m'occuper du socialisme moderne, j'ai rencontré une difficulté plus grande que tout le reste. Il y a tant de sectes, tant d'écoles différentes.'[27] As Zakarian has shown Zola offers us four kinds of socialism: Christian socialism briefly glimpsed through the character of the abbé Ranvier (though the Church in the persons of both Ranvier and the earlier abbé Joire remains distinctly separate from the real issues of the book); State socialism or Possibilism through Rasseneur; Marxist collectivism through Etienne with Pluchart as his guide; and revolutionary anarchism through Souvarine. Furthermore it is interesting to note the reasons Zola gave for having chosen the last of these: 'Je ne pense pas que le mouvement socialiste et révolutionnaire commencera en France, notre race est trop amollie. C'est même pour cela que, dans mon roman, c'est dans un russe que j'ai incarné le socialisme violent.'[28] The real problem which Zola seems to have been reluctant to acknowledge – or of which he was unaware – however, is that of the inherent conflict between the dimension of political commitment which his 'étude du rôle politique et surtout social de l'ouvrier' would almost necessarily entail, and his frequently reiterated view that naturalism merely records: 'Le naturalisme ne se prononce pas. Il examine. Il décrit. Il dit: Ceci est. C'est au public de tirer les conclusions.'[29] As in *L'Assommoir,* only to a greater degree and, in spite of what Barbusse later claimed, in a more positive fashion, Zola, through a variety of narrative and stylistic devices, gave his novel a political dimension which took it beyond his own definition of it as 'une œuvre de pitié, pas autre chose . . .'[30] and are signs that he had very much in mind the ways and means to prompt 'un frisson de terreur' in his bourgeois reader.[31]

Like most Zola novels *Germinal* at once impresses us by the atmosphere created in the opening pages.[32] As critics have often observed, the first part of the novel in which Etienne arrives at Montsou and finds employment is marked by constant references to darkness, to the voracious appetite of the mine likened throughout the novel to a monster ('un ogre [. . .] que rien ne pouvait repaître', p. 1193), and to the hellish qualities of life both under ground (specifically described on several occasions as *l'enfer*) and above where heat and the colours black and red dominate. The people who inhabit this region emerge from the darkness like animals;[33] they are conditioned by and resigned to their way of life and find relief only pathetically in promiscuity. In immediate if naïve contrast Zola presents his reader at the beginning of Part II with the bourgeois comfort of the Grégoire household highlighted by a description of the sleeping Cécile. Pastel colours, tranquility and a muted Boucher-like voluptuousness prevail: 'elle avait une chair superbe, une fraîcheur de lait, avec ses cheveux châtains, sa face ronde au petit nez volontaire, noyé entre les joues. La couverture avait glissé, et elle respirait si doucement, que son haleine ne soulevait même pas sa gorge déjà lourde' (p. 1196). In the final section of the novel Cécile is murdered by Bonnemort, an act of obvious symbolic significance, but at this earlier point Zola makes us acutely aware of the contrast between the two worlds since this particular early morning scene recalls that of the Maheu household described in Part One, Chapter 2. Again the scene is built around the daughter:

> ce fut Catherine qui se leva. Dans sa fatigue, elle avait, par habitude, compté les quatre coups du timbre, à travers le plancher, sans trouver la force de s'éveiller complètement. Puis, les jambes jetées hors des couvertures, elle tâtonna, frotta enfin une allummette et alluma la chandelle. Mais elle restait assise, la tête si pesante, qu'elle se renversait entre les deux épaules, cédant au besoin invincible de retomber sur le traversin.
>
> Maintenant, la chandelle éclairait la chambre, carrée, à deux fenêtres, que trois lits emplissaient. Il y avait une armoire, une table, deux chaises de vieux noyer dont le ton fumeux tachait durement les murs, peints en jaune clair. Et rien d'autre, des hardes pendues à des clous, une cruche posée sur le carreau, près d'une terrine rouge servant de cuvette.

[. . .]

Cependant, Catherine fit un effort désespéré. Elle s'étirait, elle crispait ses deux mains dans ses cheveux roux, qui lui embroussaillaient le front et la nuque. Fluette pour ses quinze ans, elle ne montrait de ses membres, hors du fourreau étroit de sa chemise, que des bras délicats, dont la blancheur de lait tranchait sur le teint blême du visage, déjà gâté par les continuels lavages au savon noir. (p. 1143)

The contrast between the two scenes is clear both in general terms and in matters of detail, especially those relating to the physical descriptions of the two girls, and it is a technique which Zola develops and builds into the novel on all levels. In this way descriptions are given a certain moral, social or political weight without recourse to overt authorial interference or intrusion. Thus after these two early accounts of contrasting family conditions, Maheude and her younger children arrive at the Grégoire household: 'Alors, la Maheude et ses petits entrèrent, glacés, affamés, saisis d'un effarement peureux, en se voyant dans cette salle où il faisait si chaud et qui sentait si bon la brioche' (p. 1203). The chapter closes with these words: the description has brought the previous two together and further comment is unnecessary.

Effective as this contrastive technique may be in the conveying of his point of view, Zola is none the less careful not to allow it to throw the novel out of balance. Whatever his general sympathy for the working class, over the matter of political solutions he was, as we have seen, concerned with the need to distinguish between different kinds of socialism. Similarly he resists the temptation to place all members of the bourgeoisie into a single category even though distinctions are far less clear. The *rentiers* Grégoire for all their ease of living are not as unfeeling in their treatment of the miners as is the manager Hennebeau, even though they indulge in conscience-salving acts of charity by their occasional gifts of cast-off clothes. Indeed in the opening chapter of Part Four Zola is at pains to treat them with some sympathy. The paternalistic Deneulin, whose independent mine at Jean-Bart is destroyed by rioting workers, is shown himself to be a helpless victim of a general situation in which capitalism is rampant. Even though his own class is much to blame, however, his response to the destruction firmly and ominously establishes him in the opposite camp to the miners: 'Tas de bandits, vous verrez ça, quand nous serons redevenus les plus forts!' (p. 1411).

But while a variety of possible responses to the workers' plight may be clearly indicated and examined, distinctions of this kind within the bourgeois world are all ultimately ignored. Zola rather treats bourgeois capitalism as a political philosophy allowing for little or no variation and, through descriptions of living conditions, of houses, of dress and of food, concentrates instead on reminding us that the bourgeoisie inhabits a world apart. Furthermore that it is also essentially soft and quite out of touch with 'reality' is suggested – as we have already noticed in the description of Cécile and her bedroom – by the use of references to warm, protective interiors. It is a self-contained and self-perpetuating world in which corruption and decadence lurk close to the surface. Indeed this is most pointedly expressed in the novel by the suggested incestuous nature of Négrel's affair with Mme Hennebeau which, because of their general air of self-righteousness, appears to be far worse than the animal lust, vulgarity and general promiscuity which characterize the workers' lives. (La Pierronne's adultery with Dansaert in this respect has to be seen as a pale imitation of the Négrel-Hennebeau affair, and a betrayal therefore of working-class morality.) The most bitter indictment of bourgeois callousness, however, is to be found in the prurient interest shown in the Jean-Bart disaster: 'les bourgeois organisaient des excursions, avec un tel entrain que les Grégoire se décidèrent à suivre le monde. [. . .] Lorsque, vers trois heures, les Grégoire et leur fille Cécile descendirent devant la fosse effondrée, ils y trouvèrent Mme Hennebeau, arrivée la première, en toilette bleu marine, se garantissant, sous une ombrelle, du pâle soleil de février' (p. 1556).

By such accounts of bourgeois living and morality Zola provides *Germinal* with a dimension almost entirely absent from *L'Assommoir*, and in so doing inevitably prompts a number of social if not specifically political questions in the minds of his readers. Yet what fundamentally distinguishes the two books in terms of their political weight is the much greater control Zola has in *Germinal* over symbol, atmosphere and structure. Thus, for example, in spite of certain precise details about the Parisian *quartier* in which *L'Assommoir* is set, the earlier novel fails to convey the sense of claustrophobia which is never absent from *Germinal* for long. Etienne comes into Montsou from an outside world which is only occasionally referred to and seldom (except in the case of the Belgian miners' strike or of Pluchart's visit) impinges in any direct way on life there. Similarly when at the end of the novel he leaves, Zola's emphasis is on an abstract vision of the future heavily symbolized especially in the closing paragraph by the breaking dawn, the warm sun, the approaching spring and images of germination and hidden growth. Montsou and the surrounding region are left; whatever hope there may be that the social revolution will one day come about, the mine has been reopened and is once again claiming its daily ration of human flesh. Furthermore the novel-long motif of the mine as a devouring beast,[34] and also the many direct descriptions of the miners as animals ready for slaughter, is nicely contrasted to the miners' constant demand for bread which runs as a counter theme gathering in intensity (Part Five, Chapters IV and V) as a prelude to the climax in Part Four. Similarly Zola's use of and references to time are more thoughtfully worked into the structure of *Germinal* than in *L'Assommoir*. Whereas in the earlier novel time is mentioned regularly, it merely draws our attention to the fact that matters have progressed. Weeks and months often pass by unnoticed. In *Germinal* references to time and in particular to the seasonal pattern of events are made judiciously. The strike occurs at the height of winter, and the suggestions of optimism at the close of the book are, as we have already noticed, matched by the promise of spring: 'Maintenant, en plein ciel, le soleil d'avril rayonnait dans sa gloire, échauffant la terre qui enfantait' (p. 1591).

If devices like these are not enough to persuade us that in *Germinal* Zola has set out to do rather more than provide an objective account of events, the portrayal of Etienne should leave us in no doubt whatsoever as to his intentions. Anticipating a device later to be favoured by writers of socialist realism, Zola describes Etienne as someone who has embarked on a journey, not simply of the conventional kind but more importantly of self-exploration. It has five distinct phases. The first is his arrival as an anonymous (*l'homme, un homme*) but representative member of his social class; the second takes him from an initial awareness of the miners' general conditions and of the rampant promiscuity in Montsou (the jealousy between himself and Chaval adding an extra dimension to this) through the development of his political education ('il n'en était point encore à se fabriquer un système', p. 1275) to his eventual emergence as organiser and head of the strike action: 'Désormais, Etienne était le chef incontesté' (p.1328). From this point and during the third phase Etienne's real problem begins to develop. As leader his working-class status is threatened:

> Sa popularité croissante le surexcitait chaque jour davantage [. . .] devenir un centre, sentir le monde rouler autour de soi, c'était un continuel gonflement de vanité, pour lui, l'ancien mécanicien, le haveur aux mains grasses et noires. Il montait d'un échelon, il entrait dans cette bourgeoisie exécrée, avec des satisfactions d'intelligence et de bien-être *qu'il ne s'avouait pas.* (p.1328. My italics)

While Zola's presence as commentator is here undeniable, he later uses both Rasseneur (p. 1340) and Souvarine (p. 1482) to voice identical criticisms of Etienne who 'goûtait l'ivresse de sa popularité' (p. 1381). The fourth phase is that of Etienne's withdrawal after he has lost control over the forces he has released and Zola describes him – again not uncritically – in Jeanlin's hideout, convincing himself that a career given to political theorising could be as rewarding and as effective as action: 'son ambition [. . .] lâcher le travail, travailler uniquement à la politique, mais seul, dans une chambre propre, sous le prétexte que les travaux de tête absorbent la vie entière et demandent beaucoup de calme' (p. 1460). This phase is completed by his being rejected (Part Seven, Chapter I) by those whom he now sees as 'brutes, inintelligents et barbares' (p. 1519) but whose accepted champion he had been only weeks earlier, and by the re-emergence of Rasseneur as the local political leader. Phase five, reflecting and balancing the first, records Etienne's departure.

If we were to ignore the implied optimism of the last chapter of the novel, Etienne's role charted in this way might well appear negative: individual immaturity (admittedly exacerbated by inadequate education) set against the unthinking and fickle responses of the masses. Etienne has neither the intellectual capacity to match Pluchart (though precisely how effective in the long term the latter is likely to be remains an unanswered question) nor the uncompromising single-mindedness to be able to act in the way Souvarine does. None the less he is – hence the deliberate anonymity of the opening pages – a representative of his class by whose efforts some form of revolution, if it is ever to be achieved, will come about. Only if this is accepted can the full significance of the final chapter be grasped. Resignation, especially of Maheude ('ses épaules s'affaissèrent, comme sous l'écrasement du destin', p. 1585), to the re-establishment of bourgeois control ('des files d'hommes trottant le nez vers la terre, ainsi que du bétail mené à l'abbatoir', p. 1582) *is* the natural response of the working class as a whole. Bonnemort's attitude expressed earlier in the novel – 'mais il y aura toujours des chefs, pas vrai? inutile de se casser la tête à réfléchir là-dessus' (p. 1276) – is the one which inevitably emerges in the face of the sheer necessity to survive.

What Zola successfully avoids is succumbing to the temptation to suggest any easy answers. Just as he refuses to romanticize or to idealize the working class, – except, that is, in the final paragraphs – so too does he refuse to offer any instant political alternative to the present dominant system. Yet this 'deuxième roman ouvrier . . . particulièrement politique' is more than the 'œuvre de pitié' of which he spoke in 1885. Although Etienne is in one sense shown to have failed, he has only done so personally and within the limited context of the Montsou events. His example and that of the strikes as a whole illustrate that collective action, if correctly and efficiently organized, will succeed in over-turning a repressive society. The symbolic seed of rebellion, already contained in the title and worked into the text throughout, is fully and significantly developed in the novel's final paragraph:

Maintenant, en plein ciel, le soleil d'avril rayonnait dans sa gloire, échauffant la terre qui enfantait. Du flanc nourricier jaillissait la vie, les bourgeons crevaient en feuilles vertes, les champs tressaillaient de la poussée des herbes. De toutes parts, des graines se gonflaient, s'allongeaient, gerçaient la plaine, travaillées d'un besoin de chaleur et de lumière. Un déborde-ment de sève coulait avec des voix chuchotantes, le bruit des germes s'épandait en un grand baiser. Encore, encore, de plus en plus distinctement, comme s'ils se fussent rapprochés du sol, les camarades tapaient. Aux rayons enflammés de l'astre, par cette matinée de jeunesse, c'était de cette rumeur que la campagne était grosse. Des hommes poussaient, une armée noire, vengeresse, qui germait lentement dans les sillons,

grandissait pour les récoltes du siècle futur, et dont la germination allait faire bientôt éclater la terre. (p. 1591)

A dawn of which there was no sign on Etienne's arrival ('Aucune
aube ne blanchissait dans le ciel mort' p. 1142) has now broken
and a new day is promised. The final vision of the future is here
powerfully expressed as the heavy symbolism which on earlier
occasions threatens to obscure the more objective descriptions
characteristic of naturalism now becomes Zola's dominant
narrative mode.

Although (as Zola hoped it would) *Germinal* goes further than
L'Assommoir in its examination of general issues, the problem of
offering a positive and constructive answer to the socio-political
problems which it explores is not really solved. That the
conditions of working-class existence are exposed with more force
than in any earlier novel, and that Zola describes and analyses the
collective consciousness of that class in a way which was entirely
new, are not in doubt. Yet when we examine Zola's methods it
quickly becomes apparent that for all his implied and unquestionable sympathy there remains a significant gap between himself
and his subject matter. In many ways this is attributable to his
attempted 'scientific' method: he observes, displays his facts and
leaves the reader to draw his own conclusions. The same could be
said only with more justification about the Goncourt brothers.
But there is more here than straightforward observation.[35] In both
cases facts are recorded in or retranslated into literary forms
which almost without exception reflect certain received ideas
about social characteristics and about the working class in
particular. They also anticipate readers' responses. To some
extent and despite descriptions based on carefully recorded observations this results in stereotypes: in *Germinie Lacerteux* the use of
animal imagery, in *L'Assommoir* the way in which Gervaise and
Coupeau in particular are shown as being destined to return to
and die in the squalour from which they have come. And to a
large measure it is true of *Germinal* as well, though in this novel
the process is rather more complex. That this is so is due partly to
the developed elements of class conflict and of contrasting values,
but it is due more to the fact that the working class is no longer
shown to be, as in *L'Assommoir*, the helpless victim of a socio-
economic system 'disguised' as a quasi-medical one based on a
theory of inherited physiological weakness.

We should remind ourselves, at this stage, that Zola like the Goncourts believed in the need for a stable society. Moreover whatever their sympathy for the working class and its cause and however strongly they felt they should draw public attention to it even to the extent of offering a warning, their own positions in society were secure. Such beliefs and such a position inevitably had their effect on the presentation, especially in *Germinal*, of something which could be seen as a direct challenge to and even a potential destroyer of the world to which they belonged. Thus while we find a neat alignment of various possible political alternatives, no single one proves to be either satisfactory or successful. Further, we witness a potentially revolutionary figure, Etienne, not only leaving Montsou with its problems unsolved, but having proved himself incapable of leading the rebellion to its proper self-defining end. Instead resignation – individual and collective alike – and moderate political activity are seen as truly characteristic of a working class which therefore fails in any long-lasting way to disrupt society or to challenge accepted opinions about it. However sympathetic or indignant the Goncourts or Zola may be, they are ultimately trapped by the essentially and inevitably hierarchical view they hold of society and of the place of the working class within it. This is not to say that the warning at the end of *Germinal* is to be ignored; indeed by poeticizing it in the way he does, Zola may well have attempted to put it into a language with which his bourgeois readers would be familiar. At the same time like the Goncourts at the end of *Germinie Lacerteux* he changes key with the result that something of the novel's real impact is lost.

2 Henri Barbusse and Militancy

On his death in 1953 few amongst Barbusse's supporters had any doubts that he had achieved much of what he had set out to accomplish. George Dimitrov, President of the Third International, expressed official Communist Party opinion when he remarked: 'Barbusse a clairement compris que la création artistique doit être mise au service de l'humanité laborieuse qui lutte pour sa libération du joug du capital et que le véritable artiste ne peut se tenir à l'écart de cette grande lutte libératrice';[1] in *Pravda*, Lenin himself wrote that *Le Feu* and *Clarté* were 'des confirmations particulièrement persuasives du développement de la conscience révolutionnaire des masses que l'on peut voir partout';[2] Duclos and Fréville that 'grâce à l'effort de Barbusse [. . .] le prolétariat a pu être dépeint dans les livres et qu'il s'est reconnu en eux'.[3]

Barbusse's aims, particularly during the post-war years, are nicely summarized by the title of one of his essays, *La Lueur dans l'abîme*. He sought above all to expose the injustices and irregularities from which he, like so many other left-wing intellectuals, believed post-war society to be suffering. At the same time he was eager to encourage the working class to assert itself in a revolutionary but constructive manner. Furthermore he insisted that the *writer* ('je ne suis pas un militant, je suis un homme de lettres'[4]) had a particular role to play. And while he did not share Julien Benda's view of the intellectuals' role, he regarded the writer as a privileged being whose powers of intuition and perception marked him off from many. In April 1919, the year in which his third novel *Clarté* was published, he wrote to Gabriel d'Annunzio: 'L'écrivain, le penseur, le guide, doit voir plus loin que les prétendus avantages immédiats, et plus loin que le temps

29

présent.'[5] Sixteen years later, speaking at the International Congress of Writers in Paris, he remarked: 'Le devoir de l'écrivain est d'aider, dans la mesure de ses forces et dans la voie où il s'est engagé, les progrès et les perfectionnements de la collectivité à laquelle il est mêlé'.[6] Between these two dates, by his involvement in a number of politically inspired, but non-party groups and movements, and by his writing – journalism, essays, criticism and fiction – Barbusse unequivocally demonstrated his commitment to these aims and ideals, even though he was on occasions subjected to quite violent criticism.

As we noted in the previous chapter, in 1932 Barbusse's attitude to Zola was one of admiration tempered by a feeling that the earlier novelist's work did not indicate precisely enough how the ills of society might be eradicated. Zola's concern for the individual rather than for society as a whole, Barbusse also claimed, meant that the broad social significance of his subject was missed. Only with *Trois Villes* was this emphasis corrected, attention being moved from the individual to the collective mass, from the transitory to the permanent and therefore from the present to the future. While such observations about Zola's work clearly relate to Barbusse's own ambition to 'faire entrer le collectif dans l'art', (a standard theme of a number of his earlier essays), they also serve as a commentary on his own imaginative writing and relate to the general development of an increasingly militant literature which was to find its fullest expression in socialist realism.

In terms of the influence it had upon his subsequent career few writers can have owed quite so much to a single work as did Barbusse to *Le Feu*. Born into a family with a strong radical tradition in 1873 his pre-war career was uneventful even though by the 1890s and the Dreyfus affair he was fully committed to humanist and socialist values. Direct political activity was some way off, however, and in spite of his subsequent claim that 'le cas Dreyfus [. . .]me sortit de mon inertie individualiste'[7] he seemed, not unlike Charles-Louis Philippe, to be content to divide his life between the need to earn a living and the desire to fashion a literary reputation for himself. Of his early work two volumes of poetry *Les Pleureuses* (1895) and *Les Suppliants* (1903) were strongly influenced in their form by symbolist writing and in their tone by the *fin de siècle* vogue for a rather effete aestheticism. Poetry was not likely to bring him much reward, however, and his decision to try his hand novel writing was an important one. His first novel *L'Enfer* (1908), in which a young bank clerk observes through a hole in the wall of a hotel room the behaviour of various people who frequent the one next door, is a gloomy work. Despite the tone of prurient curiosity which colours much of it, the novel deals essentially with matters of general human concern and in particular with suffering and the problems of communication. This is not to say that there are not comments of a more specific political nature, though, as Frank Field has pointed out,[8] they tend to be rather negative in nature. In this novel Barbusse appears to prefer to expose matters rather than suggest methods of correction. Thus when, towards the end of the novel, two doctors attend a person dying from cancer, the narrator overhears their conversation in which the disease is identified with the 'disease' of rampant militarism and nationalism which is killing France. Both are equally fatal and we are left with a feeling of deep pessimism with little suggestion for an alternative course of action. While there is very little in *L'Enfer* which hints at the force of *Le Feu*, it does deserve to be included amongst those works which remind us that the true picture of French society was not entirely that associated with and evoked by the 'belle époque'. In what it has to say *L'Enfer* is the work of a man whose concern for the human condition is very real, but whose indignation has yet to be channelled into more forceful and forthright forms of expression.

As for so many of his generation the coming of war had for Barbusse the effect of a catalyst. While, like Rolland, he considered France to be in some ways just as responsible for the aggression as Germany, he did see the latter as being particularly guilty of overreaching imperialist ambition. France was directly threatened and like so many others whose position was pacifist, Barbusse would, when faced by the real prospect of defeat and destruction, reconcile his pre-war attitude with one demanded by new circumstances without too much difficulty. Thus we find him echoing Péguy and writing in his *Carnet de Guerre* of 'un besoin de gloire nationale',[9] and in a letter to *L'Humanité* (9 August 1914) of 'une guerre sociale qui fera faire un grand pas – peut-être le pas définitif – à notre cause'.

Having failed to enlist as an aviator Barbusse joined the army when he was forty-one as a stretcher bearer and, before being invalided out in 1917, witnessed a considerable amount of front-line action. He was mentioned several times in despatches and in 1915 received the Croix de Guerre for bravery. Whatever his anticipations concerning either the quality of army life or the duration of the war might have been, Barbusse became, like most, rapidly disillusioned. The general inefficiency, the attitude of those in command, the ease with which many avoided what he now considered to be their duty, and above all the idea of war propagated by the national press as some kind of colourful, romantic adventure ('les descriptions à l'eau de rose')[10] are frequent themes in his early letters to his wife. Within a short time it became clear to all that hopes for an end of hostilities by Christmas 1914 had been no more than dreams. As the war moved into its long central period of attrition and near stalemate, the enthusiastic departures from the Gare de l'Est in Paris seemed to have taken place almost in another age.

As is well known *Le Feu* is based, like so many novels written during the years of the war itself, almost entirely on a personal diary containing Barbusse's observations and records of conversations with his fellow soldiers. Throughout this *Carnet de Guerre* begun in October 1915, we find passages which will eventually take their place in the novel. We also find substantial evidence of Barbusse's skill in observation, his ability to record what was ordinary in the context of war in a way which makes it appear striking to the reader – for example, one soldier 'cuirassé de boue', another 'un escargot marchant avec ses mains'.[11] By the end of the year Barbusse was already planning various parts of his novel and conceiving its overall shape. Convalescence during the early months of 1916 gave him the time and rest he needed to be able to finish the work and by August *Le Feu* began to appear in serialised but censored form in the left-wing review *L'Oeuvre*. In December it was published as a book and in the following year awarded the Prix Goncourt.[12] By the end of 1918 sales had reached nearly a quarter of a million, a success approached among the books written during the 1914–18 period only by Roland Dorgelès's *Les Croix de Bois*. Responses to it were marked and extreme particularly in the right-wing press where the novel was seen as subversive and unpatriotic.[13]

In view of Barbusse's earlier pacifism and eventual reluctant acceptance of the war as a necessary evil, it is hardly surprising that he intended to offer more than a simple exposure of the horrors of battle. It was essential that something positive should be glimpsed beyond the destruction and desolation of the battle field, something which he clearly must have hoped would be rather more accesible to the ordinary man than Zola's anticipated future at the end of *Germinal*. As a result *Le Feu* has a double focus to which some critics have objected. While it remains essentially a 'war novel' it also offers a statement about the reorganization of society along left-wing lines. Accusations of propaganda and message are, in some cases, clearly justified.[14] The opening chapter 'La Vision'[15] (added after the serialization of the novel in *L'Oeuvre*,) in which multi-national responsibility for the war is discussed, and the closing of 'L'Aube' with its symbolic dawn and lengthy discussions about equality, fraternity and freedom are features of which few beyond Barbusse's most ardent admirers would approve. The usually taciturn Bertrand's outburst shortly before the attack in Chapter 20 also seems unnatural and out of place. And there are other examples too. But such a view of *Le Feu* tends to ignore ways in which elswhere the book's two dimensions are in fact successfully fused together.

Barbusse's immediate task was to destroy the popular myth of war as an heroic adventure perpetrated by the jingoistic press – the view expressed to Volpatte by the Parisian lady in Chapter 22: 'Ça doit être superbe, une charge, hein? Toutes ces masses d'hommes qui marchent comme à la fête! Et le clairon qui sonne dans la campagne' (pp. 300, 301). In this and in his criticisms of those responsible for the war or who take profit from it, Barbusse was no exception amongst writers of anti-war novels. Examples abound: Volpatte who returns from convalescence full of indignation for those who have managed to avoid military service ('je n'aurais pas cru qu'pendant la guerre, y avait tant d'hommes sur des chaises', p. 113); the soldier whose single, tired refusal to fight any more results in his being publicly executed in spite of his otherwise impeccable war record; the civilian population which profits from billeting soldiers (p. 74). Nor was Barbusse an exception in his emphasis on the physical horror of life at the front, on suffering and on the ever present threat and arbitrary nature of death – the grotesque account of how Caron has to clear out the rotting flesh of a dead German's legs whose boots he has claimed (p. 14); the instant annihilation of Poterloo by an exploding mine ('j'ai vu son corps monter, debout, noir, les deux bras étendus de toute leur envergure, et une flamme à la place de la tête' p. 167); the sickening description of the heap of rotting corpses in Chapter 12 (p. 147).

Within such a context it is hardly surprising that the most ordinary of objects should seem to be disproportionately important – the egg in Chapter 15 or the matches in Chapter 28, for example – prompting reactions in the soldiers which are extreme or abnormal. That this should be so is due to the fact that Barbusse has moved, and is inviting his readers to move with him, from a world or context in which an easily recognized scale of values prevails, to one in which such values are distorted and in which men are obliged to exist in a way which is quite alien to them. Already the social dimension of the book is beginning to emerge and Barbusse conveys this sense of alienation by stressing two themes in particular: first that of the threatened loss of individual characteristics and the men's feeling that they are playing parts; second that of the epic proportions given to the elemental world in which the soldiers are projected.

As in so many war novels the scene of battle is presented literally in terms of a theatrical production. From the opening paragraph of Chapter 2, for example, which in terms of the action is effectively the first chapter of the book we read: 'Le désert commence à disparaître' (p. 5); 'je vois des ombres émerger' (p. 6); 'Peu à peu, les hommes se détachent des profondeurs. Dans les coins, on voit de l'ombre dense se former, puis ces nuages humains se remuent, se fragmentent' (p. 7). (Even though the theatrical element is less marked in *Germinal* we cannot fail to be reminded here of the opening of Zola's novel.) Within pages Barbusse becomes more explicit referring to war as 'le grand drame que nous jouons' (p. 12), and describing the members of the squad (and Pépin and Barque specifically) as clowns (pp. 12 and 13). Later in Chapter 19 the falling flares create 'l'illusion de grand décor d'opéra féerique et sinistre' (p. 207) and the exploding shells in Chapter 20 'un effroyable rideau qui nous sépare du monde, nous sépare du passé et de l'avenir' (p. 246). Having isolated his protagonists Barbusse is free to trace the way in which, as human beings, they gradually became modified and reduced by the role they are forced to play. From the very beginning of the novel the suggestion that they are in danger of becoming animals is strong. They are described as 'masses énormes et difformes: des espèces d'ours' (p. 6); when visited by the journalists they are likened to the animals in the Paris Zoo (p. 35), and shortly after as 'troglodytes sinistres émergeant à moitié de leurs cavernes de boue' (p. 43). The deforming, reductive influence which war experience has upon them – their lives are reduced to a basic survival pattern of eating, drinking, excreting and sleeping – is not unusual, but Barbusse is at pains to express his soldiers' resistance to it. Thus not only the idiosyncracies of uniform but the contents of kit-bags ('La Barda', Chapter 14) – like the egg and matches mentioned earlier – become important as they serve as emblems of the real world from which the men have been violently wrested. Yet Barbusse seems uncertain of allowing mere description of the soldiers' state to carry his point for him. Not infrequently one of the squad or Barbusse himself interposes a reminder that above all what enables the men to resist this process is their awareness of it. One example, with author taking over from a character, is to be found at the end of Chapter 2 with the arrival of a troop of African soldiers: 'Au fond ce sont de vrais soldats. – Nous ne sommes pas des soldats, nous, nous sommes des hommes, dit le gros Lamuse [. . .] Ils sont des hommes, des bonshommes quelconques arrachés brusquement à la vie [. . .] ce sont de simples hommes qu'on a simplifiés encore, et dont, par la force des choses, les seuls instincts primordiaux s'accentuent: instinct de conservation, égoïsme, espoir tenace de survivre toujours, joie de manger, de boire et de dormir' (p. 45). Significantly, the idea is repeated moments before they 'go over the top', their essential human-ness coming through even at this moment when they have been reduced to mere cyphers in the struggle between two massive and anonymous forces: 'Ce ne sont pas des soldats: ce sont des hommes. Ce ne sont pas des aventuriers, des guerriers, faits pour la boucherie humaine – bouchers ou bétail. Ce sont des laboureurs et des ouvriers qu'on reconnaît dans leurs uniformes. Ce sont des civils déracinés. [. . .] ce sont simplement des hommes' (p. 243). The social point is again clearly made.

Connected to this struggle for survival – physical, as well as moral and spiritual – is the use Barbusse makes of the elements, not only of fire, but also and more particularly of water and earth. Again he is not unique in this.

References to mud and rain recur with obsessive regularity in the majority of books written about this war and in some cases – for example the works of Bernanos – remain not only as symbols on a large scale, but as reminders of the indelible impression which the experience of war made on writers' minds.

Originality apart, Barbusse's skill at handling this feature is impressive, the primitive, primaeval world which he evokes being the perfect complement to the reduced existence of the 'troglodytes sinistres'. But there is as well an important development in the part such descriptions have in the structure of the book as a whole. From the opening paragraphs of Chapter II, aptly entitled '*Dans* la terre' (my italics), Barbusse sets out to evoke the atmosphere and appearance of what later in the novel he describes as an 'enfer terrestre' (p. 228). Punctuated only by moments of temporary relief or escape – sun and fine weather accompany the brief leave which the soldiers spend in Paris for example (Chapter 22) – this Dante-like inferno is ever present. But by the close of the novel it is not merely a context, however powerful. Sent to dig fresh trenches the soldiers unwittingly penetrate beyond the enemy front line; they flee and find themselves with German soldiers in no-man's land, 'au sur-naturel champ de repos' (p. 325). Here they discover from both sides men who have been drowned or sucked into the mud. Again Dante comes strongly to mind: 'Le vent s'élève. Il est glacé et son souffle glacé passe au travers de nos chairs. Sur la plaine déliquescente et naufragée, mouchetée de corps entre ses gouffres d'eau vermiculaires, entre ses îlots d'hommes immobiles agglutinés ensemble, comme des reptiles, sur ce chaos qui s'aplatit et sombre, de légères ondulations de mouvements se dessinent' (p. 327).'

Nearly twenty years after the publication of *Le Feu* Jean Giono in *Le Grand Troupeau* shows how the natural world under the impact of war becomes (to use Walter Redfern's phrase) 'out of joint'.[16] While he clearly shows a similar concern for the ravages caused by war, Barbusse does not have quite the same end in view. His point is that the natural world outraged for so long, has itself assumed the role of a common but ultimately invincible enemy, in order to convince men of the futility of their actions and to bring them to their senses.

To consider *Le Feu* merely as a piece of documentary writing – however skilful – is therefore to underestimate a number of literary qualities which contribute directly to the impact it makes upon its readers. In its depiction of the scene of war *Le Feu* is a striking mixture of small, but often poetically intense observations which remind us of German expressionist work and of large-scale accounts which clearly owe much to Zola. On stylistic grounds we might reflect as well on the novel's overall structure. René Pomeau has argued with some persuasion that many of the writers who produced novels during or immediately after the war, were still too close to events to be able to make distinctions and judgements with any degree of objectivity and, furthermore, that they lacked the perspective necessary if their work were to have a considered form.[17] On these grounds a case against Barbusse can be made readily enough, but it is also arguable that the series of disjointed, or at best tenuously connected episodes which *Le Feu* contains, constitute a highly successful method of underlining the precarious nature of the soldier's existence. Moreover, since the subtitle reminds us that the novel is intended to read like a diary, a more uniform or clearly structured account would be inappropriate. This is not to say that the order of events is totally random or unplanned. The decision to have 'La Vision' as the opening chapter in the final book version, the additions to 'L'Aube' and the central placing of 'Les Gros Mots', in which Barbusse discusses the problems of recreating the soldiers' authentic language, would all appear quite deliberate. The placing too of the title (and longest) chapter exactly three quarters of the way through the novel as a natural climax or the juxtaposing of Chapters 22 and 23, 'La Virée' and 'La Corvée' also seem to be the result of more than simple chance. Yet however impressive many of the novel's stylistic qualities may be, that there are problems created by the introduction of Barbusse's own views on war and on society has to be faced.

At this point it is worth underlining a basic distinction between works by Zola or the Goncourts and *Le Feu*. For all their documentary accuracy, the accounts of Germinie's existence, of the plight of people like Gervaise or of the Montsou strikers remain essentially outside the experience of many people who, in the late-nineteenth century, would be likely to read them. However successful these authors were in prompting some kind of positive reaction, their books did not invite the degree of personal indentification necessary for positive response. With war as the 'subject' of Barbusse's novel this limitation disappeared. An event of unprecedented proportions in terms of the ravages done to the land and people of France alike, the 1914–18 War genuinely made an impact in some way upon the lives of millions. Although statistically not entirely proven, the feeling that the working class in particular was providing the vast proportion of infantry men, whose chances of survival were virtually nil, was influential in persuading a reading public to consider why and how matters might be improved. But to arouse indignation about the war – or even, as Dorgelès claimed he was doing, about war in general – would not necessarily lead to an active expression of concern for social conditions as a whole, especially once the war had ended. Furthermore the question 'For *whom* was Barbusse writing?' was a nicely relevant one. Was it for those of the working class in an attempt to encourage them to translate their sense of justice into purposeful action, or was it for the bourgeoisie to make them aware of a state of affairs of which they had long been in ignorance or to which they had wilfully closed their minds? These were all issues which were to become increasingly important to militant writers in general as the century progressed. *Le Feu* is therefore an important book in that in it Barbusse is asking and attempting to answer some of these questions in the knowledge that in so doing he is addressing himself to an audience of quite different proportions and sympathies from the one in which Zola had aimed to prompt his 'frisson de terreur'. As a result we find significant changes not only in the attitude of Barbusse as a writer, but in the ways in which a number of stylistic devices are used.

Perhaps the clearest indication that Barbusse was aware of some of the attendant dangers in what he was attempting to do is to be found in the central chapter 'Les Gros Mots'. This ostensibly is about trench language and the question of authenticity. As Barque remarks: 'tu n'entendras jamais deux poilus l'ouvrir pendant une minute sans qu'i's disent et qu'i' répètent des choses que les imprimeurs n'aiment pas besef imprimer. Alors, quoi? Si tu ne le dis pas, ton portrait ne sera pas r'ssemblant' (p. 169). The point is a sound one, and even when the narrator assures Barque that 'je mettrai les gros mots à leur place' the latter is not convinced: 'Veux-tu mon opinion? Quoique je ne m'y connais pas en livres: c'est courageux, ça, parce que ça s'fait pas, et ce sera très chic si tu l'oses, mais t'auras de la peine au dernier moment, t'es trop poli!' (p. 169).[18] The discussion remains without conclusion or agreement; indeed it is arguable that there can be none.

What is clear, however, is that it raises more than the simple matter of foul language. Basic to it is the question of the different levels or registers of language which are appropriate not simply for the events or characters which Barbusse wishes to describe, but also for the extrapolation of the social and political values of which he wishes his readers to become aware.

As a prelude to this concern for language, Barbusse makes his intentions clear early on by the way he emphasizes the fact that his squad of men is intended to be representative both of France as a whole and of a single class. They belong to 'la multitude compacte d'hommes qui, depuis des saisons, vide la France pour s'accumuler au Nord-Est. Laboureurs et ouvriers pour la plupart. [. . .] Pas de profession libérale parmi ceux qui m'entourent' (pp. 16, 17). Only Bertrand the corporal, who in civilian life is a foreman, remains rather distant – 'un peu à l'écart, taciturne et correct' (p. 16) – and appropriately so in view of the purpose he serves later in the novel. It should also be noted at this stage that as in so many anti-war novels, commissioned officers are considered to be of middle-class origin and to avoid action. As a representative himself of that class Barbusse is quick to dissociate himself from it: 'Nous sommes des soldats combattants, nous autres, et il n'y a presque pas d'intellectuels, d'artistes ou de riches qui, pendant cette guerre, auront risqué leurs figures aux créneaux, sinon en passant, ou sous des képis galonnés' (p. 17).

Even though he has taken some care to prepare his ground in this way, however, the problem of linguistic register still remains. It would have been instructive had Barbusse given some indication in his 'Carnet de Guerre' or in his letters that he had been aware of this problem in advance. Apart from anticipating that the role of Bertrand would be in some measure that of a spokesman, Barbusse seems to have had no particular scheme in mind, even though 'Les Gros Mots' suggests that at least in the process of writing the novel it became a matter of some concern. Basically four methods can be discerned: in the observations made by the men in their 'own language'; in the use of individual characters and of Bertrand in particular as spokesmen for Barbusse himself; and above all in Barbusse either as interpreter of what his fellow soldiers have to say or as a commentator in his own right. Of these the first requires little comment; the soldiers' brief and simplistic remarks about German officers (p. 32) or about German nationalism and the causes of war (p. 263 and p. 336) are entirely in keeping with their roles in the novel. The second is less convincing. Through Volpatte's indignation about methods of selection and conditions generally behind the lines in Chapter 9, 'La

Grande Colère', or through the airman's account of the Sunday mass in Chapter 21, 'Le poste de secours', Barbusse's own feelings are too easily glimpsed. As a result the uniformity of the novel at these junctures is threatened in spite of his attempt to retain the everyday language of the soldiers in their descriptions. With Bertrand the transparency is total, the corporal being used unequivocally by Barbusse as his spokesman. This is apparent in remarks like 'Quand le pays, quand la justice et la liberté sont en danger, ce n'est pas en se mettant à l'abri qu'on les défend' (p. 125). Or shortly before the attack his statement of faith in the future and his rejection of militarism: 'L'avenir! l'avenir! L'œuvre de l'avenir sera d'effacer ce présent-ci, et de l'effacer plus encore qu'on ne pense, de l'effacer comme quelque chose d'abominable et de honteux. Et pourtant, ce présent, il le fallait, il le fallait! Honte à la gloire militaire, honte aux armées, honte au métier de soldat qui change les hommes tour à tour en stupides victimes et en ignobles bourreaux' (p. 259). Normally a silent figure Bertrand's passionate and politically coloured outbursts are impressive, but the fact that he is also a marginal character tends to render them unconvincing and, like Barbusse's own direct interventions, extraneous to the main fabric of the book. Ultimately therefore Barbusse is obliged to explore the possibilities which his own role in the novel offers him to explain and to exhort. As character-novelist he allows himself to be both observed and observer at the same time. Not infrequently his personal involvement in events is conveyed with some success – his pleasure when Paradis gives him the egg or the manner in which his share in the frenzy and apprehension of the attack is recorded for example. But all too often he remains quite detached – 'Je contemple encore une fois ces créatures qui ont roulé ici . . .' (p. 186) – and is willing to expand or interpret inadequately expressed thoughts quite bluntly without effecting the kind of transition Zola achieves between two levels of language. For example: ' – Oui, c'est ça. la guerre, répète-t-il d'une voix lointaine. C'est pa'aut'chose.'

> *Il veut dire*, et je comprends avec lui: Plus que les charges qui ressemblent à des revues . . . (p. 330. My italics)

And in the closing pages of the novel not only does he introduce his personal views on the superiority of equality over fraternity and liberty ('La liberté et la fraternité sont des mots, tandis que l'égalité est une chose' p. 341), but has his soldiers begin to articulate in a language which is foreign to them, concepts whose significance they are beginning to grasp only for the first time: 'Leurs yeux sont ouverts. Ils commencent à se rendre compte de la simplicité sans bornes des choses' (p. 348).

We have already noted Barbusse's objection to Zola's failure to offer a solution to the socio-political malaise of France with enough force or conviction. Once again, however, we have to consider the questions of context and in particular of audience. By 1925 Barbusse repeatedly emphasized the need to 'faire entrer le collectif dans l'art', by which he meant not simply a reflection in art of mass situations, but an analysis of shared, common problems and an indication of a collective solution to them. In addition he believed that many of these problems were permanent and that individuals served in a way as depositaries for the past, a process which he termed 'l'éternel recommencement avec les noms différents'. Writing at the time of *Les Enchaînements* (1925) he remarked: 'je veux montrer la persistance effrayante des situations historiques, le parallélisme des grandes crises humaines, la similitude ou plutôt la monotonie de l'exploitation de l'homme par l'homme depuis qu'il existe des sociétés'. Essentially this basic idea was already present in the elemental and epic aspects of *Le Feu* and with his third novel, *Clarté*, Barbusse consciously set out to develop it still further. In words which almost anticipate Lukács' theory of the novel as the modern epic Barbusse wrote in 1918: 'Le roman est la forme moderne du grand poème. [. . .] Il faut que le poète romancier pense au drame de la vérité, aux grandes questions émouvantes du passé, de l'avenir et du devoir et qu'il ne recule devant rien pour exprimer ce qui est.'[19]

Having been declared unfit for further action in 1917 Barbusse devoted himself to a new novel which would be a corollary to *Le Feu*. In it he hoped that the progressive movement and anticipated future of the earlier novel would be better integrated, but he seemed to be unaware of the potential danger to the work's literary qualities. *Clarté* was written in 1918 and published a year later.[20]

The most immediately noticeable difference between *Clarté* and *Le Feu* is one of overall structure. Whereas the earlier novel is basically and often appropriately irregular and disjointed, *Clarté* is much more ordered and considered. It can be divided into three sections of approximately equal length: the first (Chapters 1–10, 96 pages long) covers Simon Paulin's pre-war life and experiences; the second, the war and his brief spell at the front (Chapters 11–16, 96 pages); the third, his return home and his growing political and social awareness (Chapters 17–23, 90 pages). There is as well within this overall structure an attempt to tighten the action by having the third section reflect the first in a number of very precise and specific ways all of which illustrate the change which Paulin has undergone. A second significant difference between the two books concerns the role of the protagonist. In *Clarté* Paulin's progress towards the enlightenment of the title is carefully charted; his experience is an educative one and like, for example, Simon Bordes in Courtade's *La Place rouge* he moves from uncertainty and passivity to conviction and action. But in spite of various attempts to maintain a balance between Paulin's public role and his private life, and in spite of the first person narrative technique – a device which potentially at least should have enabled Barbusse to avoid the uncertainty of his own role in *Le Feu* – Paulin is never very convincing.

In the first and in many ways most successful section of the novel he is shown to be utterly passive, allowing his life to follow well established patterns and routines: 'Tous les jours de la semaine se ressemblent, du commencement à la fin. [. . .] je me laisse emporter par tout le monde' (p.1) and 'La même existence complexe et monotone m'emporte comme elle emporte tout le monde' (p. 45). An orphan, he has been brought up by an aunt. He works unthinkingly as a clerk, his petit bourgeois existence reflected in his need to save money ('comme tout le monde' p. 57), in his attitude to relations between the sexes and eventually to marriage with Marie. Even his local political role is shaped for and accepted by him without question: 'Je me trouve désigné pour la succession de Crillon au Conseil municipal. J'arriverai sans doute tôt ou tard à ce but. Je continue à devenir quelqu'un par la force des choses, sans m'en apercevoir, sans que personne, autour de moi, s'intéresse vraiment à moi [. . .] Mon avenir ressemblera à mon passé; il lui ressemble déjà' (p. 74). In keeping with this passivity and appropriate in view of his future enlightenment ('je vais vers ma lumière' p. 3), the majority of Barbusse's descriptions of Viviers (itself already containing perhaps the idea of a teeming, unthinking insect world) are dark or dull. It is a world where most, and those of the working class in particular, are kept in ignorance, and where the distinction between *les rois* and *le peuple* is maintained at all costs. The stag hunt ('L'animal était agenouillé par terre, écrasé, diminué' p. 77) or the killing of the captive bear by the visiting Austrian prince are clearly symbolic. Barbusse's description of the onlookers' acceptance of these brutal actions which only the drunken Brisbille dares question, contains an obvious condemnation. Paulin who challenges him expresses the average revanchist attitude and his reflections on his action are full of the kind of right-wing rhetoric made popular by Maurice Barrès: 'Je revins à la maison exalté par mon acte d'énergie, tout frémissant encore, fier et joyeux. J'ai obéi à la voix du sang. C'est le grand instinct ancestral qui m'a fait serrer les poings et m'a jeté tout entier, comme une arme, contre l'ennemi de tous' (p. 86).

Yet for Paulin's eventual conversion not to appear totally unconvincing or miraculous Barbusse needs also to suggest that he already has a potential for self-awareness not shared by others. His attitude to working-class people – 'la cohue noire, la foule' (p. 61) – is hesitant. Certainly they frighten him, and he has a momentary vision of future revolution: 'L'étendue immense d'hommes s'ébranle, crie, et roule dans le même sens le long du faubourg. Un inépuisable écho de clameurs nous entoure; c'est comme un enfer en activité encerclé dans un horizon de bronze' (p. 61). His own description of the effect he has on the one worker he gets close to is also revealing: '(il) me fait l'effet d'un animal qui fuit, en sautelant, dans les pénombres' (p. 61). However envious he may be of 'la pauvre fraternité des pavés' (p. 58) he is temperamentally quite unable to establish any kind of real contact with the working class. The anonymity which he is abliged to accept when he joins the army is important therefore ('Nous nous sommes habillés tous pareillement' p.98); so too is the enforced passivity ('On sait pour vous!' p. 100) which is an ironic comment on his earlier attitude in civilian life. Initially his patriotism holds firm and he is deeply impressed by Marcassin's outburst about 'la gloire de la France' full of right-wing rhetoric culled again from Barrès or Déroulède. But gradually his preconceptions are challenged and his initial feeling that he has in some way been treated unjustly gives way to a general uncertainty about the war. He discovers that people profit from it, that infantry men are kept in ignorance of developments and are required to take part in 'useless' manœuvres. He is introduced to the internationalist and pacifist ideas of Termite and is unable to explain with conviction to a fellow soldier – or more significantly to himself – why war should exist at all. For three chapters, symbolically entitled 'Les Ombres', 'Où vas-tu?' and 'Les Ruines', Paulin experiences the horrors of action. Much recalls the descriptions of war in *Le Feu*: forced marches and exercises, executions for indiscipline, the inadequacy of provisions and of ammunition, the appalling conditions of the trenches, the unremitting movement towards enemy lines at whatever cost, and so on. The same moments of shock and horror are also captured – barbed wire strewn with corpses or a body unexpectedly blown up: 'le soldat fut emporté par le vent en fragments immenses, enterré dans le ciel' (p.133). And the warscape as a whole is again evoked as though it were hell.

Although Paulin is shown to become increasingly indistinguishable from his fellow soldiers, he obstinately refuses for a while to be turned from his belief in and admiration for the war. For the wider socio-political dimensions of the book to be understood this attitude must change. Unlike the narrator in *Le Feu*, or indeed any of the characters in that novel, Paulin must realize – and be seen to realize – that not only the war, but the attitudes and interests which have caused it and which he is guilty of supporting, are wrong.

There are, as we have noted, suggestions in the first third of the novel that Paulin has the capacity for the conversion which is later to occur. His moment of truth finally arrives when, trapped in a shell hole, he is wounded: 'Un coup de lumière me remplit les yeux; toute la lumière. Je suis soulevé, je suis brandi sans cesse, par une lame inconnue au milieu d'une sphère de clarté extraordinaire [. . .] je tombe fantastiquement hors de ce monde, ayant eu le temps de me revoir dans cette cassure d'éclair, de penser à mes entrailles et à mon cœur jetés au vent, et d'entendre des voix qui, tout bas, se répètent au loin, au loin: Simon Paulin est mort à trente-six ans' (pp.171, 2). Given the first person narrative which Barbusse employs in *Clarté*, the kind of problems which confronted him in *Le Feu* might be thought to be reduced. But Barbusse clearly feels that the significance of Paulin's conversion requires a new, elevated language if it is to be fully appreciated. Thus the hint of St Paul's religious conversion, already implicit in the narrator's name, is made explicit in this passage. Furthermore his recovery, recorded at the end of Chapter 15 – 'je me réveille en poussant un léger cri comme un enfant qui naît' (p. 198) – and in the opening sentence of Chapter 17, 'Matin', is clearly more than physical: 'Je me suis rendormi dans le chaos puis je me suis réveillé comme le premier homme' (p. 199). What Barbusse resorts to in fact is a technique adopted by many religious novelists who accommodate the supernatural workings of faith, by moving their characters temporarily beyond the limits of normal referential experience. In Chapter 15 'De profundis clamavi' Barbusse's narration shifts between Paulin's delirium and explicitly religious visionary experience and open comment. Here the stress on the elemental nature of the war which we find in *Le Feu* and Barbusse's view of historical development merge. Initially Paulin's vision is of the formation of the earth and of the advent of man with his gradual awareness of the need for community: 'se réunir pour être plus forts, pour être tranquillisés, et même pour pouvoir vivre' (p. 175). This is followed rapidly by reflections on the common identity of man and on his being exploited in times of war. At this point Barbusse interposes his address to the universal soldier, the 'esclave moderne' (p. 183), whose error has been to accept unquestioningly the values and instructions of those in authority. And coupled with this is a criticism of the kind of literature – in particular the epic poem – which has glorified war. In fact the whole central portion of this chapter from which Paulin, even in a state of delirium, is almost completely absent, is given over to a violent anti-Barresian denunciation of 'la magie du passé et l'empoisonnement de la tradition' (p. 195). The chapter closes with Paulin's vision of Christ, 'l'homme de lumière et de simplicité' (p. 197), forbidding the rebuilding of churches and the reintroduction therefore of institutionalized christianity – the greatest of all mascarades according to Barbusse by which men have been regularly duped, and equally the greatest cause of conflict and war. And finally just as at the beginning of the chapter the situation in which Paulin found himself dissolved into the unreality of delirium, so too at the end does the hospital ward break into the subconscious world to re-establish him firmly among the living, converted and ready to begin his apostolic mission.

Whatever our reactions to *Clarté* as a whole this particular episode is in some respects rather more effective than, for example, the airman's account of the two masses or Bertrand's outburst in *Le Feu*. As the account of a delirium, with the presence of Paulin's immediate environment – the mud, rain, sound of shells, or the hospital bed – prompting new turns in his wandering mind, it is convincing. Where Barbusse's hand does become apparent, however, is not only in passages of direct address, but in the way Paulin also 'recalls' specific incidents and remarks from the past, each one signifying an attitude which he will subsequently reverse: for example, the references to Termite (p. 182), to Marcassin (p. 183) and importantly to Marie and her words: 'C'est magnifique comme on est belliqueux' (p. 186). Similar interference is also to be seen in the general control of style in this chapter: in the literary allusions, particularly to Dante (p. 190 and p. 191), and in the incidence of words indicating Paulin's growing enlightenment – *clarté, lumière, soleil, aube, blancheur, éclair*. But whereas in *Le Feu* similar features indicate the author's 'corrective' role, in *Clarté* the language in which the 'new' Paulin and Barbusse express ideas is basically the same. What Barbusse appears to imply therefore is that a certain level of language is essential if the kind of socio-political awareness he is trying to encourage is to be adequately presented. Working-class people have for too long been kept 'dans l'ignorance bestiale' (p. 187); worse still they have passively accepted this position. Even those characters like Brisbille and Termite who threaten to express an alternative view are unable to sustain it, so conditioned have they become by the role expected of them. Enlightenment, and in particular the expression of such enlightenment, will not occur overnight; leadership and instruction are vital before the 'enchaînement des mensonges' or the 'illusions qu'on entasse au-dessus de nous' can be destroyed. Paulin is brought to understand this. He accepts the invitation to become 'un de ces grands crieurs', and the final third of the novel is an account of his gradual realization not only of how his own life is assuming a new direction and purpose, but of how he can assist and influence others as well.

From the beginning of Chapter 17, symbolically entitled 'Matin', Paulin's physical and 'spiritual' recovery follow the same course: 'J'ai dormi. Je vois plus clair que la veille. Je n'ai plus ce voile qui était devant moi' (p. 201); 'lavé, simplifié, lucide [. . .] je voyais tout avec netteté, sans voile (p. 205); 'Il me semble [. . .] que je vois les choses comme elles sont [. . .] Je n'ai plus d'illusion qui déforme et qui cache' (p. 207). As mentioned earlier, this final section of the novel is a mirror image of the first: Paulin is faced with the same events and experiences as those described in the first eight chapters, in particular local celebrations in which religion and patriotism become mixed ('la communion en patriotisme' p. 237) and his own marriage. Thus at the village remembrance service with its eulogisms of war ('une si magnifique floraison d'heroïsmes qu'il ne faut pas la regretter' p. 230) he remains an outsider and for the first time actively voices – though to no immediate effect – his new spirit of rebellion:

> Solitaire au bord de cette foule, je me suis assis sur une borne qui est là. Je me sens glacé au contact des ces paroles, de ces commandements, qui enchaînent l'avenir au passé et le malheur au malheur. Je les ai déjà entendus retentir à jamais. Tout un monde de pensées gronde confusément en moi. A un moment, j'ai crié sourdement: Non! Cri difforme, protestation étranglée de toute ma foi contre toute l'erreur qui s'abat sur nous. Ce premier cri que j'ai hasardé parmi les hommes, je l'ai jeté presque comme un illuminé, mais presque comme un muet'. (p. 231)

Subsequently when Brisbille again expresses his anger and threatens the priest, Paulin now approves (p. 240) even though he does nothing to assist. A little later he refuses to salute the national flag at the march-past (p. 247). Similarly with the opening of the local war museum Paulin finds himself quite outraged by the familiar rehearsing of the standard attitudes about heroism or German militarism and aggression. Yet however well formulated his sense of revolt may be, he fails to translate it into action, a fact which he finally recognizes in the title chapter, 'Clarté'. The alternative is to encourage awareness in others through writing, and while Paulin protests his inability to do so – 'Ce n'est pas moi qui ajouterai sur cette blancheur l'écriture comme une lumière' (p. 265) – the chapter develops into an address to 'le peuple universel'. Reflective prose is now replaced by a series of exhortative paragraphs encouraging vigilance and action. Statements like 'L'humanité est le nom vivant de la vérité' (p. 251) or 'La vérité n'est révolutionnaire qu'à cause du désordre de l'erreur. La révolution, c'est l'ordre' (p. 288), have an aphoristic ring to them more suited to the manifesto or political essay than to the novel.

That Barbusse was perhaps aware of this is suggested by the

way in which during the final chapter in particular he refocuses attention on Paulin's marriage. The change in his relationship with Marie reflects in miniature one which should occur in society at large: 'Autrefois je t'aimais pour moi; aujourd'hui, je t'aime pour toi' (p. 288). This use of the personal and private to give pointed illustration to matters of wider social or political concern is something we find later in the work of Nizan and Vailland in particular. Barbusse, however, fails to find the right formula. The couple's relationship is over sentimentalized and, for all that he is shown to be a changed man, Paulin ceases to be consistent as a character. Earlier in the novel in 'De profundis clamavi' Barbusse usurps the role of his protagonist albeit only temporarily; by the end of the novel he does so completely, with the result that the dominant tone changes. In spite of Paulin's disclaimer of his own ability to convince through writing, *Clarté* develops into a statement of Barbusse's faith in the power of words and in books as actions. In this sense it is significantly different from *Le Feu*; control and schematization are much more apparent, and implicit in much of the novel's style is an acknowledgement that illustration alone is not sufficient, however powerful.

After *Clarté* Barbusse turned to fiction less frequently, but when he did, as in the volumes of short stories *Les Enchaînements* or *Faits Divers* (1928), passages of sharply observed realistic description are overshadowed by a moralizing tone and an emphasis on the plight of the enslaved individual and the absorbing power of bourgeois society. Caute's evaluation of *Clarté* can in fact be equally applied to all of Barbusse's subsequent imaginative writing: '(he) found himself unable to fashion an action from which the ideas, however tendentious, might seem to spring naturally'.[21] Throughout the twenties and until his death Barbusse practised his belief that as a left-wing intellectual he should be positively involved. Unlike Rolland he held that inactivity was a form of political conservatism. Frequently, through the columns of his journals *Clarté* and later *Monde*, he repeated the view that only within a collective organisation could the intellectual and the artist have the kind of constructive and positive impact which it was his duty to make. In his *Manifeste aux Intellectuels* (1927) for example we read: 'l'individu nous intéresse moins que l'ensemble, et nous laissons le particulier pour nous consacrer au collectif' (pp. 19, 20).[22] Yet for all his commitment and pursuit of this aim Barbusse could never bring himself to accept the narrowly orthodox and hard-line positions established by the Communist Party towards the end of the twenties. As a result both he and in particular *Monde* met with considerable opposition and criticism at the International Conference of Revolutionary Writers held at Kharkov in November 1930.

In Nizan's last novel *La Conspiration*, set in the late-twenties, the character of Régnier is generally recognized to be based on Barbusse. Whether or not his attitude was as disillusioned and as cynical as Nizan's description suggests is impossible to say, though there is no doubt that Barbusse was considerably hurt by events. With the changing political climate of the mid-thirties, the development of the European Peace Movement of which he was a leading member and the foundation of the Association des Ecrivains et Artistes révolutionnaires, Barbusse returned to favour. Yet however respected, he remained very much, like Rolland, a man of an earlier generation who, in spite of his anger about the war, was never fully able to share the more militant attitudes of people like Aragon or Nizan. As an imaginative writer too his emphasis on liberal humanist values and on idealistic visions of a new society suggest that he belongs to a nineteenth-century tradition rather than with the newly developing climate of socialist realism.

3 Sentimentality and Resignation: Charles-Louis Philippe

The son of a cobbler, Charles-Louis Philippe was born in Cérilly in 1874. In spite of his humble background and some ill-health, he enjoyed a successful school career until he failed the 'concours de Polytechnique et de Centrale' in 1894. Thereafter he lived in Paris, earned his keep by working in various clerical jobs for the city council, and devoted as much time as possible to literature. In 1894 he had some poems published in a Belgian review *Stella*: in 1897 the short stories, later grouped together as *Quatre Histoires de pauvre amour*, appeared in Lumet's review, *L'Enclos*. Two *nouvelles* (*La Bonne Madeleine et la Pauvre Marie*) were published at his own expense a year later, and between 1901 and his death in 1909 five full-length novels. A sixth unfinished one based on his father's life, *Charles Blanchard*, was published posthumously in 1912.[1]

From his letters, his life appears to have been somewhat unsettled, punctuated by a series of unhappy or ill-fated love affairs. Although not a prominent figure himself, he could name Mallarmé, Gide, Giraudoux, Jammes, Mirbeau and Lucien Jean amongst his acquaintances. His work, however, despite having been twice considered for the Prix Goncourt, never appears to have enjoyed a particularly high reputation. By comparison with Barbusse, of whom he was almost an exact contemporary, he could hardly be considered a socially or politically engaged writer; and even Mirbeau, to whom in temperament he was much closer, emerges as someone who had a much clearer social point to make in his books, however idiosyncratic. Yet Philippe's work is far from negligible. By both choice and treatment of his subjects, he offers a much more low-key alternative to the weight and militancy of Zola or Barbusse and, in so doing, anticipates the non-militant proletarian and populist writing of the post-wars.

To commemorate the fiftieth anniversary of Philippe's death, *Europe* devoted part of its September 1960 issue to a short memorial tribute compiled by Albert Fournier: 'Charles-Louis Philippe, cinquante ans après sa mort'. The attitudes and tone are what we might expect them to be. Almost without exception contributors refer approvingly to his having been unaffectedly 'of the people'. Giraudoux claims that Philippe is 'le seul de ces écrivains qui, né du peuple, n'eût pas trahi le peuple en écrivant'; Valéry that 'ce qui nous paraît surtout important c'est que Philippe ait voulu rester un homme du peuple'; Marcel Ray that 'il n'avait pas besoin d'aller au peuple, il en était'. Statements like these support what Philippe himself says in the only published work in which he discusses his attitudes towards novel writing or indeed life in general, the collection of letters to his Belgian friend, Henri Vandeputte. Yet in these, even though he repeatedly stresses his working-class origins and preferences, he claims to be quite apolitical. Of socialism for example and in connection with his collaboration since 1895 with the review, *L'Enclos,* he writes: 'cela ne m'inspire pas énormément; je suis le mouvement, voilà tout. Peut-être n'est-ce pas en ma faveur, mais j'aimerais beaucoup mieux rester chez moi à penser à ce que je veux écrire' (30 May 1897).[2] But he was not always so withdrawn. In the course of the following year, while studying prostitution in Paris – the subject of his next novel, *Bubu de Montparnasse* – we find him writing with an anger which reminds us of Mirbeau: 'quand on voit certaines choses de trop près on est plein de douleur comme un chien. On est tout en larmes. *On a des colères contre la Société et l'on devient anarchiste*' (4 December 1898. My italics).[3] Yet the fact remains that, however strong his feelings may have been, they did not lead him into any form of social or political action. This apparent reluctance to commit himself publicly is also reflected in his attitude to writing. Like Dabit or Guilloux in later years for whom social problems were a cause for grave concern but who similarly preferred, at least initially, to observe rather than to act, Philippe considered that his position as a writer should be entirely independent of movement or faction: 'L'artiste ne doit pas participer à une école. D'ailleurs une école, c'est un homme qui, plein d'orgueil, croit avoir trouvé la pie au nid, et la gueule partout. Quelques bonnes gens qui veulent le suivre y perdent leur personnalité. L'artiste est un bon ouvrier qui s'écoute et, dans son coin, avec candeur d'âme, écrit ce qu'il entend' (9 February 1897).[4] His claimed preference for simplicity and independence, however, did not always result in objective detachment. In his private life, Philippe appears to have wavered between resignation and revolt, between acceptance and rejection of the plight of the underprivileged, an uncertainty which is reflected in his novels and especially in the portrayal of certain characters. Furthermore, much, if not all, of what he wrote is characterized by sentimentality – 'je suis heureux et gai, heureux surtout quand je suis triste' (12 December 1896). As we shall see, this leads him to resort to a number of stylistic devices, all of which tend to romanticize the situations with which he deals and diminish the full impact which such issues as exploitation and victimization might otherwise have had.

Whatever its weaknesses, Philippe's early published writing, *Quatre Histoires de pauvre amour*, in some ways promised more than he proved himself able to sustain. Despite a clear sexual obsession (which he shared with Mirbeau and which his admirers and critics have either played down or ignored altogether), these stories strongly suggest that society is responsible for the problems or crimes with which they deal. In 'La Chair des Troix Gueux' for example, the account of a rape committed by three tramps, Philippe suggests that 'normal' feelings have so often been suppressed by the demands and pressures of family life or of society, that as in this case people have become perverted. In this, he strongly echoes both the tone and preoccupations of Mirbeau whose novels *Le Calvaire* (1886) and *L'Abbé Jules* (1888) deal with much the same theme. No doubt it was because of the promise of this early work that Lumet accepted these stories for publication in *L'Enclos*. But with *La Bonne Madeleine et la Pauvre Marie* published a year later,[5] Philippe only too clearly indicated the direction that most of his subsequent work would follow.

These, ostensibly, are simple tales: case histories almost of two village girls, one of whom dies through lack of love, the other who fails to find it on account of her ugliness. As will often be the case, Philippe clearly intends to demonstrate that there is a beauty in suffering, that the two girls should be seen as martyrs of their situation. But the pathetic and religious sentimentality suggested by the title breaks through on almost every page destroying any attempt Philippe may make to introduce more straightforward or serious observations of a social nature. The description of the carpenter who replaces a pane of broken glass in Marie's window is brisk, the syntax of Philippe's sentences in one way nicely reflecting the man's workman-like attitude to the job: 'Il vint le lendemain matin, celui qu'on espère, avec une vitre, une règle et quelques outils. Il vint, comme il faut pour travailler, avec ses vêtements de chaque jour et son visage d'ouvrier' (p. 118). But the tone is wrong; the carpenter is rendered impersonal and almost abstract by the repetition and by the messianic ring of 'celui qu'on espère'. Also typical of his style is his commentary in the closing pages of the book on the fate of all young women in Marie's situation. Here the recourse to religious and pastoral imagery, the use of direct address to character and reader alike, and the way in which Philippe both withdraws from Marie and yet voices her thoughts for her, result in a dilution of any impact which the passage may have had:

Mais, passé vingt ans, les jeunes filles s'ennuient parce qu'elles ne sont pas faites pour travailler sans but à leurs robes de couturières, parce que leur sein devrait concevoir et parce que leur cœur devrait chérir. Un peu plus tard, il y a un soulèvement de leur vie qui veut, ah! qui veut violemment goûter à l'amour. C'est la dernière palpitation de leurs forces, c'est le cramponnement suprême, pauvre naufragé, à l'épave de bois qui peut le mener au port. Marie fut rejetée loin du salut par une petite vague.

Jeunes filles qui aviez seize ans, vous devenez des vieilles filles noires et ridicules. Petit troupeau rieur, vous devenez le troupeau de vieilles bêtes dociles et vous mangez sans joie l'herbe de la prairie, en attendant la mort brutale comme un boucher.

Et Marie a eu vingt-cinq ans, vingt-six ans, elle a maintenant trente ans. Chaque jour sa vie est ennuyée comme je vous l'ai dit, et chaque jour passe. Les années sont faites avec de gros morceaux de jours et passent aussi. Chacune d'elles apporte une ride à un visage et déssèche un cœur. [. . .] Marie a compris la vie comme elle devait la comprendre. [. . .] Marie s'est résignée à la sienne, mais non sans avoir fait des réflexions amères. Est-il possible de ne pas se plaindre de ce qui blesse? Marie s'est dit: La vie est faite de grosses actions matérielles, aussi les grosses âmes peuvent parcourir le monde en y trouvant des joies, mais les âmes délicates ont beaucoup à souffrir'. (pp. 135, 5)

Suffering is indeed what the book is principally about, but nowhere does it even remotely resemble that of a Cathérine Maheu or a Germinie Lacerteux. The pastoral setting for the whole story, and such details as the long description of Madeleine's voice as that of a bird (p. 54), or the absurd address to a bowl of soup (p. 80) – all of which may remind us of the writings of another of Philippe's preferred authors, Francis Jammes – ensure that bitterness is always tempered. In addition, Philippe's account of events remains pastel in hue (the adjectives *blanc, rose, blond* and above all *bleu* dominate) and mild in tone (*pur, humble, simple, suave, tranquille, délicat, doux*) characteristics of his work as a whole, attributed by some commentators to the influence of the symbolist poets.

While it would be misleading to pretend that such limitations in both subject and style do not continue to be characteristic of Philippe's work, three novels in particular deserve some attention for the ways in which they illustrate the development in his attitude towards the poor and underprivileged amongst whom, we should not forget, he liked to count himself: *Bubu de Montparnasse* (1901), *Le Père Perdrix* (1902) and *Croquignole* (1906). Of these the first, dealing with prostitution, is Philippe's most overtly 'social' novel. It is also the only one for which he appears to have relied extensively on some kind of elementary research and documentation.[6]

The idea for *Bubu* came to him as the direct result of a brief affair he had with a flower maker turned prostitute, Maria. To judge from his correspondence with Vandeputte his attitude towards her appears to have been one of condescension: 'Je m'intéresse à sa souffrance, j'aurais du plaisir à la former, comme j'ai du plaisir à former des petits enfants' (8 September 1898). Later in the same year (26 October) he recounts how, having suffered from ill health (presumably from venereal disease) and given the miserable wages paid for such piece work, Maria has decided to become a regular prostitute ('elle l'est déjà un petit peu'). His remonstrations seem to have had little effect, and he is left deploring the fact that she has been forced into the situation by circumstances. His words could again easily have been those of Mirbeau and remind us once more of his early short stories: 'Lorsque la Société pervertit certaines âmes, on sent qu'on est en présence d'un crime.' His decision to write a novel 'où l'on verrait tout au long une jeune ouvrière devenir une prostituée' (4 December 1898) is prompted therefore not only by first-hand experience ('Marie [. . .] est un trésor de documentation'), but by indignation and anger as well.

Throughout 1899 he repeatedly refers to his attempts to document himself on the world of prostitution, yet all the while his comments are coloured and modified by certain preconceived ideas and values. As we might expect the prostitute is seen as a helpless and above all innocent being, 'une pauvre créature chaste que la Destinée a choisie pour faire le mal. Elle n'est plus elle-même, mais une partie du Destin' (15 February 1899). While in *Bubu* we do not find the kind of emphasis which Zola might place on the workings of an anonymous destructive force, we do have prostitution presented as *economically* unavoidable for many and, once accepted, inescapable. Philippe is quite direct and open in his accusations, even though the emphasis on inevitability does alleviate the responsibility of those like Bubu who lives by prostitution: 'Bubu devint souteneur parce qu'il vivait dans une société pleine de riches qui sont forts et déterminent les vocations. Ils veulent des femmes avec leur argent. Il faut bien qu'il y ait des souteneurs pour leur en donner' (pp. 64, 5). And as Pierre Hardy observes quite without irony later in the novel: 'Nous vivons dans un monde où les pauvres doivent souffrir' (p. 154).

This last view would seem to be essentially that of Philippe himself, and much of the book describes how the poor, individually or as a class, respond to the conditions of their existence passively and even instinctively like animals. The final description of prostitutes as 'des bêtes passives que l'on mène au pré communal' (p. 192) is typical of many. The older prostitutes are 'les vieilles à pas lourds comme des vaches qui font station aux coins des rues' (p. 144); Berthe is 'lasse comme une bête rendue' (p. 158) or 'une bête abattue' (p. 169); the mother of the street singers has '(des) seins bouffis de bête usée' (p. 63) and so on. In addition – and here Philippe differs somewhat from others like Huysmans, the Goncourts or Zola[7] who had also written about prostitution – he endows such resignation with a sense of religious dignity. Paraphrasing Dostoievsky he writes: 'Celui à qui il a été donné de souffrir davantage, c'est qu'il est digne de souffrir

davantage' (p. 108).[8] The result of this is not only that the full
shock of the exploitative nature of prostitution is actually presented as a form of inverted virtue. Like that of the girl of the
early short stories, and indeed like that of nearly all Philippe's
female characters, it is Berthe's lot to be exploited. This impression is further accentuated by some of the descriptions of Paris.
Throughout Philippe's work the contrast between the inherent
corruptive influence of the town and the pastoral innocence and
purity of the countryside is marked. In *Bubu* (and in a way which
extends the use of animal imagery elsewhere) Paris is described as
being both superficially theatrical and animated by lust:

> Les arcs voltaïques s'entouraient d'un halo et, de l'un à
> l'autre, éclairant l'air entre les maisons, formaient un grand
> canal lumineux qui débordait les toitures, montait jusqu'au ciel
> et lui jetait son feu. Cette atmosphère vous baignait dans un
> fluide subtil, dans un bain électrique et pénétrant. Puis des
> vents chauds, l'exhalaison d'une nuit d'été faisaient Paris
> comme une bête hurlante, avec des sueurs et des yeux fous, et
> qui soufflait son haleine jusqu'à en défaillir. Un cri répondait à
> l'autre, un passant éveillait un désir, les lumières l'allumaient
> comme un fétu, chaque vie se gonflait sur le boulevard et criait
> aussi, comme la bête d'amour, jusqu'au fond des cœurs
> défaillants. (p. 62)

Elsewhere we find it likened to an animal systematically
devouring the poor. In Chapter 1 the street singers are typical
victims: 'Paris les avait pris dans sa main qui broie et tous quatre,
les bons et les méchants, les avait broyés' (p. 64); and in a later
description of prostitutes at work the streets are 'fortes et [. . .]
mordent la vie avec leurs machoires' (p. 150).

Were Philippe's account of prostitution as one admittedly
marked form of exploitation and suffering to be limited to such
features as these, *Bubu* would have considerable weight. In many
respects the novel rings true; as Poulaille was to claim later,
Philippe gives the impression of writing not as an observer but as
a participant.[9] But Philippe's position is not quite so clear. While
he may quite successfully convey the idea that there is no real
economic alternative to prostitution, he also suggests that if this is
the prevailing system, then those who are able to use it should do
so in order to give some purpose to their lives. The result is a

moral ambiguity which colours the whole book. Criminal activity of all kinds is simply not to be judged by 'normal' standards. Thus stealing is condoned (pp. 109, 110 and pp. 132–4), and Le Grand Jules, who is both burglar and murderer, and for whom imprisonment is an accepted part of life, is described in terms befitting a romantic hero: 'Il agissait fermement selon sa volonté. Il savait briser une serrure et pouvait tuer un homme avec simplicité. Les femmes l'entouraient d'amour comme des oiseaux qui chantent le soleil et la force. Il était un de ceux que nul ne peut assujettir, car leur vie, plus noble et plus belle, comporte du danger' (p. 77). The 'agents de mœurs', responsible for the maintenance of law and order are also, without apparent cause, described as 'malpropres comme leur métier' (p. 51). And most disturbing of all is the fact that such ambiguity is reflected in Philippe's undisguised admiration for Bubu himself who, despite his limitations, has bourgeois ambitions (p. 80) and believes in the rights and natural superiority of the strongest (p. 79).[10]

The presentation of the issue in *Bubu* is further obscured by certain aspects of Philippe's style. As we have already noted the use of animal imagery is particularly noteworthy. So too is the description of Berthe's room in the opening paragraphs of Chapter 4, with its repeated emphasis on dullness and squalor contrasting sharply with the earlier description of the brightly lit streets. And, again, structurally the novel is not without merit. As in most, characters and situation are presented the first half, the plot is developed in the second; chapters dealing with Bubu and Louis alternate with one another. But it is in his attempt to dignify his characters and in his own role of narrator that Philippe reveals his uncertainty. Thus while suggestions of martyrdom may indeed be appropriate in certain descriptions of Berthe, elsewhere attempts to add stature by reference to historical or biblical characters and places – Charlemagne (p. 78), Adam (p. 101), the Nile (p. 135) – are merely out of place. Particularly noticeable is the scene in Chapter IV in which Jules and Bubu sit outside a café and discuss syphilis: 'Les passants défilaient devant eux qui, pour s'occuper, les regardaient et les jugaient d'une phrase brève et souvent ironique. Cela rappelait le jour de la Création, alors qu'Adam, le roi du monde, assis au pied d'un chêne, voyant passer les animaux, les examinait et les nommait' (p. 101).

Even if Philippe's admiration for such characters is responsible for inflation of this kind he seems generally incapable of conveying dignity through simplicity. And closely related to this is his shifting role as a narrator. As Bruno Vercier has observed the principal male characters in *Bubu* (and indeed in all his novels) reflect in different ways aspects (real or imagined) of Philippe's own nature: reflectiveness (Louis), weakness (Pierre), strength (Bubu). But this 'multiplicité du "je"'[11] does not justify the manner in which, in an attempt to ensure that his points are clear, Philippe leaves objective description in order to explain his characters' thoughts (p. 177), address them directly, identify himself with them (pp. 95 and 104) or involve the reader (p. 75). His narrative is also punctuated by statements which read all too often like maxims. The result is a book which hovers indeterminately between an imaginative account of a real social problem, a vehicle for a number of Philippe's reflections on life in general and a projection of his own inner contradictions and ambitions.

However, even if ultimately *Bubu* has more to tell us about Philippe than about prostitution, it remains his most social novel in the sense that it deals with an issue of public concern. In no other work did he venture beyond the bounds of his own immediate experience, and certainly did not rely on the kind of documentation which had provided its framework. Instead in his next two novels, *Le Père Perdrix* amd *Croquignole*,[12] he turned to worlds with which he was more directly connected – Cérilly in the first and his life as an office worker in Paris in the second. Once again we find the same debate between resignation and revolt, accompanied, especially in the first novel, by a number of open reflexions on class conflict. This is not to suggest that they are more militant novels – indeed each in his own way is decidedly resigned and pessimistic – more so even than *Bubu* – in that they offer no real alternative to the kind of life which the characters are obliged to endure.

Set in his own region of France and based partly on his own father's life (a subject more extensively treated in *Charles Blanchard*) *Le Père Perdrix* gives the impression of being a much more controlled piece of writing than any of his earlier works. This is particularly true in the way Philippe describes local society. The neat divisions into *ouvriers pauvres, ouvriers aisés, bourgeois républicains* and *bourgeois réactionnaires* come across as being those which the poor believe exist and avoid an oversimplified worker-bourgeois contrast which might otherwise have developed. With more success than in *Bubu* Philippe observes from the inside. Although he continues to identify himself with a number of different characters he frequently achieves a nicety of observation, often marred in other novels by his search for effect. Thus the poverty of the Perdrix family is simply but well conveyed by the description of an ordinary meal: 'Ils mangeaient très vite, avec de gros couteaux en fer de dix sous, qui pouvaient couper de grosses bouchées de pain mais ne coupaient que de petites bouchées de fromage' (p. 64). Similarly captured is the father's *sense* of social distinctions: 'Lorsqu'un bourgeois passait, il le sentait d'avance à son pas plus léger, à ce pas qui a l'habitude des parquets cirés' (p. 87).

In terms of theme what Philippe again sets out to do in this novel, and in *Croquignole*, is to establish a context in Part One and explore the consequences of it in Part Two. Thus in the opening five chapters, social divisions, the influence of money, the question of care for the elderly and sick, attitudes to work and to professional qualifications are treated sympathetically, but with few signs of excessive indignation. Thereafter, however, we find a distinct change. Each of the last five chapters deals in turn with a specific event and bears implicitly or explicitly a strong social or moral comment. Chapter 1 contains Jean's return to the village after his support for the workers against the management; 2 contrasts the grossness of bourgeois living epitomized by Edmond Lartigaud with the growing emancipation of Perdrix; 3 deals with Jean's revolt against his family and his father's advice to accept (resign himself to) life on terms dictated by the bourgeoisie; 4 recounts the death of Perdrix's wife and his growing inability to cope with life; 5 contains his death in the alien environment of Paris. As in Part One Philippe is at his best when he deals with something of which he has direct experience himself. His descriptions of Lartigaud may at times verge on caricature, but they are also convincing as projections of Perdrix's own thoughts, and, often by being registered through the impersonal *on*, become as well a general observation on social distinctions: 'L'autre [Lartigaud] avait tellement mangé depuis un an que les couches de graisses s'amoncelaient et que, jour par jour, on aurait pu, les compter. On le roulait comme cela, assis dans une petite voiture, dans les allées de son jardin. Il s'était mis aux fleurs et jamais on n'aurait pu supposer, lui qui était un bourgeois, qu'il montrerait tant de patience et tant de minutie' (pp. 163, 64). Such grossness is sharply contrasted with and directly echoed within a few pages in the description of Perdrix's own failing health and in particular of his varicose ulcer: 'une pourriture intérieure qui sortait par couches et s'accroissait, pareille à une mauvaise fortune qui s'accroît en mangeant les pauvres' (p. 167, 68).

Contrasts of this kind are worked into the second half of the novel quite extensively and to effect. Unlike *Bubu* or *Croquignole* in which bourgeois values are glimpsed by some as goals to be aimed for, *Le Père Perdrix* suggests that even if they are not to be destroyed, neither are they to be admired. The fact remains, however, that they do exist and in the main dominate the social and economic pattern of life in the village. Resignation again prevails, and it is tempting to see Perdix's failing eyesight (references to this open and close the novel) as a symbol of his class's ultimate failure to recognize the extent of their plight. Furthermore the one attempt at revolt is only temporarily successful. Whereas in *Bubu* there is a sense in which Bubu gets the better of the society to which he belongs by exploiting it, Jean Bousset merely causes temporary unrest and leaves having in the long term, it is suggested, achieved nothing.

Although for his next novel *Croquignole* Philippe relied less on recollection and drew instead, as in *Bubu*, on his immediate environment of Paris he continued to explore the same problem. *Croquignole* deals with the repetitive and stifling nature of certain kinds of work. Philippe presents us with two groups of characters. First four office workers and second two women, one a prostitute, the other a shirt maker who uses her garret room as her workshop. Resignation to the pattern and conditions of work is pronounced. In the office Paulat rarely speaks and is frequently referred to by Philippe and by his fellow clerks as an animal; Félicien works out of a sense of family responsibility ('J'avais besoin de gagner honnêtement mon pain quotidien' p. 41); Claude Buy, who closely resembles Pierre Hardy in *Bubu*, feels that it is his lot in life to work and that society suffers from too many who act irresponsibly (p. 53). Of the two women Angèle has allowed her work to dominate her life to such an extent that her only alternative occupations are the necessary ones of eating and sleeping, and even these are reduced to a bare minimum. Her sewing machine too symbolically blocks the view (over the Montparnasse cemetery) from her window. Typically her resignation to work endows her with a kind of religious dignity: 'Elle apparaissait toute modeste, toute honnête et comme entourée par l'amour du travail. Parfois elle posait ses deux mains l'une sur l'autre, en croix, à la hauteur de ses seins, s'inclinait un peu vers la droite et battait des paupières, en silence' (p. 62).

These attitudes are further reinforced by descriptions – the office with its furniture and equipment (pp. 3–10) and the tenements in which each floor indicates in a particular way – by the style of the doors or by the absense of carpeting for example – various social distinctions (pp. 55–8). This is the familiar passive world of Philippe's novels against which are set the two remaining characters both of whom succeed in breaking away from it: Mme Fernande through prostitution, Croquignole by virtue of an unexpected and large legacy. The two groups of characters are also interconnected through the relationships which develop between Croquignole and Mme Fernande, and Louis and Angèle. In addition Croquignole finally seduces Angèle whereupon she is abandoned by Claude and, full of shame, commits suicide. Croquignole himself uses all but his last few francs on high living and, having revisited the office after an absence of two years and having found its atmosphere intolerable, shoots himself. Claude, Félicien and Paulat are left to their routine, mundane existence: Mme Fernande to a life of parasitism.

Bruno Vercier has described *Croquignole* (which he sees possibly as Philppe's masterpiece) as '(une) exaltation de la libération'.[13] His assessment, especially in the light of the two previous novels, might be challenged, however. In Part Two, Chapter 3 in which Croquignole seduces Angèle, Philippe introduces into his text the image of a captive zebra in the Jardin des Plantes. Now while there is no doubt that the animal is in an alien environment, Croquignole is not. His attempt to escape does not indicate a qualitative difference between him and his class of the kind which exists between the zebra and prison-like atmosphere of his compound. (At this point in the narrative Philippe introduces an incongruous and fanciful image of the zebra leaping over the zoo wall.) Certainly Philippe has stressed Croquignole's carefree and generous nature from the outset (p. 29), but his rejection of a working-class life style is only made possible by an external factor – money. Furthermore his ambitions when realized are both superficial – sex, food and clothes – and short-lived. If Philippe is exalting freedom there is nothing in this novel, any more than in *Bubu*, to show how the restrictive social and economic forces which control the lives of such people can be altered other than by recourse to those very factors which impose the restriction initially. In their attempts to escape Croquignole and Mme Fernande, like Bubu before them, 's'embourgeoisent'.

The difference between *Croquignole* and the earlier works, however, is in the two suicides. In the case of Croquignole himself it is implied that no matter how it has been realized, freedom, once tasted, allows no alternative. With Angèle the implication is rather different. For her the moment of escape which she enjoys with Croquignole is subsequently considered by her to have been a betrayal of her class's values, and death is the only possible answer. If this is so then Philippe appears to be saying that true freedom may indeed be possible but only at a price. In *Bubu* the strongest are shown to be capable of manipulating the prevailing system for their own benefit even though there is no suggestion that they thereby escape from it. In *Le Père Perdrix* Jean Bousset's show of political strength is short-lived and ultimately without effect, while his disappearance from the novel suggests that he too will be reabsorbed by society. In *Croquignole* so strong are the pressures to conform, that a refusal to do so allows for no alternative other than death. If indeed *Croquignole* is the exaltation of freedom which Vercier sees it to be, it is so only in a very limited sense. What emerges much more strongly (and continues to be apparent in Philippe's remaining works) is the way in which pressure to conform results in witting resignation on the part of the majority. From Berthe and Louis to Claude and beyond to Charles Blanchard the pattern remains essentially the same.

This particular aspect of Philippe's work is equally central to the whole concept of proletarian writing as it develops in the late 1920s – hence Poulaille's admiration. Philippe is rarely content to convey the dignity of humility and resignation by an appropriately simple style – an equally important consideration for Poulaille. Instead the apparently indiscriminate attempts to heighten the tone of his narrative or to poeticize certain features of it – all of which tend to diffuse the social point of *Bubu* – are to be found throughout his later works as well. This is not to suggest that there are not signs of increasing control and of an awareness that style and theme might be more carefully matched. As we have noted the structure of *Le Père Perdrix* works well; so too does that of *Croquignole*, in which having introduced all his characters and relevant information in Part One Philippe resolves his intrigue neatly in Part Two. The use of *on* to embrace both the old man's reflection on society in *Le Père Perdrix* with his own, or the introduction of images especially those relating to animals or to the crushing power of Paris are frequently successful. The routine nature of clerical life is suggested by the list-like description of the office furniture, and Angèle's small world is similarly evoked with effect. But all too often the use of an inappropriate image disturbs the tone of the narrative. In *Le Père Perdrix* brandy is described as 'un ange aux ailes étendues' (p. 116); in *Croquignole* a *vermouth-cassis* has similar unlikely religious associations: 'le vermouth attaque l'estomac et développe en lui on ne sait quelle amertume qui fait que l'on va jusqu'à souffrir. C'est à ce moment qu'arrive le cassis, avec la douceur, avec le baume, avec le mot de Jésus: "Bienheureux ceux qui souffrent, parce qu'ils seront consolés!"' (p. 99). We also find the same Jammesian appeal to or use of objects and weather, and a preference for pastel colours. And as narrator, even though his intrusion is less apparent than in *Bubu*, Philippe frequently moves from one position to another to moralize, to address character and/or reader at will, or even to introduce himself. When, in *Croquignole*, Claude and Angèle spend a day in the country on the outskirts of Paris, Angèle's impressions are recorded (in a way which recalls Germinie's excursion in *Germinie Lacerteux*) in a language which, though effective, is clearly not her own. Indeed Philippe for once explains: 'Angèle pensait à de grandes choses qu'elle ne savait comment exprimer' (p. 189). Similarly in Chapter 3 when Croquignole entertains his colleagues to lunch, Philippe's reflections on nature (compared to the Garden of Eden, p. 95) or the manner in which it is given a voice of its own (p. 97), do much to detract from an otherwise quite striking account of the men's pleasure and, above all, sense of escape.

Philippe's premature death in 1909 closed a career which, if only in quantity, promised much. Already in the course of a period of twelve years he had published seven volumes (of which five were novels) together with articles and short stories in *La Revue blanche*, *Le Canard sauvage* and *Le Matin*. Whether in terms of range or quality there would have been any substantial development in his work must remain a matter of speculation, but on the evidence which exists it seems likely that he would have continued to write much in the same vein. The suggestion that his discovery of Nietzsche in 1900 ('un remède à mes maux, un grand cordial qui me fait très fort') encouraged him in his depiction of strongminded individuals who rebel against society seems to have little foundation. Whatever private fantasies he may have had Philippe seems ultimately to have been incapable of writing convincingly about anything other than the lives of the poor and about their resignation to the conditions of their existence. The signs of anger in his early work remain at best muted and criticism of society tends to be implied rather than directly stated. He rarely if ever matches the satiric bitterness of Mirbeau and clearly lacks the massive vision of Zola. Had he survived the war of course, and had he seen the decimation of his own class, his attitude might well have changed, but it is difficult to imagine that he would have been even remotely tempted to follow the path taken by Barbusse.

Yet however apolitical and asocial he and his work may have been, he does have links with some of his contemporaries and anticipates certain kinds of writing in the post-war years. Historical authenticity – to become an important consideration of socialist realism for example – is unimportant for Philippe; instead what matters is the need to convey a sense of intimate involvement, of treating his subjects from the inside and of identifying with them. In spite of the often inflated and inappropriate style with which he then seeks to give stature to his characters, these are aspects of his works which link him with both proletarian and populist writing in general and with the early Guilloux or Dabit in particular.

Part II

Introduction

In 1919 in his essay 'Crise de l'Esprit' Paul Valéry wrote: 'toutes les choses essentielles de ce monde ont été affectées par la guerre, ou plus exactement, par les circonstances de la guerre'.[1] Such a view was scarcely an exaggeration. After four years of savage destruction, a huge area of France had been laid waste, and families almost without exception had mourned the loss of at least one of their number. Society, it was felt by many would never be the same again, values had been destroyed, fragmentation and decay seemed inevitable, a Spenglerian[2] gloom was expressed in phrases like 'la décadence de la civilisation', 'la fin d'une culture', 'l'effondrement du monde', 'la fin de l'humanisme'. Within this climate – what Marcel Arland neatly defined in his essay 'Littérature et politique' (1924) as a modern 'mal de siècle'[3] – new forces and attitudes began to emerge. In particular it was the period when the intellectual – *le clerc* as he became known – came into his own and when literature too was increasingly expected, as Nizan was to argue in 1935, to be 'responsible'.[4]

The idea of the writer becoming involved with and expressing opinions about social and political issues was not new of course. But in the memories of many there was still the turmoil surrounding the Dreyfus Affair of the last years of the nineteenth century. It was during these years that the noun 'intellectual' had first been used by Maurice Barrès as a derogatory term for those like Zola or Anatole France who had expressed their support for Dreyfus in the name of freedom and justice for the individual, irrespective (in Barrès' view) of any concern for the security of the state.[5] After the war, such involvement and indeed partisanship were much more usual, and intellectuals responded in a variety of specific ways not only to individual events, but to the social, political and cultural climate as a whole. In very general terms, the two basic kinds of response can be seen. On the one hand there were those who, whatever their political persuasions, believed it to be their duty not only to express an opinion but to be active in attempting to give society a new direction and purpose. On the other there were those (far fewer) who considered that the intellectual should be apolitical and remain apart from such activity. For the latter, Julien Benda with his essay *La Trahison des clercs* (1927) was the principal spokesman.[6] Although he later turned to the Left, as a self-confessed platonist Benda believed throughout his career that, like the Guardians of *The Republic*, the intellectual was a privileged creature enjoying a divine right of pronouncement. He belonged, Benda claimed, to 'une classe d'hommes qui [. . .] glorifie des biens qui passent le temporel'.[7] A similar view had already been expressed in 1915 by Romain Rolland who, in his essay 'Au-dessus de la mêlée', had written: 'L'esprit est la lumière. Le devoir est de l'élever au-dessus des tempêtes et d'écarter les nuages qui cherchent à l'obscurcir'.[8] Emmanuel Berl too argued that the intellectual had a duty: 'd'abord de rester intellectuel, et de rester dans le monde moderne, ensuite de bien résister aux tentations diverses qui le guettent . . .'.[9] And even Henry de Montherlant, whose taste for action and authoritarian attitudes ultimately pushed him towards the Right, could see the dangers only too clearly: 'Un homme qui tient à son intelligence, quand il sent prendre l'action trop à cœur, doit avoir le même réflexe qu'a un homme qui tient à sa qualité morale, quand il se voit acquérir de la popularité: il doit se devenir suspect et se surveiller'.[10]

In the main, however, the temptation to become involved precisely in the way these writers believed to be a danger proved to be irresistible. On the Right, the influence of Barrès and of the Action Française (despite its being condemned by the Catholic Church in 1926) were important, as in a more precise way was the development from the late-1920s of the quasi-fascist Ligues (Jeunesses patriotes, Le Faisceau, Orde Nouveau, for example). Individuals like Henri Massis, Drieu la Rochelle and Robert Brasillach championed law and order, turned to tradition and the past for inspiration and in several cases were seduced by the mystical appeal of Hitler's national socialism in the 1930s. But as a whole the French Right lacked a clear political direction, with the result that its intellectuals tended to act and write more as individuals than as party members. On the Left the situation was quite different, especially with the creation in 1920 of the French Communist Party. However various the strands of pre-war socialism and vague the Left's growing concern for humanitarian values in general had been, the war in particular had been responsible for the growth of a clearer sense of common purpose than on the Right. And for many left-wing intellectuals the emergence of a firm political discipline (whatever the subsequent vagaries of Communist policy) was welcome, providing a direction hitherto lacking. Not surprisingly, not all were willing to conform to the extent demanded of them, even when revolution was apparently a shared objective. The most notable examples perhaps were the Surrealists. In the *Second Manifeste du Surréalisme* (1930), André Breton wrote: 'Tout est à faire, tous les moyens doivent être bons à employer pour ruiner les idées de *famille*, de *patrie*, de *religion*'[11] – all, we might recall, vital ingredients for the maintenance of Barrès nation. But of those Surrealists who enthusiastically applied for Party membership in 1927 only Aragon remained after 1933. Not all allowed their individualism (or self-indulgence) to have such influence. The equally radical Philosophies group of Friedmann, Politzer, Lefebvre and Nizan expressed views similar to those of the surrealists, but unlike them remained faithful (with the exception of Nizan) and were responsible for spreading Party directives in various ways.

But it was not simply the matter of political discipline which caused problems for some. Equally disquieting in a different way were the questions of socio-cultural allegiance and betrayal. For the intellectual of bourgeois origins, acceptance of Communism automatically demanded espousal of working-class values and causes. This in turn inevitably raised the question of communication with that class. To what extent was it possible for someone from the bourgeoisie to respond, however sympathetically, to the problems of those of a lower class and, moreover, in a language which was accessible to them? Conversely the danger for those of working-class background who managed to penetrate the dominant institutions of the educational system, was that their original identity and simplicity could be damaged if not lost altogether. Jean Guéhenno was one who felt this problem acutely: 'Dans la réalité, je m'appliquais de toutes mes forces à retrouver l'unité de mon âme plébienne. Ce fut longtemps en vain. [. . .] On ne lit pas impunément les livres. [. . .] La culture a quelquefois d'abord cet effet de détruire en nous le caractère.'[12]

Whatever personal feelings or even awareness about such subtle interplay may have been, there was also, as Marcel Martinet echoing Trotsky pointed out in the 1953 Preface to his *Culture Prolétarienne*, the simple fact that French society had not undergone a revolution of the kind experienced in the USSR and in consequence remained divided by class. In addition, he went as far as to say that, in terms of culture, a specifically working-class one was impossible, as long as French society remained essentially bourgeois in character. This was only marginally less pessimistic than the more pragmatic view of Victor Serge expressed seven years earlier in *Monde* (3 November 1929): 'Il n'y a pas, il ne peut pas y avoir dans la société capitaliste d'écrivains ouvriers; l'apprentissage du métier d'écrivain est incompatible avec le travail à l'usine: huit heures par jour pour gagner de quoi vivre médiocrement.'

Even from these few examples it is obvious that the whole relationship between intellectuals, writers and the Left was a complex one from the beginning, and that individual responses were many and various. For the purpose of this study, however, two facts in particular are to be stressed. The first is that not only did the PCF provide a new political discipline, it also eventually acted as a channel for a number of directives concerning art and literature which originated in the Soviet Union. The second is quite simply that through the activities not only of Party members, but of sympathizers as well, the presence and conditions of working-class society were reaffirmed.

The influence of the Soviet Union on literary and cultural matters in France led in particular from 1934 onwards to the debate concerning the development of socialist realism. This was not the only 'contact' however. The whole attempt in the newly-formed Soviet to establish during the early 1920s a genuine proletarian culture (the *proletcult*) also made its impression. Influences of this kind were not of course immediate, but regularity of contact between France and the Soviet Union was maintained in various ways. In August 1920 Raymond Lefebvre defied allied blockades in order to be the French representative at the ten-nation Proletcult conference in Moscow and in 1927 Barbusse and Francis Jourdain attended the one at which the International Union of Revolutionary Writers (RAPP) was formed. In 1930 Aragon and Sadoul went to the second Soviet Writers' Congress at Kharkov; in 1934 Aragon, Nizan, Malraux,

Bloch and others were present at the conference which was almost entirely responsible for the formulation of the principles of socialist realism. And so on. Contacts such as these together with many individual private visits or, for example, official placements like that of Victor Serge as *Clarté*'s Moscow correspondent between 1922 and 1926 ensured a regular transmission of information and did much to maintain a level of interest which in turn led to considerable debate.

For our present purposes four areas of this activity are of particular interest and importance. First, the role of Barbusse and especially of his two reviews *Clarté* and *Monde* as forums for discussion; second, the development of populism under the guidance of Léon Lemonnier and André Thérive; third, that of proletarian literature and the influence of Henri Poulaille; fourth, the establishment of the Association des Ecrivains et Artistes révolutionnaires (AEAR), of its journal *Commune* and the response to the theories of socialist realism. The interplay of these elements is far more complex than such a simple division indicates, but in them it is possible to discern both the continuation of the kind of nineteenth-century tradition we have already examined, and the beginnings of a new politically inspired and militant literature which was to develop even more vigorously after the Second World War.

4 Proletarian and Populist Writing

1 DEBATE

(a) *Barbusse, 'Clarté' and 'Monde'*

As we have already noted Barbusse's career as an imaginative writer faded during the 1920s when, having joined the PCF, he assumed the role of one of the leading left-wing intellectuals of his generation. His reputation as a vigorous spokesman and essayist developed rapidly, his ideas and theories being expressed in pamphlets like *La Lueur dans l'abîme* (1920), *Lettre aux intellectuels* (1921), and *Manifeste aux intellectuels* (1927). And perhaps even more important is that through the two reviews of which he was founding editor, he provided a public forum for much of the literary debate with which we are concerned.

In the years immediately following the war, the first of these, *Clarté*, noted for its pacifist and internationalist character, turned its attention to the question of the social utility of art and literature. On 8 November 1919 Jean-Michel Renaitour wrote: 'L'art social, c'est l'art justifié utile. L'art est dit superflu [. . .] quand il s'adresse plutôt au cerveau'. He carefully distinguished between *social* ('qui signifie strictement "qui concerne la société"') and *socialiste*, proposing Zola as an example of a writer who had managed to include a politically and socially relevant dimension in his work without damage to his artistic achievement. Other contributors went further and held that an undisguised element of didacticism or even propaganda was an essential ingredient in a work of art. An unsigned article about projected 'Bibliothèques populaires' (27 December 1919), for example, envisaged that these would contain 'des ouvrages ayant un sens nettement moralisateur et susceptibles de fortifier, chez ceux qui les liront, la volonté de réaliser l'ordre nouveau, pour lequel nous luttons avec une même foi'. Almost a year later (20 October 1920) the review published a translation of the manifesto issued by the 1920 Proletcult conference and in which it was categorically announced that the proletarian cultural movement should be 'pénétré de l'esprit actif du Communisme'. Works should not only be the creation of the proletariat itself, but vigorously revolutionary in tone: 'L'art, la poésie prolétarienne, le roman, le chant, la création musicale, le théâtre, tout peut servir comme un moyen de propagande magnifique. L'art dirige les sentiments comme la propagande développe la conscience et comme la pénsée renforce la volonté d'action'. What is particularly noticeable about this manifesto is the implicit assumption either that the artistic qualities of such works would somehow remain automatically at an acceptable level, or that their political ends more than justify the artistic means employed to achieve them. Clearly the statement related – as indeed it acknowledged – to the Soviet Union more than to France, and Lefebvre's name amongst the signatories may be no more than an acknowledgement of his presence at the conference. Certainly it would be unwise to see in it an acceptance of such a policy in France, either by the *Clarté* group as a whole or by Barbusse in particular – a fact which was to become clear ten years later. Yet it is tempting to speculate that had Lefebvre not been drowned in the Baltic Sea on his return journey to France, further information would have become available and might have led to a more informed debate, at least between him and Barbusse. Clara Zetkin would also appear to have been a likely participant when, in March 1921, she wrote (with words of which Barbusse must surely have strongly approved) that: 'La révolution est l'acte des masses, et l'art le plus élevé restera toujours l'expression de la vie spirituelle de la collectivité.' Statements of this nature were rare, however, and when they did occur were too vague to have any practical application. Although it was felt by some that proletarian literature should be directly illustrative of the Proletcult's ambitions, the fact remained, as Bernard has observed,[1] that in France no specific recommendations were forthcoming. But debate continued and the publication in 1928 of *Monde* was an important event.

Monde (Hebdomadaire d'information littéraire, artistique,

scientifique, économique et sociale) owed its existence to the 1927 Proletcult conference which Barbusse had attended in Moscow. It was intended to provide an opportunity for experiments in proletarian literature in France as well as a forum for theoretical debate. In view of its origins, Barbusse was quick to underline his review's independence from the first issue: '*Monde* ne dépend ni financièrement, ni idéologiquement d'aucun parti, d'aucune organisation politique. [. . .] *Monde* ne prendra part à la polémique politique' (9 June 1928). In various essays and either openly or tacitly, Barbusse had already expressed his own views about the role of literature in general and about proletarian literature in particular. These stem from his ideas concerning an 'art collectif' which, as he wrote in 'Un nouvel Elan', (*L'Humanité*, 28 April 1926) 'allume et [. . .] soutienne, en même temps qu'il exprime, le grand cri des masses vers l'affranchissement'. Such remarks no more amounted to a definition than did earlier ones in *Clarté*, of course, but in the autumn of its first year, in order to arrive at a more precise assessment, *Monde* launched an 'enquête sur la littérature prolétarienne'.

The two questions which people were invited to consider were not only of the most general kind, but also clearly a reflection of Barbusse's own position:

1. Croyez-vous que la production artistique et littéraire soit une phénomène purement individuel? Ne pensez-vous pas qu'elle puisse ou doive être le reflet des grands-courants qui déterminent l'évolution économique et sociale de l'humanité?

2. Croyez-vous à l'existence d'une littérature et d'un art exprimant les aspirations de la classe ouvrière? Quels en sont selon vous les principaux représentants?

Not surprisingly responses varied considerably. Some contributors like Benjamin Peret (17 November 1928) were completely dismissive: 'La littérature prolétarienne d'aujourd'hui? Un arrivisme comme un autre.' Victor Serge, anticipating an issue which was to become central within a few years, suggested that some bourgeois writers could be genuinely sympathetic to the proletarian cause, even though their value and use would be limited: 'Ils peuvent être de quelque utilité au prolétariat; ils ne font beaucoup plus souvent que de lui inoculer les façons de sentir et de penser de la bourgeoisie radicale. Sensibilité, pensée, talent, modes d'expression, les intellectuels sont formés par la culture bourgeoisie' (3 November 1928). E. J. Finbert (22 December 1928) claimed that 'proletarian' was too restrictive a description, that 'popular' would give a clearer indication of the nature of such literature and, echoing Barbusse, that it should '(faire) éclater l'âme même de la masse'.

Barbusse's own response (20 September 1928) recalled his remarks of June: 'La littérature prolétarienne c'est la forme actuelle et vivante, précisée, intensifiée et imposée par l'évolution historique de ce qu'on appelait la littérature populaire'. Already in an earlier article (23 June 1928) he had acknowledged that it was the duty of the proletarian writer to make his readers more aware of life and 'les rendre sûrs de leurs propres forces'. There also emerged from his comments in October a concern for style which, strikingly Marxist in conception, marked a major difference between his views and those of Poulaille: 'La forme doit être organiquement liée au fond comme le corps est automatiquement et physiologiquement lié à la vie. [. . .] L'écriture est devenue une peau plutôt qu'un habillement.' Yet even such an apparently orthodox view as this did not find favour in the hardening political climate in the Soviet Union in the late twenties. While Barbusse, perhaps because of his status and influence, was probably spared a good deal of personal attack, his views together with those of Poulaille and the whole idea of proletarian literature in France were heavily criticized.[2]

The general tenor of this criticism was set by Selivanovski in an article 'La Littérature prolétarienne de Monsieur Poulaille' published in the third issue of *Littérature de la Révolution mondiale* in 1931.[3] What was wrong, Selivanovski claimed, was the general socio-political climate in France: 'Nous assistons sans conteste à un abaissement général du niveau idéologique et artistique de la littérature française qui est alimentée par l'état d'esprit d'apaisement et de satisfaction du bourgeois français d'après-guerre' (p. 87). Similar views had already been expressed at the Kharkov conference and were subsequently reported in a special issue of the review. While *Le Feu* was recognized as a valuable and important book, Barbusse's involvement with *Monde*, and his open sympathy for Poulaille (their differences appear to have been ignored), were deplored. S. Gopner interpreted this development as 'une déviation de droite' (p. 28), but both he and Bena Illès confirmed that Barbusse would receive every assistance in 'reeducating' himself in order to stay 'dans les rangs de la littérature de la révolution prolétarienne' (p. 19). In two resolutions – the first on proletarian writing in France in general, and the second on *Monde* in particular – the intolerance of the 'new' orthodoxy soon became evident. Already in a previous resolution true proletarian literature had been defined as 'rien d'autre qu'une arme de la lutte de classe' and the writer as 'un homme de pratique révolutionnaire' (p. 90). In France all was not well: 'La France reste tellement en arrière qu'il est impossible de dire en ce moment qu'il existe dans ce pays le moindre embryon de littérature révolutionnaire prolétarienne' (p. 102). All other literature was rejected as degenerate, reactionary or fascist; *Monde* had fallen into 'le réseau des illusions bourgeoises' (p. 107), and Barbusse himself had been compromised.

Unable to attend the conference because of ill-health, Barbusse none the less sent a message, read out on the morning of 15 November and in which, while attacking bourgeois art for its 'désordre, incohérence, abstraction, artificialité' and 'préciosité' (p. 244), he claimed (as Aragon had done a week earlier) the fundamental difference between French and Soviet society. Further, in a statement which could hardly have endeared him to the official conference organisers, Barbusse warned against the potential dangers – admittedly within the context of France only – of an over-politicized literature: 'si l'on fait intervenir le principe politique, la lutte des classes, les adhésions s'envolent et il ne reste qu'une toute petite minorité' (p. 246).[4] In the principal response to Barbusse's communication Jasienski accused him of idealism and of paying insufficient attention to the reality of class conflict. In many ways of course this was true. Barbusse fully shared neither the new political orthodoxy nor the Party views about literature. His concept of proletarian writing, most fully expressed in *Russie*, and already partly illustrated by *Clarté*, was of something which was a natural outgrowth of the epics, mystery plays and 'chansons populaires' of the French literary tradition. Of the appropriateness for France of a militant and proselytizing literature he remained unconvinced.

Within the next few years the climate was to change. By 1933 *La Littérature internationale*, as the review was then called, devoted noticeably less space to theory, and carried an increasing amount of writing by people like Pearl Buck, Hemingway, Giono, who only shortly before had been dismissed as reactionary. Barbusse's case was reviewed and the earlier attacks upon him – and indeed those upon Poulaille as well – made especially by Jasienski, were deemed invalid and to have been inspired by Trotskyist extremism. Even so, in a tribute 'Ecrivain-combattant', published in 1937 on the second anniversary of Barbusse's death, no mention was made of either the idealist or the religious aspects of his work.

(b) *Poulaille and proletarian literature*

In the April 1931 issue of Poulaille's review *Nouvel Age* (the year after Kharkov but before the publication of the conference's proceedings) Suzanne Engelson, reviewing the translation of Fedor Panferov's novel *La Communauté des gueux*, wrote: 'il est pénétré de la conception marxiste [. . .] pénétré du sens profond de l'unité des efforts humains et de la solidarité fraternelle, qui sont la philosophie et la psychologie du prolétariat en tant que classe historique'. For these reasons, she argued, the novel was a good illustration of politically motivated proletarian literature. Poulaille's response was immediate and predictable: 'M'est avis qu'il faudrait une fois pour toutes ne demander au marxisme que de jouer sur son plan propre, car il n'a rien à faire dans le domaine artistique.' In spite of changes in the political and cultural climate and of accusations levelled against him, this was a position from which Poulaille was not to move.

Throughout the 1930s Poulaille continued, with seemingly boundless energy, to express his views and attempt to gather others to his side in a variety of reviews and groups.[5] (Association was a word he was unwilling to use since it smacked too strongly of organisation and control.) From March to June 1932 the *Bulletin des Ecrivains Prolétariens* appeared, *Prolétariat* from July 1933 to July 1934, *A Contre-Courant* (July 1935–October 1936), *L'Equipe des Arts et des Lettres* May–July 1939). In addition, in February 1935 the Musée du Soir opened. The previous May Poulaille had outlined his plans in an article ('Musées du Soir') in *L'Homme réel* in which both through the conception, especially that of natural growth, and the language in which it is presented the influence of Martinet can be identified: 'Il s'agit moins d'un lieu de distraction, même élevée, que d'un lieu de réunion. On aurait vite créé un noyau actif dans chaque quartier et, peu à peu, tous les indifférents reprendraient goût à la vie collective, cristallisation du sens de classe que les mots d'ordre de lutte de classe ne sauraient remplacer.'[6] His plan remained unrealized, but with some financial support from the Union des Syndicats de la Région parisienne a single 'musée' was established whose membership grew from 75 in 1935 to 450 by the declaration of war.[7] The short duration of the reviews and the relative lack of impact made by the 'musée' did nothing to dampen Poulaille's enthusiasm. His position remained the same even though collaborators like Marc Bernard, who was principally responsible for Ecrivains Prolétariens, occasionally expressed views with which he could not wholly agree. It is, however, rather curious that in September 1935 Poulaille should reject Lemonnier's call in *L'Oeuvre* (14 May) for a 'Front littéraire commun' when, as Loffler has observed, there was a case for some kind of reaction on the part of the non-politicized literary left to the AEAR's acceptance of the principles of socialist realism.[8]

Although Poulaille's principal statement about proletarian literature appears in his *Nouvel Age Littéraire* (1930), he had (like Barbusse) concerned himself with the matter for some years already. On 17 December 1925 in a Bordeaux newspaper *Le Progrès*, he wrote an article entitled 'La Littérature et le Peuple'. In this, in which the influence of Martinet can again be glimpsed, the basis of all Poulaille's subsequent pronouncements can be found – the need for proletarian writers to remain as close to their true origins as possible, and above all for such literature to be not only humanist in tone, but authentic in its depiction. When *Monde* published the results of its *enquête* Poulaille was annoyed; the majority of the opinions merely served to prove, he argued, that a large number of people judged proletarian literature either by its political dimension or by the inappropriate and irrelevant matters of style and form. And when within the following twelve months four of Lemonnier's articles on populism appeared, Poulaille's response was both immediate and massive – an essay in Georges Valois' series 'Les Cahiers bleus' on Charles-Louis Philippe (29 March 1930) – 'Charles-Louis Philippe et la littérature prolétarienne' – followed shortly after, in July, by his *Nouvel Age Littéraire*.[9]

From the opening pages of this long work Poulaille attacks the claims made in the name of populism. It is, he argues, nothing new: the depiction of working-class life by 'braves bourgeois' writers like Zola, the Goncourts, Sue, Hugo, France and

Huysmans is evidence enough. Moreover the idea of examining the working-class in this way ('aller au peuple') is typical of those late-19th century examples of social concern – the Universités populaires, the Equipes sociales or Marc Sangnier's social Catholic movement, Le Sillon – all of which caused the worker to become alienated from his social and cultural origins. To support his argument Poulaille quotes Michelet and in so doing anticipates Guéhenno: 'Presque toujours ceux qui montent y perdent parce qu'ils se transforment, ils deviennent mixtes, bâtards, ils perdent l'originalité de leur classe, sans gagner celle d'une autre. Le difficile n'est pas de monter, mais en montant de rester soi' (p. 19). Despite considerable admiration for both Lemonnier and Thérive, Poulaille claims that populism is a label invented and used by critics in order to conceal the existence of true proletarian writing at a time when literature in general continues to be dominated by bourgeois ideology. Art and literature produced for a guaranteed audience of 'les bourgeois, les oisifs, les riches' (p. 142) is not only sterile and divorced from true experience ('une littérature de chambre' p. 101), but a sign too of a decadent society.

Poulaille's discussion of and claims for proletarian literature contain two essential points. First (and he quotes from his 1925 article in *Le Progrès*) there is a need to introduce working-class people to works of literature which owe their greatness to their treatment of eternal human problems: 'S'il y a un art pour le peuple, c'est l'art humain. C'est la littérature des plus grands maîtres, la grande littérature' (p. 143); second, a new literature is required which, maintaining this quality, will take the working class and its problems as its subject matter. Such literature will not only be authentic ('elle amasse et dispense d'observations, d'expériences vraies' p. 101), but useful as well: '(elle doit) dégager les grandes lignes des problèmes de la vie. Avoir une utilité en somme' (p. 104).

Like Barbusse, Poulaille suggests in his essay that such literature has developed in France, as elsewhere, instinctively; not even in the Soviet Union is it written 'to order'. Its origins lie in what he defines somewhat vaguely as 'la littérature dite "sociale"', best exemplified in England by the work of Hardy and in France by that of Ramuz. With the notable exception of *Le Feu* or the end of *Clarté*, their works are more important than others by Barbusse or Rolland which are, he claims, too directly inspired by specific, and therefore limited, ideas and issues. More significant still, especially in view of his claim that literature should not serve political ends, is the point he makes in his essay on Philippe: 'La littérature prolétarienne [. . .] est l'expression d'une classe, elle est spontanée. [. . .] Elle n'a pas la prétention d'être le but de l'Art, *mais un moyen de combat*' (my italics). Despite statements to the contrary, it is difficult not to feel that this is what he frequently believed; that, even if only incidentally, such writing was intended to make its contribution to some kind of social revolution. The same point is made again in *Nouvel Age Littéraire*: '(La littérature prolétarienne) est l'expression d'une classe et dit les aspirations, les volontés de cette classe souvent, car la plupart de ses manifestations sont des œuvres de combat. [. . .] (Elle) répond à un besoin d'une classe sous le joug d'une incertitude continuelle du pain quotidien' (p. 47). But such statements were not enough. While the criticism which Poulaille, like Barbusse, received at Kharkov may have stemmed from specific political circumstances, it is unlikely, in view of his confessed 'absence de bases idéologiques', that his recommendations for proletarian literature would ever have found favour even in a politically more tolerant climate. Like the populists (though for different reasons) and indeed even like Barbusse, what Poulaille had to offer was basically unacceptable to a new generation of left-wing critics and writers who believed that literature did have a central role to play in the realization of social revolution.

(c) *Populism*

While as we would expect populist literature was condemned at the Kharkov conference as reactionary, it was rejected in France by both Barbusse and Poulaille as unauthentic and gratuitous. In December 1931 (and we should not forget that this therefore postdates Kharkov) it was described in *Monde* for example as 'une excursion parfaitement gratuite à travers la vie de la classe ouvrière vis-à-vis de celle-ci'. For those who shared Poulaille's views on proletarian literature, the idea that such writing should concern itself with observation and description, rather than identification and sympathetic understanding was quite unacceptable.

Populism had its roots in an article 'Plaidoyer pour le

Naturalisme' by André Thérive published in *Comœdia* (3 May 1927) in which he expressed the already familiar objection to literature which took bourgeois mores as its staple subject matter. What was needed, he argued, was a literature which described 'le soin de gagner sa vie, par les traces professionnelles, par la vie pratique, la vie tout court'. One example he quoted was Léon Lemonnier's *La Femme sans péché*, a story set in the 18th *arrondissement* of Paris about a working-class woman's courage in the face of considerable personal adversity. Lemonnier was grateful to Thérive for his review and from their association the idea of populism gradually evolved. On 27 August 1929 *L'Œuvre* carried an article by Lemonnier entitled 'Un manifeste littéraire. Le roman populiste'. Lemonnier's reaction was one of doubt and shock. According to him, the actual formation of 'populisme' was the outcome of much discussion, and was certainly not intended to carry the weight and significance normally given to a manifesto:

> Il fut d'abord question d'humilisme; mais humiliste ressemblait fâcheusement à humoriste, et il avait tort, selon Thérive, d'évoquer les livres bêlants et larmoyants de Charles-Louis Philippe. Il fut ensuite question de *démotisme*, mais le mot me parut trop savant, et obscur pour la plupart des gens. Alors, le terme *populisme* nous séduisit: il était clair et frappant.[10]

However unwilling Lemonnier may have been to launch a literary movement with strict guidelines to which writers would adhere (and he refers to populism both as a movement and as a school), it is clear that he and Thérive were not so uncertain about their general intentions. Like Barbusse and Poulaille, and indeed like writers as radically different, for example, as Nizan or Bernanos, they objected to a literature which merely entertained. Referring specifically to the Surrealists, they claimed that since the War, the public had been fed 'une littérature d'inquiétude et de débilité, un style de jeunes bourgeois qui [. . .] cherchaient à se chatouiller l'âme pour se faire frissonner. [. . .] Une réaction commence. Elle doit s'inaugurer par une modification du genre le plus populaire, le roman' (pp. 9, 10). For inspiration they looked – as Thérive's earlier article suggested they would – to Zola and the Naturalists, and while Lemonnier objected to Zola's occasional sentimentality and to his scientific theories in particular, he saw in him the originator of the kind of novels he wished to encourage: '(des romans) sur le peuple, des romans que lit le peuple, et qui ne sont point de naïves histoires artificieuses, mais de grandes œuvres d'art (p. 23).

From various statements it is clear that Lemonnier had a number of general guiding principles in mind for this new novel. It should be objective in its depiction of life ('cette soumission au réel' p. 99); it should not attempt to 'prove' anything; models for characters should no longer be taken from the 'beau monde' but from 'les gens médiocres qui sont la masse de la société (p. 201). 'Faire revivre l'âme populaire, tel est l'un de ses buts' (p. 188). Populist quite simply denotes 'of the people'. Alert to the expectations of those who considered that literature should have a clear socio-political dimension to it, Lemonnier frequently stressed the apolitical nature of populism, and emphasized a concern for style – albeit with a rather different end in view from that of Barbusse. In an interview with Frédéric Lefevre,[11] he claimed that populist writers were 'de purs gens de lettres, nous ne nous mêlons point de politique' (pp. 121, 2); and 'Nous ne songeons pas, comme l'on dit à élever le peuple, à éduquer les masses. Nous prenons le peuple tel qu'il est, nous le peignons tel qu'il vit. Nous l'aimons en lui-même et pour lui-même' (p. 126).[12] Here according to Lemonnier was the basic difference between populist and proletarian writers whose principal aim, he claimed, was to defend the rights of the working-class. While as we have seen implications of this kind are to be found as well in Poulaille's manifestos, and while many of the works produced by proletarian writers do have a socio-political dimension to them, the distinction is perhaps rather less clear cut than Lemonnier would have us believe. His concern for a *sympathetic* account of working-class life and his acknowledgement that a work of art contains a moral (even though 'elle doit être secrète, non point apparente' pp. 97, 8), suggest that his apolitical (or even asocial) stance is also rather unsteady. Furthermore, when he speaks of the value and necessity of depicting 'les petites gens, les gens médiocres [. . .] dont la vie, elle aussi, compte des drames' (p. 102), he reminds us not only of the preface to *Germinie Lacerteux*, but also of Zola's words in 1869 when he claimed that a truthful, factually accurate depiction of working-class life must inevitably result in 'de l'air, de la lumière et *de l'instruction* pour les basses classes' (my italics).

Lemonnier also claimed distinction from the proletarian school on two further counts – the author's own background and his works' intended audience. First, it was no more necessary for the populist writer to be of the people himself (a view shared by Barbusse and Serge), than it was for someone writing about women to be a woman. Second, while populist literature was written *about* working-class people, it was not necessarily written *for* them. Poulaille in particular was quick to argue that such criteria implied a degree of distance and hence condescension, and, despite Lemonnier's claim for objectivity, of incompleteness and distortion.

2 PRACTICE

In the second part of *Nouvel Age Littéraire* Poulaille lists more than fifty contemporaneous authors whose works, in his view, are unmistakably proletarian; Lemonnier, somewhat less ambitiously, mentions rather fewer representatives of populism. More recently, in the latest version of his survey, Michel Ragon lists well over two hundred writers who meet the requirements of his rather more general criteria. To offer anything resembling a comprehensive survey of these works – even of those written during the interwar years alone – is clearly impossible. Even more so would be an attempt to examine the range of novels which have been considered for the all-embracing Prix Populiste, still awarded today fifty years later. In order to understand more clearly what kind of works best illustrated the theories at the time when they were being expressed most vigorously therefore, what follows is a brief examination of a few illustrative texts. Some, like those by Vincennes, Hamp or Poulaille himself, can be readily placed in one category rather than the other; others, like a number of early works by Dabit and Guilloux, defy such easy (if superficial) definition.

(a) *Pierre Hamp,* Le Rail (1921)[13] *Henry Poulaille*

Whether or not we accept Poulaille's claims that true proletarian literature could be produced by the working-class writers alone, and that whatever such literature disclosed of working-class conditions it did not seek to make a direct political point, there is no doubt that his own works, or those of Hamp, do have a quality and tone to them which distinguishes them quite clearly from much populist writing.

Pierre Hamp's panoramic survey of various aspects of working-class life, *La Peine des Hommes*, is perhaps the best illustration of proletarian literature other than Poulaille's own works, even though many individual novels in this series pre-date the latter's attempts to formulate any theories. In *La Peine des Hommes*, Hamp describes and attempts above all to dignify work and workers – glass blowers and those associated with the wine-trade in *Vin de Champagne*, those in the textile industry in *Le Lin* or railway workers in *Le Rail*, for example. This last novel in particular with its account of the gap between officials in Paris and local representatives, of the conflict between man and technology, of strike activity and demonstrations, and of the final disintegration of the union (Cordier being symbolically crushed by a railway carriage) as the company survives, recalls much of Zola's work, especially *Germinal*. By its style it also reminds us of much Naturalist writing – the welter of detail in the first fifty pages of the novel concerning time-tabling, technicalities and relationships between various groups of employees, or the creation of a sense of panic and distress after the accident (pp. 85, 6). Employers and superiors, like the mine owners in the earlier novel, are described as though by employees: thus, for example, Qualin the station officer: 'Il sortit de la gare, avec son air de messe, le nez tourné à droite et les yeux à gauche. Aucun office du soir ne le sonnait à l'église, mais il subissait l'appel de la maison de tolérance' (p. 41). And elsewhere the evocation of the Jewish Bank which runs the company contains that same animal image which haunts *Germinal*: 'Un colosse silencieux et mauvais personnifiait l'injustice qu'ils éprouvaient par trop de travail et manque de pain. Ce Dieu étranger, vorace de leur peine, vivait pour leur imagination dans une ombre armée de mystère et blonde du reflet de l'or' (p. 138). Already in such a passage as this, Hamp's own position can of course be glimpsed, just as it can in the expression of a hope for the future voiced by Gossens at the end of the novel: 'Le souvenir de notre souffrance donnera la rage de vaincre aux hommes de la prochaine grève. Il ne nous a peut-être manqué, pour nous créer une âme de victoire, que les morts à venger' (p. 225). Passages like this might cause some[14] to object quite legitimately that Hamp's own values and theories intrude too much upon his plot. But he does succeed in describing vividly and authentically the conditions of working-class existence in a way which far exceeds anything offered by the populists. The sense of (if not actual) personal experience reduces the impression of clinical observation which we find in much populist writing and Poulaille's description of Hamp, on account of his later career as a business man and economic advisor, as one of the 'prolétaires douteux'[15] does seem somewhat ungracious.

Poulaille's own contribution to proletarian literature was substantial. His four principal novels (all to some degree autobiographical) cover the period 1903 to 1920 and fall into two pairs – *Le Pain quotidien (1903–1906)* (1931); *Les Damnés de la Terre (1906–1910)* (1935) and *Pain de Soldat (1914–1917)* (1937); *Les Rescapés (1917–1920)* (1938) – to which should be added the earlier experimental volume *L'Enfantement de la paix* (1926).[16] Together, largely by virtue of the unifying role of the Magneux family and of a series of cross references and links, they depict a block of working-class experience.

Poulaille aims to describe the lives of his characters sympathetically from within. For much of the time he succeeds; routine, the daily pattern of a life which has to be and is endured, gives a certain rhythm to the works. Working-class existence is shown to contain an infinitely repeatable pattern of births, deaths, injuries, marriages, strikes, political meetings and so on largely observed through the characters. Thus when, in *Le Pain quotidien*, Magneux breaks his leg and becomes bed-ridden, the passage of time depends almost entirely on *his* attitude to his condition – irritation, boredom, contentment. Similarly in the first part of *Pain de Soldat*, Poulaille's account of Magneux's early life from his pre-war apprenticeship to action in the trenches is essentially conveyed through anecdote and dialogue, with the result that the sense of movement and above all of authenticity is strong. In as much as Poullaille argued in *Nouvel Age Littéraire* that prole-tarian literature should 'amasse et dispense d'observations, d'expériences vraies' (p.101), these five novels achieve no small measure of success. Society during a period of some fifteen years is viewed very largely through the optic of Magneux and his family; but their values, hopes and fears remain those of an entire class.

Principally Poulaille's aim, like Hamp's, is to emphasize the dignity of work. In an age when the machine was encroaching more and more upon the territory hitherto occupied by the artisan, Magneux, a carpenter by trade, still manages to retain an attitude to his work which marks him off from many of his fellow labourers. Even though he has anarchist sympathies and likes to quote Reclus, Kropotkine and Grave, and has decorated his workshop with cuttings from radical papers like *La Feuille* and *Gil Blas illustré* and with photographs of Zola and Kropotkine, politics fade before the beauty of his work: 'La politique s'effaçait devant la joie de blanchir cette planche que le rabot avait prise rugueuse' (*Le Pain quotidien*, p. 163). And on the building site the collective work on the house ('la carcasse d'une immense tête endormie', p. 89) also has for Magneux a lyrical quality about it: 'Les coups de marteaux sonnaient clair leur chanson rude, les hommes s'interpellaient. Un jeunot s'occupait au treuil à la montée de madriers. Il sifflait comme un pinson' (p. 89). There is of course much idealism and nostalgia in such descriptions, just as there is in that of Hulot in *Les Damnés de la Terre* who, having spent his life decorating porcelain, dies pen in hand at his work table. Yet a more immediate concern is not far away. Idealism or indeed the dignity of work will not pay bills; and, while it is true that Poulaille refrains from offering any Marxist-based critique of society, his concern (like Hamp's) for the workers' lot is clear.

Characteristically, the representatives of the bourgeoisie are viewed with suspicion or contempt: political rhetoric is dismissed by Magneux in *Les Damnés de la Terre* as 'de la mascarade' (p. 150), by Louis in *Les Rescapés* as 'le jeu papillonnant des phrases toutes faites' (p. 300) (a commentary also made by Poulaille as narrator in *'L'Enfantement de la paix* (p. 128)). Magneux is also critical of the lack of political action, but fails himself to take any initiative. His is an individualist position. Although in *Les Damnés de la Terre* after the strike has succeeded, he speaks in favour of collective action ('Ceux qui ne sont pas avec nous sont contre nous', p. 156), he is, like his fellow workers, content to rediscover and be reabsorbed by the regular pattern of work. Only by the end of *Les Rescapés* when he is shown as having a sense of doubt, and even guilt that he too has somehow had his anarchist spirit eroded, does a rather different feeling of resignation overcome him. Clearly Magneux's personal odyssey through these novels is intended to be that of the 'working-class man'; he illustrates both what Poulaille considers to be most noble and admirable in the working class, and what he sees as its inevitable lot in a capitalist society. In this sense, therefore, the novels are 'useful', the moral lesson is conveyed through the description of situations which working-class people would recognise as their own.

Yet while he claimed that the writer should remain apart from his work allowing it to make its point through the weight of description, Poulaille cannot – any more than Hamp – prevent his authorial presence from intruding at times upon his narrative. In *Pain de Soldat*, Poulaille voices Magneux's thoughts for him: 'La souffrance muette des gosses, Magneux connaît cela. Il sait combien elle est pénible; il sait qu'elle reste à jamais incomprise, qu'elle est niée. Et même l'enfant qui paraît insouciant, peut cacher une plaie douloureuse et incicatrisable. Déjà il connaît des centaines d'enfants que la guerre a mutilés dans leur âme' (p. 45). Elsewhere in the same novel, in a description of the soldiers' reactions as they pass a signpost to the field hospital, he comments omnisciently: 'Ils tentaient de fixer en leur mémoire ce petit coin de bois qui était le carrefour du salut. Combien peu devaient y revenir pourtant' (p. 206). In *Le Pain quotidien* when food is in short supply during the strike, Poulaille describes not only Loulou's response to the situation but, like Barbusse, interprets it for him: 'Loulou ne comprenait pas cette transformation soudaine chez lui. . . . Porquoi son père ne travaillait-il plus? Il n'était pas d'âge à voir le rapport qu'il y avait entre le repos de son père et la nourriture frugale dont on était obligé de se contenter tous ces jours' (p. 188). In *Pain de Soldat* he directly addresses new recruits who are unwilling to move rotting corpses: 'Allons! Plus tard vous ne serez pas si dégoûtés. Vous vous abriterez derrière les macchas sans qu'on vous le dise . . .' (p. 223). And in some places, he attempts to disguise his own views by expressing them in the vocabulary and syntax of working-class speech. Thus in *L'Enfantement de la Paix*, on the occasion of the 14 July celebrations we read: 'Tous s'en foutent. Ils ne savent pas au juste de quoi. . . . Mais c'est royalement qu'ils s'en foutent. Ce qui est une façon comme une autre d'être heureux' (p. 264). Despite some uncertainty utility is not, however, Poulaille's principal concern. The true hallmark of successful proletarian writing is, as he frequently claimed, its simplicity and its ability to depict the wholly absorbing nature of work and the manner in which a way of life, however unjust, is shown simply to be accepted. It offers a view from the inside, glimpses of actual experience without the constant and overt commentary or moralizing observations of a privileged narrator.

(b) *André Thérive,* Le Charbon ardent *(1929); Jean de Vincennes,* De Pauvres Vies *(1927)*[17]

Thérive's novel was hailed by Lemonnier as a populist novel of the first rank. In it, he claimed, Thérive had explored and authentically portrayed 'la vie intérieure et mystique des personnages humbles'.[18] Certainly external features like setting or physical descriptions are of little importance in this tale of a humble bank clerk's existence. Jean Soreau is a passive creature ('Nul n'aura eu moins que moi le goût de commander' p. 94; 'Il n'avait aucune énergie pour se révolter' p. 275) who resigns himself to fate – 'La Force' as he terms it – without question. The story is simple and sentimental. Returning home after the First World War, he marries. His wife, who has pretensions to scientific learning, leaves him for a while and he becomes friendly with another girl who momentarily offers what he imagines will be an opportunity for escape. This fails, the girl becomes a prostitute, and his wife eventually returns. We have the impression that their life together will continue much as it had done before their separation. The implication of the novel is that such people are totally conditioned by their class and origins; escape, it seems, is impossible except through death.

In terms of its completely inconsequential nature *Le Charbon ardent* does indeed merit the populist label. Yet, like so many of its kind, the book displays major inconsistencies. For all his humble origins, Soreau in three chapters (3, 8 and 12) is made to indulge in a form of self-examining interior monologue which both disrupts the narrative flow of the novel and, because of the quality of language used, creates the impression that it is Thérive who is talking for him. 'Interference' of this kind is also apparent elsewhere: in the images found for example in Jean's recollections of his war experiences with La Provenchère ('la plainte chromatique d'une balle qui semblait se perdre vers l'éther' pp. 114, 115) or in the narrator's direct observations of and comments on his characters: 'ils sentaient la fierté exquise d'être deux, deux comme tout le monde, deux comme les hommes et femmes non maudits, deux comme ceux qui ont accepté de s'aider à vivre' (p. 106).

Thérive does, it is true, achieve some success in conveying the sense of aimlessness and resignation of his working-class world. But he is also too intent on drawing moral conclusions, on attributing to his characters thoughts and expressions of which they are incapable, and in general of providing the work with some kind of structure. Unlike Zola – and indeed Poulaille to a great extent – whose authorial pressure and gloss is at least in part masked by a use of characters' language, Thérive is never absent for long.

This particular weakness of much populist literature is also well illustrated by Jean de Vincennes' *De Pauvres Vies*, a collection of short stories which earned him Poulaille's unflattering assessment of being 'le plus parfait modèle de ceque peuvent réaliser de pire les visées populistes'.[19] To be fair to Vincennes, he makes no claim to be other than a privileged observer. In the preface to his book, he maintains that his bourgeois position in life ('Je porte en effet des gants et un chapeau melon [. . .] des signes notoires d'existence bourgeoise', p. 1) has caused him to lose the comradeship which he had enjoyed during the war. In an attempt to rediscover it he disguises himself and sets out to investigate through personal experience a number of different working-class occupations, becoming in turn a porter at Les Halles, a waiter, a sandwich man and a shoe cleaner. His aim is unambiguous – to observe and report: 'J'ai voulu être objectif et vrai' (p. 239) – and certainly at this level the stories are not unimpressive. His descriptions of the bustle of Les Halles with its 'véritables édifices de légumes' (p. 12) are conveyed in particular by his attempt to reproduce the workers' language phonetically, by an accumulation of detail, and a series of sharply focussed *instantanés*: 'Têtes inquiétantes et bizarres, grosses paysannes rougeaudes et gonflées, charretiers à veste de fourrure, le fouet autour du cou, jeunes fermières adossées à un mur de choux, les cheveux coupés à la 'garçonne', en bas de soie, les mains sur les hanches, une sacoche à la ceinture' (p. 15). Here life in this part of Paris is reflected in the abrupt syntax. Elsewhere dullness and misery are conveyed differently as in the description of the sandwich-man in which clauses are longer and sounds less brittle: 'On traîne un ennui monotone parmi la foule inattentive. Les collègues sont peu nombreux et tellement épuisés qu'ils ne parlent guère. Leur silence est fait de plus de vieillesse et d'usure que de méfiance. Il n'y a rien à tirer de ces débris qui s'effondrent' (p. 72). In this account, even though *on* is used inclusively, and in spite of the obvious care for assonance, the observation remains acceptably objective. Elsewhere, however, personal response can result, as in

Le Charbon ardent, in clumsy even pompous commentary, as for example when he abandons his job as a waiter: 'N'ayant malheureusement qu'une capacité limitée, je suis obligé d'arrêter assez vite ce genre d'investigations comportant l'ingurgitation de liquides variés' (p. 46).

In much of *De Pauvres Vies* Vincennes, like Thérive, meets Lemonnier's criteria. His accounts of these jobs are for the most part sympathetic, objective and apolitical; yet his moral is always made and not, as Lemonnier would wish 'secretly'. While occasionally a character will express indignation ('Nous ne sommes pas des hommes, nous: nous sommes des bêtes' p. 51), it is more usually Vincennes' own voice which is heard: 'Je devine une poussée de colère, contre une société qui abandonne des êtres jusqu'à les obliger à voler pour vivre' (p. 53), or 'Assis près du sol, on finit par souffrir d'une impression de lassitude et d'isolement extrêmes' (p. 89). Such comments as these, like Thérive's manipulations of language and plot, illustrate the gap which exists in both books between the author and the world they set out to depict. The result, argued Poulaille, was a loss of authenticity and sincerity which all literature which truly set out to depict the lot of the working class should possess.

(c) *Eugène Dabit*, Petit Louis *(1930)*, Hôtel du Nord *(1931)*; *Louis Guilloux*, La Maison du peuple *(1927)*, Angélina *(1934)*[20]

Distinctions between proletarian and populist works were not always quite so clearly made, however. Not surprisingly there appears in some cases to have been genuine confusion, but in others it is difficult not to feel the authors were quickly claimed as much for the general literary qualities of their work as for their strict observation of the guidelines of one side rather than the other. Two authors who fall into this category are Dabit and Guilloux.

In his preface to the 1977 edition of Dabit's *Hôtel du Nord* Jean Freustié writes:

Théoriquement du moins, le 'populisme' est un phénomène irréalisable. Comment existerait-il une littérature prolétarienne quand la culture bourgeoise qui en permettrait l'expression est interdite à ceux qui connaissait vraiment le peuple? Et pourtant il existe un 'prix populiste'. En choisissant pour premier lauréat *Hôtel du Nord* d'Eugène Dabit, André Thérive et Léon Lemonnier, qui lancèrent le premier Manifeste en faveur de la peinture vraie des petites gens, venaient de couronner un chef d'œuvre dans un genre qui en fin de compte en donnerait très peu.

Freustié's confusion here is typical of the responses to Dabit's early work. In 1953 Maurice Pernette classified the same novel as 'un des plus beaux, un des plus marquants de la littérature prolétarienne';[21] before that Poulaille had claimed the novel as being 'nettement d'inspiration peuple'[22] and therefore proletarian; Lemonnier had classified it as a populist work 'puisque l'auteur y décrit les mœurs du peuple'.[23] Louis de Sidener also considered Dabit to be an 'écrivain par excellence populiste'.[24]

Dabit himself expressed disquiet at attempts to classify him one way or the other: 'Ils veulent que je sois un romancier populiste! Qu'est-ce que c'est que le populisme? Il faut toujours qu'ils vous classent, qu'ils vous mettent sur le dos une étiquette'.[25] And in his private diary for 1933 we read: 'Je suis bien incapable d'obéir aux exigences d'une esthétique'.[26] Instead, he often maintained, his sole concern was simply to write about his own direct experiences which, in early works like *Hôtel du Nord* and *Petit Louis*, were those of working-class Paris during the early years of the century. He looked, he said, to Vallès, Huysmans and above all to Philippe as his guides, aiming not only at objectivity, but at effectiveness and utility as well. In a grateful letter to Lemonnier (in which he none the less rejected the label of populist) he expressed his wish to write 'avec des soucis simplement humains. Ce monde auquel vous vous consacrez est le mien, je ne pense le quitter jamais. [. . .] Et tant mieux si mon travail peut avoir quelque utilité'.[27] Like so many others, including Poulaille, Dabit felt moved to reveal the plight of working-class people by his experiences during the War. These he records in a muted fashion in the second half of *Petit Louis*. Yet, as his later work was to prove, Dabit was not committed to his class in quite the same way as Poulaille, and in spite of continued protestations that he was no artist, he attempted to move closer to writers like Gide and Martin du Gard.

That Poulaille should have greeted *Hôtel du Nord* with enthusiasm is not difficult to understand. The story is based on the lives of Dabit's own parents. Apart from Chapters 1–5 describing the Letourneurs' decision to buy the lease of the hotel and move in, and Chapters 32–5, their removal after the take-over by a property developer, there is little cohesion or sequential pattern. Thus, while we are allowed to follow the fate of the maid Renée who after the death of her illegitimate child turns to prostitution (Chapters 10, 15, 16, 17, 21), we are denied further information about Adrien the homosexual (Chapters 32, 33) or Bénitand the political agitator (Chapter 29). Superficially *Hôtel du Nord* is not unlike Poulaille's novels, in that such irregularity might be seen to reflect the way in which life is episodic and irregular. But Dabit has no character to fill the role of Magneux. Further, given the enclosed nature of the hotel, the novel strongly conveys the impression that Dabit, as omniscient author, is merely taking samples of working-class life without having to give that sense of movement conveyed by Poulaille or of unanimist acceptance and resignation by Hamp. He also adopts this position of observer to interpret his characters' unexpressed feelings and thoughts: 'Pour elle (Louise) le bonheur, c'était vivre avec les siens sans chômage ni maladie' (p. 16).

In *Petit Louis* the use of a first person narrative may suggest that Dabit had been aware of such problems. Louis' contented resignation to his lot ('J'ai dix-huit ans, comme mes parents je suis un ouvrier, ma vie ressemblera à la leur', p. 10) in a way, sounds more convincing than the description of Letourneur's feeling of satisfaction behind his polished *zinc* in the later novel. Similarly the political hopes of Louis' fellow soldiers are recorded in passing without authorial gloss as something which is incidental and, above all, natural to their condition. Yet each novel in its own way rings false. In *Hôtel du Nord*, the *style dépouillé* much admired by Poulaille, at first appears to be appropriate: rarely does a sentence contain more than three clauses, the present tense dominates, and *et* and *puis* are the principal conjunctions. But only occasionally does Dabit introduce slang or attempt to reproduce the syntax of working-class speech, with the result that the style as a whole is uniform and subdued. In *Petit Louis* despite the advantages of the first-person narration, we find forced literary images not altogether unlike those in Philippe's novels. Nature is 'Un bourdonnement fait d'un murmure d'insects, du frémissement des buissons, des caresses du vent' (p. 133); Louis records his reflections on life: 'Je tends le bras pour saisir la vie et je ne trouve que son ombre' (p. 139).

Such examples are interesting, not only in terms of the notional requirements of proletarian or populist writing, but also for what they suggest about a writer like Dabit. Despite his working-class background and lack of literary training, they give the impression that Dabit was moving towards becoming, or at least had ambitions to be, a professional or in Poulaille's terms, a bourgeois writer. When in 1931 he was awarded the first populist prize, he accepted it with some reluctance. Not surprisingly, Poulaille considered that he should have refused it, acceptance being a sign of betrayal of his true class. But once awarded, the definition of Dabit as a 'romancier populiste' remained with him. Without exception his position in subsequent works is one of detached observer. In *Villa-Oasis ou les faux bourgeois*, he describes the dangers run by working-class people who try to rise in society; in *L'Ile* his descriptions of fishermen he came to know in Menorca and in *La Zone verte* in which he deals with his experiences as an inn worker at Montlhéry, he is equally detached. The tendency in *Hôtel du Nord* to describe a number of 'case histories' is now fully developed and all sincerity and authenticity have disappeared.

During the early thirties Dabit claimed that he needed freedom in order to mature as a writer, and that systems of any kind restricted him: 'Mon désir d'individualité cadre mal avec tous ces systèmes' (19 January 1932).[28] Eventually he moved away from Poulaille and joined the AEAR, but his association with it was predictably short-lived and freedom brought little improvement in his development as an imaginative writer. Unlike Guilloux whose work, while retaining its early qualities, broadened in scope, Dabit remained very much a writer of the second rank.

In his turn Guilloux also received the Prix Populiste – in 1942 for *Le Pain des Rêves* – an award which gave him no great satisfaction. He too was wary of being neatly assigned to one literary group or another, and his early works in particular are, as Jonathan King has remarked, 'born of an allegiance to the world of his childhood, not of allegiance to a literary tradition'.[29] But two facts do set him close to Poulaille, if only during this early part of his career. The first is precisely the use he makes of his working-class childhood at Saint-Brieuc (his father was a cobbler and his grandmother an umbrella maker); the second is his belief in the artist's freedom. In January 1929, in response to a review by Marc Bernard of Guéhenno's *Caliban parle* in *Monde*, he asked: 'La littérature prolétarienne est-elle nécessairement marxiste, dogmatique, sans liberté?' – an attitude which must clearly have met with Poulaille's approval.

As most of Guilloux's critics have stressed, his development as a writer has increasingly justified this statement. Certainly the subjects of his work, while becoming increasingly abstract and metaphysical, have largely been set in working-class society; and the kinds of liberal and humanitarian values in which he has always expressed belief could broadly be termed 'left-wing'. But schematization or evidence that he is willing to accept theoretical directives for writing are quite absent. From the simple, almost parable-like quality of *La Maison du peuple*,[30] through the tight control of time and episodes in *Le Sang noir*, to the apparent random nature of the structure of *Jeu de Patience*, Guilloux remains, in terms of style, essentially independent. Yet his early work does have qualities which place it, like *Hôtel du Nord* and *Petit Louis*, in the context of proletarian and populist writing.

The world Guilloux describes in *La Maison du peuple* and *Angélina* is a simple one in which the ordinary is what matters, and in which the inarticulateness of his characters and their naïve enthusiasms are entirely appropriate. Through characters like Quéré or Camille Fouras he also creates the portrait of the archetypal worker whose honesty and dignity is reflected in brief, but idealised descriptions of them. Quéré: 'De larges épaules, des bras robustes, un pas souple et précis, c'était un homme tout d'une pièce. Ses cheveux blonds taillés en brosse, restaient soyeux au-dessus d'un front large, encore sans rides' *(La Maison du peuple*, p. 29). Fouras: 'Un beau regard bleu, profond et tendre, plein de sourire' *(Angélina*, p. 130). As King rightly argues, in creating a physical and class archetype in this way Guilloux has also created a *moral* archetype.[31] (This, interestingly, becomes a ploy of later, more militant writers for whom Stalin and even Thorez become idols.)

Like *Hôtel du Nord* and the early part of *Petit Louis*, *La Maison du peuple* covers the two decades preceding the outbreak of the First World War, a period which witnessed the foundation of the CGT in 1895, the unification of the French Socialist Party in 1905 and the series of important strikes in 1909. With the exception of the bakers' strike none of these is mentioned, even though growing political awareness, however naïve, is one of the book's key issues. And while *Angélina* (even though Nizan dismissed it in 1934 as 'une histoire intemporelle')[32] has a much sharper socio-political point to make both books remain essentially local in emphasis.

Another device which Guilloux uses to create the impression of simplicity and authenticity in *La Maison du peuple* is to have a child as his narrator. The illusion is not always successfully sustained however. Like so many writers who attempt this he not infrequently slips into a position of (adult) omniscience:

– Alors François qu'est-ce qui va arriver?
– Comment, dit mon père, j'espère bien que la révolution n'est pas loin.
Elle leva les bras au ciel.
– Bien sûr que oui, dit-il, la Révolution.
Qu'est-ce qu'il racontait là! Avait-on besoin de la Révolution? Et la misère qui viendrait. On était bien assez malheureux sans cela (p. 35).

In general, however, the impression of authenticity is well maintained. As in Poulaille's *Le Pain quotidien*, the linear development in *La Maison du peuple* is irregular; the reader only registers events as they impinge upon the lives of the characters, and the passing of time is only imprecisely recorded – *un jour, quelques semaines plus tard*. What dictates the rhythm of existence instead is the availability of work, the threat of illness, the need to provide for children and an educative dimension as characters slowly move towards political awareness. There is also, as in, say Phillipe's *Le Père Perdrix*, an unchallenged rightness about views expressed by Quéré and Le Bras (*La Maison du peuple*) or by Esprit and Fouras (*Angélina*). The attitudes of Mlle Bapier or M. Le Moël, both representatives of bourgeois society in the earlier novel, are only 'assessed' by Quéré's naïve, but realistic, response to them. Similarly in *Angélina* the description of the bourgeois church-goers who after mass make their way to the pâtisserie is given without commentary. But in this case, when the family's own Sunday meal is described by a sympathetic omniscient author, an additional, delayed bitterness emerges: 'quoi qu'on va manger? Des pommes de terre avec des patates frites dans l'eau, festin de Balthaser? Oui-da! c'est dimanche jour Seigneur. A la gloire du Seigneur, on rongera un petit bout de plat de côte aux choux, avec beaucoup de sauce . . .' (p. 19). Points of detail too contribute to the attempted evocation of working-class lives: once again we find the use of working-class speech with its disjointed syntax and popular expressions, the close identification (as in

Poulaille's work) of characters with their work, hints of absolute poverty – the wooden cradle which has had to be used for fuel (*Angélina*, p. 12) or dried cabbage as substitute tobacco (p. 51). Occasionally, like Philippe and Dabit, Guilloux exaggerates in his search for effect. To some extent the parable-like quality of *La Maison du peuple* in particular allows this: for example, the lamp which Quéré brings during the workers' political discussion (p. 139). Elsewhere, however, the results are distinctly out of key with the tone of the book as a whole – the attribution of life to tools (*La Maison du peuple*, p. 116; *Angélina*, Chapter 1), the lyrical description of Esprit's hands (*Angélina*, pp. 136, 7) or of Angélina's response to the countryside (pp. 123, 4).

Where Guilloux does differ from Dabit, and indeed to a considerable extent from Poulaille, is in the much clearer political direction to be found in both novels. For this to emerge depends on the successful evocation of the social conditions of his families, but it also results in a degree of oversimplification and even caricature. Thus each of the workers in *La Maison du peuple* is instantly recognizable by some characteristic of dress or physique; members of the bourgeoisie too are categorized. But the situation depicted is not merely static. In *La Maison du peuple* the grandfather advises caution and acceptance; in *Angélina*, Esprit (also of the older generation) is less hesitant: 'Mais à present [. . .] ce prolétariat prend conscience de lui-même, il sort pour ainsi dire de sa nuit et cherche à s'organiser. [. . .] Entre eux (les bourgeois) et nous, c'est une lutte à mort' (pp. 134, 5). But it is amongst the younger generation that political awareness develops with most vigour, and, while it may not result in the formulation of a precise programme, its direction is unmistakeable.

Despite some suggestion in these early works that he might develop into a more militant writer, Guilloux in fact remained essentially apolitical. His real concern, subsequently as then, was always for the individual's struggle against an oppressive and often frustrating universe. (It is not by chance that Camus admired his work so much.) His stance against fascism in the 1930s, his love of Russia which he visited with Gide in 1935, his Resistance activities, his involvement with local cultural affairs and his view of television as a means of taking culture to the masses, all relate to the early formative influence of a socialism inspired by Jaurès, and to which his father (himself the secretary of the socialist section at Saint-Brieuc) introduced him. In May

1962 he claimed in an interview with Guy Belleval: 'Je suis le fils d'ouvrier et ouvrier de lettres, en plein accord moi-même et resté ce que j'étais au commencement' (*Arts*, no. 870, p. 3). This fundamental position from which he has never shifted, combined with genuine humility and considerable flexibility as an imaginative writer are the distinguishing qualities of Guilloux's work and ones which give his work a dimension not to be found in Dabit's or Poulaille's.

In his 'Présentation' to *Les Temps modernes* in 1947,[33] Sartre dismissed populism as 'un enfant de vieux, le triste rejeton des derniers réalistes'. The same remark could, to a large extent, be applied to proletarian writing as well. Made at the time when he was also producing *Qu'est-ce que la littérature?* and when he believed in the potential of literature to shape peoples' social and political awareness, it is not surprising of course that Sartre's evaluation should be so unenthusiastic. But there is no doubt that even allowing for their non- or apolitical nature most of the works produced under either banner have a distinctly jaded look about them. With the notable exception of Guilloux, only Poulaille can be said to have had reasonable success in producing novels in which the essence of working-class life is convincingly evoked. Even so the writing is rarely better than inconsequential and anecdotal, and lacks both depth and vision. In literary terms this, together with lengthy and sometimes unclear and self-contradictory discussions concerning the criteria for and qualities of such writing, ensured ultimate oblivion. Yet it would be unfair not to acknowledge or to dismiss the efforts of Poulaille, Lemonnier and others as most literary historians of the period have done. Certainly socialist realism emerged for some in the early 1930s as a formula promising much (though in fact achieving quantitatively little), and giving rise to a more wide-ranging and significant debate. But as a purely historical phenomenon the presence of these two 'movements', at a time when left-wing writing was becoming increasingly militant, usefully modifies the usual account given of this period.

5 The Beginnings of Socialist Realism

Whereas both populist and proletarian writing continued to have their advocates during the 1930s, socialist realism gradually emerged in France as the first coherent attempt to wed political ideology to a cultural programme. It was a new and influential doctrine, the effects of which, especially in literature, would go beyond the Second World War. Initially, after the attitude of the Kharkov conference, socialist realism appeared as though it would have a liberating influence. In the Soviet Union the dissolution of the RAPP in April 1932 and the creation in its place of a single Union of Soviet Writers with the claimed intention of removing central authoritarian control over literature was welcomed. And in France this apparent relaxation could not have come for the PCF at a better time. After a period of marked isolation and loss of popularity, Thorez in particular recognized (at the national Party conference in July 1931) that one vital way of reforming links with the mass of working-class people was through cultural activities of various kinds. Furthermore the mounting concern on the Left generally at the growth of Fascism, and the threat of another war, produced a climate of political tolerance – the period of the fellow travellers – during which various writers, who would eventually be rejected as bourgeois, were welcomed.[1]

The broad aims of the Union of Soviet Writers and the principles of socialist realism were outlined in 1933 in the first issue of *La Littérature internationale* – which now replaced the former *Littérature de la révolution mondiale* – by Vladimir Kirpotine.[2] As far as subject matter and its treatment are concerned, the liberalizing intentions of the Union are clear; in particular the danger of schematization seems to be recognized: 'La création artistique est

98

compliquée et variée. On ne peut transformer le mot d'ordre du réalisme socialiste en recette schématique. Différents artistes peuvent y arriver de différentes façons' (p. 126). Even so there is, not surprisingly, an insistence in Kirpotine's article on the need to have the principles of the socialist revolution emerge from such writing unambiguously.

> Lorsque nous parlons de réalisme socialiste, cela ne signifie pas que le romantisme révolutionnaire lui soit opposé, soit en conflit avec lui. Au contraire, nous vivons à une époque héroïque [. . .] L'héroïsme, l'exploit, le dévouement plein d'abnégation pour la révolution, la réalisation de notre rêve réaliste, – ce sont là les traits essentiels extrêmement caractéristques de notre époque, de nos jours. [. . .] Lorsque nous parlons de réalisme socialiste, nous avons en vue ce qui dans l'art représente le monde objectif, non seulement dans ses détails superficiels ou voire même dans des détails essentiels, mais encore dans toutes les circonstances fondamentales, et à l'aide de caractères typiques essentiels. Nous avons en vue ce qui représente la vie véridique avec ses côtés négatifs et positifs, avec l'élément triomphant des forces de la révolution socialiste. Nous avons en vue le caractère anticapitaliste, le caractère antipropriétaire de nos œuvres qui éduquent chez les lecteurs la volonté de lutte pour un avenir meilleur de l'humanité. (p. 127)

Whatever the initial reaction to this programme the insistence on the exemplary and even didactic nature of such literature would present considerable problems. Indeed on examination the shift in emphasis from the old to the new policy proved to be rather less substantial than Kirpotine's words led people to believe.

As far as the French intellectual Left was concerned the publication of Kirpotine's article was interestingly timed. In March 1932 in the wake of Thorez's appeal, the *Association des Ecrivains et Artistes Révolutionnares* (AEAR) had been formed with Vaillant-Couturier (who was to become the editor of the French language edition of *La Littérature internationale*) as its general secretary. On 22 and 29 March the group's manifesto was published in *L'Humanité*; its tone was distinctly militant and may indeed remind us of the tenor of the Kharkov debates:

> D'abord propager autour de nous notre conception de la

littérature et de l'art révolutionnaire prolétariens; souligner devant la classe ouvrière la nécessité et l'urgence de la création d'une littérature et d'un art prolétariens révolutionnaires en France; dénoncer tous les camouflages et toutes les manœuvres de la bourgeoisie dans ce domaine.

But by July of the following year (1933), in which the first issue of the AEAR's review *Commune* was published, signs of an apparent relaxation more in line with the new directives from Moscow could be seen. The editorial team was composed of Vaillant-Couturier, Guéhenno, Barbusse and Rolland, with Nizan and Aragon as secretaries. Society was seen by *Commune* to be suffering from an 'ideological crisis', and in the editorial statement contained in the first number a pledge that intellectuals would join the working class in the struggle against economic oppression was issued: 'Nous les [les intellectuels] persuaderons que leurs intérêts sont solidaires de ceux de la classe qui est opprimée et exploitée comme eux, sous des formes différentes, à un degré supérieur, mais pour les mêmes raisons, en vertu du même mécanisme économique'. Yet despite both the presence of Barbusse and Rolland on its editorial board, and its total commitment to the anti-fascist campaign, many of the statements and debates published by *Commune* during the six years of its existence, betray an adherence to ideological directives emanating from Moscow. Nowhere was this covert activity more clearly encouraged than in the 'Lettre à l'AEAR' by Illès, Ludkewicz and Nizan published in the third number of *Littérature internationale* in 1934. Having surveyed the AEAR's activities and policy of recruitment, they return with some force to the matter of ideological direction: 'il est clair que la discussion ne doit pas cesser d'être fraternelle: il faut que les nouveaux venus aient l'impression que l'AEAR est une organisation où l'on respire et ne se sentent pas en présence de tel dogmatisme vaniteux, mais la discussion ne doit à aucun moment être faible' (p. 123). Not only should the AEAR work for the 'reconstruction' (p. 122) of those whose origins are in the 'petite bourgeoisie intellectuelle' (p. 121), but should concentrate on 'la question de la création littéraire et de ses formes, dans le mouvement révolutionnaire' (p. 123).

Commune had already shown that the idea of literature as a revolutionary activity which Vaillant-Couturier had voiced in *L'Humanité* was one of its principal concerns. The first issue (July

1933) contained a poem by Aragon 'La prise du pouvoir' which openly champions the Communist Party and celebrates the violent destruction of bourgeois society in a way which recalls his earlier 'Front Rouge':

Saute volcan colonial
Craque empire français craque haillon tricolore craque
Et l'immense corps opprimé se soulève rejetant
un ruissellement de bourreaux et de monstres
à l'appel du Parti Communiste

Similar in tone is Pierre Unik's 'L'Ennemi' (October 1933), which is addressed more generally to the proletariat:

Debout les damnés de la terre
pour abattre la bourgeoisie
notre sang les fleurs et la terre
sont à nous   debout   allons-y

Also in the second issue is a short story 'Fonderie d'Acier' by Pierre Bouchot which relies for its impact on a somewhat naïve contrast between the living conditions of foundry workers and management which, in one respect, recalls some of Pierre Hamp's work. However obvious its theme, there is in this story a not unsuccessful attempt, especially in the syntactical patterns of the sentences, to create the impression of the oppressive monotony of a work which reduces men physically: 'Tous ils ont maigri. Mais la fortune du patron, malgré la crise, enfle comme une panse'. Even from these three illustrations it is clear that there is little of the resignation and acceptance which Poulaille saw as an essential feature of proletarian literature and that the tone is a more aggressive and revolutionary one which will be characteristic of socialist realism.

Kirpotine's article we should remember was published in 1933. Between December of that year and April 1934 *Commune* published the results of an *enquête* conducted by Aragon, 'Pourquoi écrivez-vous?' Like those to Barbusse's *enquête* in *Monde* six years earlier, replies were various ranging from the openly militant ('j'écris parce que je sens le besoin impérieux de faire connaître certains faits et de déranger certains mensonges', Henriette

Valet, No. 7–8, p. 769) to the dismissive and totally apolitical ('Il n'existe pas de roman fasciste ou communiste; il n'y a que des bons et des mauvais romans', Alfred Mortier, no. 4, p. 328). As we might expect this latter view was not allowed to pass uncriticized: 'Les œuvres *apolitiques* sont des œuvres militantes pour la conservation du régime au pouvoir' (ibid., p. 329). Yet while the issue of a work's political weight and intention is frequently discussed, that of style is rarely mentioned. Occasionally a reference is made. Jean Audard touches upon it in his response in the fourth issue admitting that attempts to write in a way which would give pleasure to working-class people have all too often failed. And in support of an anonymous *rabcor*, who shows no hesitation in writing for the proletariat, *Commune* editorially raises, but fails to answer, the very question: 'Comment écrire pour le prolétariat? la question de *qualité* de la littérature prolétarienne' (p. 344).

In the wake of Aragon's *enquête*, *Commune* published a number of related articles during the early months of 1934: Vaillant-Couturier's 'Avec qui êtes-vous artistes et écrivains?' (January–February), an attack on the current 'hypocrite esclavage de la neutralité dans l'art et la science' (p. 484); Armand Bour's 'Théâtre prolétarien' in which he argues that 'l'art ne se développera noblement, splendidement, que lorsqu'il sera délivré du règne de l'argent, qui est à la base de notre civilisation actuelle' (p. 627). As we can now see with hindsight, articles like these together with the *enquête* were preparatory to the dissemination of the theory of socialist realism in France which was about to occur.

Although the Moscow Congress did not take place until August 1934, already in the May–June issue of *Commune* Aragon had described Nizan's first novel, *Antoine Bloyé*, as an example of socialist realism. In the same number an article by Youdine and Fadeev also appeared, 'Le Réalisme socialiste. Méthode fondamentale de la littérature soviétique' (pp. 1025–30). This article, written about a post-revolution culture, predictably describes it as something already *naturally* achieved:

> Le réalisme socialiste n'est pas un dogme, un recueil de lois limitant la création artistique, réduisant toute la diversité des recherches et des formes à des commandements littéraires. Au

contraire, le réalisme socialiste est l'expression naturelle des nouvelles relations socialistes et de la conception révolution-naire de monde. (p. 1025)

Ideologically secure such a literature will offer 'la peinture véridique et historiquement concrète de la réalité dans son développement révolutionnaire' and 'peut exposer la réalité dans son mouvement historique, peut montrer comment l'avant naît dans le présent' (p. 1026). Here we find an important aspect of the new doctrine which potentially at least contains certain impli-cations for style. Realism which merely depicts will always be sterile: 'une photographie, dépourvue d'importance sociale et éducatrice' (p. 1029).[3] In socialist realism, socialism will penetrate the very fabric of the work and will appear to be 'l'essence même de l'œuvre, incarnée dans ses images' (p. 1028). The same, rather imprecise claim for artistic rejuvenation, is also made in a selection of the statutes and guide-lines prepared by the Union of Soviet Writers for the August conference, a selection of which was published in the same issue of *Commune*: 'Le réalisme socialiste assure à l'artiste une possibilité exceptionnelle de manifester son initiative créatrice, de choisir des genres, des formes et des méthodes variés [. . .] Le but de l'Union des Ecrivains Soviétiques est la création d'œuvres d'art dignes de la grande époque du Socialisme' (pp. 1150, 1).

The principal speeches made at the Congress, which opened on 17 August, were by Gorki, Radek and Bukharin.[4] Zhdanov, later to become Stalin's Minister of Culture, and already, at the age of 38, an influential member of the Party's Central Committee, welcomed the delegates and set the tone. Expanding Stalin's idea of writers as 'engineers of the soul' he argued that literature should offer a combination of 'truthfulness and historical con-creteness [. . .] with the ideological remoulding and education of the toiling people in the spirit of socialism'. Gorki, who had been largely responsible for the removal of RAPP and who was now hailed as the main torchbearer for these new precepts, spoke on Soviet literature. Like many he dismissed bourgeois literature for its decadence, its 'creative feebleness' (p. 34), and praised only those whose works might be defined as examples of 'revolutionary romanticism' (p. 41) since they illustrated how it was possible to break away from the 'suffocating atmosphere in which their class lived' (p. 41). Even so, mere critical exposure was not enough

Gorki claimed; it lacked that instructive dimension and, more important, the opportunity for the writer to 'participate directly in the construction of a new life' (p. 67). Radek broadened the context by discussing 'World Literature'. He took the 1914–18 War as his starting point, predictably seeing it as an imperialist and bourgeois inspired event in which the working-class masses were exploited. The writer's duty, he argued, is to encourage the masses to rebel against war and proletarian literature should – and will – reflect such a rebellion. Again in terms of the anticipated subject matter and aims of socialist realism Radek's speech was predictable. With capitalism moribund, literary realism must reflect a new reality, that of socialism (pp. 156, 7); furthermore 'socialist realism means not only knowing reality as it is, but knowing whither it is moving' (p. 157). Unlike Gorki, however, Radek did take more account of the purely literary dimension of the debate. He acknowledged that proletarian writers could and indeed should learn from the 'treasury of past literature' (p. 146), and that with bourgeois writers now changing positions as they come to understand that their true social and political allegiance lies with the working class (the point already made earlier by Serge and by *Commune*'s own manifesto), certain literary skills must be noted and absorbed. Although in its present form naïve and artistically immature, proletarian literature, he claimed, will eventually produce 'great' works (p. 166). In the third major speech Bukharin, while accusing the Russian Formalists of divorcing art completely from its social context and of offering an interpretation of literature which was 'dry, vapid and lifeless' (p. 207), none the less saw much technically that could be gained from them. He cited examples of contemporary writers Bedny and Mayakovsky whose work already showed an appropriateness of form to its revolutionary content. Diversity of content Bukharin maintained must be matched by diversity of form, the whole being infused with the spirit of socialist realism. Sensory images should predominate and replace any that smack of the 'supernatural, mystic [and] other worldly idealism' (p. 251). Like Gorki he accepted 'revolutionary romanticism' (p. 253), seeing it as a challenge to bourgeois conformity, and justified a lyrical portrayal of the *individual*, on the grounds of its being part of an evolutionary process leading towards a description of the wakening collective conscience.

The French representatives at the Congress were Aragon,

Malraux, Bloch and Pozner. (Nizan, who was already resident in the Soviet Union also attended though there is no record of his having contributed to discussions.) The spirit in which they went was indicated by *Commune*'s editorial in July–August 1934 which pointed to the need to establish in France 'la culture socialiste des Soviets en France', and of thereby revitalizing the national cultural heritage. In September, extracts from the speeches by Radek and Bukharin were published, and in the following issue others from Malraux's address, 'L'Art est une conquête'. Bloch's speech was reprinted in the September issue of *Europe*. On 23 October Malraux and Gide – the latter had not gone to Moscow but his current sympathy for the Party was well known – both spoke at a public meeting in the Palais de la Mutualité in Paris. As historians like Caute have suggested the publicity given to these non-Party writers (Malraux had also given an interview to Aragon for *L'Humanité* in September) was deliberate, forming part of the general attempt to convince as many as possible of the Party's new conciliatory attitude. What emerged from the remarks of all three writers, as being of significance for the literary debate, was a concern for the failure to give adequate consideration to the literary merits of socialist realist writing, both by its Soviet proponents in Moscow, and by some of its supporters in France. All three saw through the apparently liberalising attitude of the party to the real prospect of another form of controlled writing. Bloch, in spite of his admiration for the Soviet Union, pleaded for diversity in style and form, and warned against the 'notions de masse' (*Europe*, September 1934, p. 106) once applied to literature. In his interview with Aragon, Malraux pointed to the consequences for the novelist of ignoring individual psychological portrayal.[5] Most succinct of all was Gide: 'J'estime que toute littérature est en grand péril dès que l'écrivain se voit tenu d'obéir à un mot d'ordre' (*Commune*, November 1934, p. 162). In the middle of the following year, Bloch and Rolland drew attention to what was perhaps the most intimate aspect of the whole problem – language. Those who claimed to be fellow travellers of the proletariat should, Rolland argued, 'parler un langage qui soit accessible à leurs compagnons' (*Commune*, May 1935, p. 931), but as Bloch pointed out rather more acutely in the same issue, this was more easily said than done:

Dans neuf cas sur dix, l'écrivain révolutionnaire doit encore sa formation aux humanités et à l'enseignement des lycées. Le problème qui se pose à lui est de rompre avec le système des complicités savantes, des métaphores entendues à demi mot et des allusions distinguées, sans verser pour cela dans une affectation dégoûtante de style "peuple". (p. 1064)

We know that this particular matter was one which, in a slightly different way, had been central to the doubt and anxieties of people like Guéhenno. In the context of the discussion surrounding socialist realism it was virtually ignored. Even Nizan, whose commitment to the Party and to revolutionary literature was at this time absolute, drew for much of his central imagery in *Aden Arabie* and even in *Le Cheval de Troie*, on the world of classical antiquity with which only a bourgeois education would have allowed him to become familiar. Against this the argument elaborated earlier by Trotsky, Fréville and Serge remained valid; in a society which had not undergone the kind of revolution experienced by Russia, the dominant influences and modes of expression would necessarily remain those of the bourgeoisie. Léon Moussinac, writing in *Europe* (June 1936) observed with some pertinence: 'Le réalisme socialiste pose donc, pour nous écrivains d'un pays où la révolution reste à faire [. . .] des problèmes particuliers, comme il exige le renouvellement, avec le contenu originel du roman, de la pièce, du poème, de la forme même du roman, de la pièce, du poème' (p. 188).

Apart from such reverberations from the 1934 Congress as these, the only major statement directly concerning socialist realism as it might develop in France was Aragon's *Pour un réalisme socialiste*, published in 1935,[6] and in the main comprising five talks given between early April and late June of that year. Not surprisingly Aragon's case rests on his belief that society is changing. The proletariat's rise to power would bring about 'la rééducation de l'homme par l'homme, [. . .] la transformation du singe social de notre temps en l'homme socialiste de l'avenir' (p. 8). Already his own development has demonstrated this. The Surrealists he claims have failed since they have been incapable of taking advantage of the full 'material consequences' of their actions (p. 80), and have become too obsessed with the need to 'renverser ce monde qui nous révoltait' (p. 50). Aragon's moment of change came when he met Mayakovsky whose own work had shown him how art could become a weapon in the struggle for social justice (pp. 61, 2). Restating *Commune*'s message, he claims that, as in the Soviet Union, intellectuals and workers are 'frères égaux [. . .] des constructeurs du socialisme' (p. 27); moreover writers have a responsibility towards society as a whole, not only by questioning their own roles and by coming to recognize this link, but by illustrating within their works the benefits to be gained from socialism. To anyone who had followed the socialist debate during the previous 18 months or so his message must have been a familiar one. Once again the emphasis is on content rather than on form, on ideological direction rather than on expression. In fact virtually the only observation which Aragon makes about style is offered without illustration – a Soviet writer who, having worked with peasants and soldiers, has, he claims, created a 'langage de l'avenir, compréhensible pour tous, sans abaissement de sa qualité technique' (p. 29). Were it not for the political gloss of this statement, these words might have been written by Poulaille.

Aragon's general view that socialist realism could create its own modes of expression every bit as rich and worthwhile as its bourgeois forerunner found some support, in particular from Nizan. In a review of *Pour un réalisme socialiste* Nizan, having praised Aragon for his personal and exemplary evolution, also wrote about the 'capacité de perspectives' which socialist realist literature possessed. It was this he claimed which took it beyond bourgeois realism, a 'réalisme-critique [qui] décrivait amèrement la réalité. Mais il ne voyait point d'issue à cette réalité'.[7] Once again, however, style is disregarded. In a tribute to Eugène Dabit which appeared in *L'Humanité* the following year, Nizan did suggest that the task of the 'new' writer was to 'faire passer la révolte dans l'art, sans détruire l'art'. And in 1937 he further suggested, in a review of André Philippe's *L'Acier*, the first winner of the Prix Ciment, that what was important was the novelist's ability to communicate with the reader: 'le rapport de l'écrivain au peuple, auquel il se sent uni'.[18] Both of these points are undoubtedly central to any programme of ideologically motivated or, as it became fashionably called, committed writing. But like those made by Aragon and indeed by other theorists, French and Soviet alike, they remain tangential. Questions like 'How stylistically are works of socialist realism distinguishable from other examples of so-called realist writing?' or 'What are the characteristics of successful socialist realist writing which ensure its status as literature?' remain not so much unanswered as largely unasked. To be fair there clearly was, in France at this time, a good deal of uncertainty. Ideas imported from the Soviet Union were, if not ill digested, not always sufficiently well modified to suit national circumstances. For all that a new climate of political tolerance on the Left was apparent, and despite the participation of non-Party members in various discussions concerning cultural and literary matters, socialist realism as such was debated by relatively few and consciously practised by even fewer. The continuation of populism and of Poulaille's proletarian literature also ensured that distinctions were less clear than the militant Left would have liked. However, the 1930s did witness the beginnings of a literary programme which was to reappear in a much more vigorous and controlled form in the late 1940s and 1950s when it would coincide, of course, with a political climate of a different nature.

(a) *Aragon:* Les Cloches de Bâle *(1934)*[9]

When Aragon reviewed Nizan's first novel Antoine Bloyé in *Commune* (March–April 1934) he defined it as 'non pas seulement un ouvrage naturaliste, mais l'expression de ce réalisme socialiste (pour reprendre la terminologie de nos camarades soviétiques) où la réalité a son visage de classe, où le réel n'est pas une fin, mais un moyen de transformation, sa propre transformation' (p. 826). When his own *Les Cloches de Bâle* appeared, Georges Sadoul greeted it in much the same spirit. It was, he wrote, 'un roman qui peint à travers les individus leurs classes, à travers l'action, la lutte de ces classes, et qui fait entrevoir, par sa peinture de la réalité d'hier, la réalité socialiste de demain . . . [c'est] l'une des premières œuvres à laquelle le terme de réalité socialiste pourra s'appliquer' (*Commune*, January 1935, p. 503). Other critics and reviewers, French and Soviet alike, however, expressed some reservations, especially about the firmness of the novel's ideological position. René Garmy in *L'Humanité* (31 December 1934) saw in *Les Cloches de Bâle* 'une sorte d'idéalisation inconsciente de l'anarchisme'; and while it was warmly reviewed by D. Mirski in the Soviet journal *Litteratournaya Gazeta*, the same critic, in another article published in *L'Humanité* (22 January 1935), expressed more concern for what the novel revealed to be lacking from the French political left than for its literary qualities.

Galperina in *La Littérature internationale* (December 1935) praised it for the brilliance of Aragon's 'réalisme critique traditionnel', but considered it to be much more hesitant 'dès qu'il passe au réalisme héroïque qui est en train de naître en France'.

Aragon's own intentions are most clearly stated in the Epilogue of the novel which is largely devoted to 'la militante allemande' (p. 436) Clara Zetkin when she appears at the 1912 Bâle peace conference. As the last of the women presented in the book she is the projected ideal, 'le nouveau type de femme [. . .] la femme de demain, ou mieux, osons-le dire: elle est la femme d'aujourd'hui. L'égale' (p. 437). But whatever she is meant to represent, her introduction at this point is barely credible, and it is hardly enough to claim as one of Aragon's leading apologists, Roger Garaudy has done, that she has to be accepted as a symbolic figure.[10] In spite of the extremely varied manner in which the bulk of the novel is written, not only does Aragon's presentation of her disrupt the narrative flow, even at this late stage, it also suggests that he is not entirely certain that what he has previously written conveys his ideas about the future, equality, responsibility and so on with sufficient clarity and positiveness.

Critics are almost unanimous in the view that of the four parts of *Les Cloches de Bâle*, 'Diane', the first, is the most successful. Indeed if Malraux's idea that revolutionary writing in France could at best only be directed 'contre la bourgeoisie', is valid, then this section of the novel must rank very highly. In essence it is a vast, extended image.[11] The overriding bourgeois concern for material possession and appearances is expressed through a series of events and situations in which superficiality and uncertainty are everywhere apparent. This tone is established from the opening paragraph with the suggestion in the first sentence of Guy's illegitimacy, the hotel setting and false, holiday atmosphere, the search for social advantage and concern for fashion and reputation. Moreover Aragon presents this in a style in which thoughts, speech and descriptive narrative alternate and merge, in which sentences are often short and expressions popular, and in which, as a result, there is an impression of pace and breathlessness. For example, the introduction of Mme Melazzi:

le père de Mme Melazzi avait été tué à Gravelotte. Et une cousine à elle avait dansé avec Antonin Mercié. Ou peut-être

qu'elle n'avait pas précisément dansé. A une fête de charité.
Mais qu'est-ce que Mlle Judith lisait donc là? Mlle Judith lisait
Oscar Wilde. Mme Melazzi hésita un peu. Oscar Wilde. . . .
(pp. 15, 16)

Having created this impression in the opening chapter Aragon
carries it forward through the rest of the section. The world he
sets out to depict for us is one of duplicity, social manœuvring and
profiteering, in which people use and discard one another
wittingly and at will like so many disposable objects. Nowhere
does Aragon more successfully achieve this than in his portrayal
of Diane herself, already divorced – and therefore already
used – at 19, whose standard of living is maintained by a series of
lovers, and whose sole concern is for the effect she has on others.
Aragon's irony is harsh:

' – Même quand elle se tait [. . .] elle a l'irrésistible esprit de
son sourire qui éclaire toutes les conversations, jusqu'aux plus
fastidieuses'. Précisément, Diane souriait, de trois quarts.
Diane était exactement l'idéal des premières pages de
magazine.
    Très grande, très blonde, les yeux noirs, la peau blanche,
très blanches, une beauté. (pp. 19, 20)

The full extension of this which is her ability to play any part
required of her, is best exemplified in her handling of Jacques de
Sabran after his brother's suicide. In this scene (Chapter 8)
gesture, setting, language and emotional control are skilfully
combined to give a performance both of the highest quality and
completely successful. Sabran is immediately trapped by the
carefully prepared atmosphere of tragedy and high-minded
seriousness:

Diane lisait,[12] très pâle dans ses oreillers, sans fard. [. . .] Elle
était manifestement épuisée par l'élan qu'elle venait d'avoir.
Silence insupportable. [. . .] Jacques remarqua au-dessus du lit
[. . .] une vierge espagnole tout habillée, très brune avec des
yeux clairs, et des bijoux. Diane lui en parut plus pure, presque
déjà d'un autre monde. (pp. 71, 2)

Gradually he is seduced. The teasing movements in the bed

('. . . et le geste disjoignait la berthe de dentelle passée pour cacher la chemise', p. 73), the melodramatic gestures ('Diane cacha ses yeux dans ses mains', p. 73), and Diane's increasing insistence on her responsibility in what has taken place, all culminate in the final confession: 'si je l'ai poussé au désespoir [. . .] c'est parce que je l'aimais' (p. 77). When he eventually leaves, Sabran is a changed man. As a precise, highly distilled example of the way in which this society customarily works, this scene carries much of Aragon's indictment of it quite simply by the way in which he presents it. (Indeed in this respect it is worthy of comparison with the scene of Rosenthal's death, and of his family's reaction, in Nizan's last novel *La Conspiration*.) Aragon also underlines the falseness and immorality of the scene from the beginning by the impression Sabran has that he is being shown into a brothel, and in particular by the hypocrisy of Diane's self-castigation: 'Une abomination comme toute cette comédie de vertu et d'honorabilité qui m'entoure et qui me fait horreur. Une abomination comme votre monde, vos mensonges, vos conventions. Pauvre Pierrot!' (p. 77). The ironic use in this outburst not only of *comédie* but of 'Pierrot', not simply an affectionate diminutive, but an unwitting (on Diane's part) allusion to the archetypal clown–scapegoat figure of pantomime, carries considerable weight.

Pierre's suicide remains without adequate explanation and receives only passing reference in the press (p. 394). It too has been like an excerpt from a play – when Guy comes upon it unawares it has the quality of a *tableau vivant* – in which all those concerned have played the roles required of them. Thus when Dorsch writes to Brunel about the matter expressing his private concern, he chooses the language of outmoded patriotism which befits his character:

> Il ne faut pas que la fin de Pierre Sabran puisse permettre de salir le drapeau, de compromettre l'armée, de traîner dans l'ordure avec le vieux nom alsacien des Dorsch l'honneur, le prestige des généraux français, qui mèneront un jour ce peuple de frondeurs et de chansonniers à la glorieuse revanche de ce Sedan, dont le seul nom nous fait gémir. (p. 66)

For most of the opening section Aragon concentrates on this general idea of established role playing. In the case of Guy, however, he shows (as does Sartre in 'L'Enfance d'un chef') how people are moulded. In the Brunel household Guy is simply one more object to be admired. No thought is given to his natural development, as Aragon's syntax partly indicates: 'Il était habillé en satin blanc et noir avec un béret de marin anglais: *H.M.S. Victoria*. On lui faisait apprendre le violon, et il récitait des poésies. 'Ce sera un prodige', disait Diane' (p. 24). Having been kept and tutored at home he is friendless, but Aragon allows little sympathy, the implication being that such conditioning is unthinkingly accepted by the child. Like his uncle Robert, Guy too will in time become a parasite (p. 28). Although his role in the novel is never developed, it is through Guy that Aragon does make one of his most overt socio-political comments, but his brief skirmish with the working-class boy (p. 47) appears both out of place in the general tenor of the opening section, and carries too little weight to be particularly effective.

After completing 'Diane' Aragon gave the section to Elsa Triolet to read. In the context of the debate surrounding left-wing literature her response – 'Et tu vas continuer longtemps comme ça?'[13] – was interesting. 'Diane' does indeed seem to be precisely an example of what Galperina and Nizan described as 'réalisme critique', written with subtlety and destructive verve. But the question of a positive alternative remained, and the subsequent sections of the novel must be read as an attempt by Aragon to answer it.

Although we know from the details of Guy's age that the opening section covers seven or eight years there is little sense of forward movement. Nor are there many signs that the 'real world' outside their insulated existence – an emphasis worth comparing with Zola's portrayal of the bourgeois domestic world in *Germinal* – has much meaning for the Brunels and their associates. ('Diane ignorait qu'il y avait eu des grèves' p. 72). These two aspects are very deliberately worked into the rest of the novel. The second part 'Catherine' begins in 1912, moves back in time to the 1890s after the opening chapter, and returns to the 'present' in the final chapter of Part Three, 'Victor'. And just as the opening section focussed on Diane as someone entirely characteristic of her class, so the next two concentrate on Catherine's attempted rebellion as she gradually undergoes a social and political education.

The first and perhaps most constant feature of this education concerns the emancipation of women. Catherine is fascinated by but wary of men: 'elle avait peur de se voir définie par l'homme à qui elle se donnerait' (p. 147). (Ironically her freedom at the end of the novel is manœuvred by Jean Thiébault, now a high ranking army officer, to whom she had first given herself, and whose advances and proposals she had subsequently rejected.) Like Diane she takes a series of lovers, not as a form of socially acceptable prostitution, but as a deliberate challenge to conventional bourgeois morality. Closely following this personal development is the growth of her political awareness. Aragon carefully illustrates how her personal response to society gradually changes by introducing Catherine to a series of politically motivated groups, each of which seems to her, for a while at least, to make sense of her privately conceived scheme of things in which 'les travailleurs étaient du côté des femmes' (p. 151). Thus social catholicism is followed by anarchism which in turn gives way to socialism; but unlike Victor through whom she is introduced to the last of these she is unable to commit herself absolutely. Even when at the end of Part Three the coal miners' strikes remind her of Cluses, where she had made the first and vital step forward in her political education, we know that Catherine has developed as far as she is able to go. 'Cette impossibilité à se déclarer véritablement' (p. 211) which she had experienced during her discussions with Libertad has not changed.

At the time of the Cluses episode, Aragon gives no indication that Catherine will ultimately fail to reject her past completely. These few days in 1904 are preceded by the 'parenthèse champêtre' (p. 163) of the holiday which she and Jean spend together. It is a period of innocent self-indulgence which looks back to and is contrasted with the oppressive and febrile atmosphere of the hotel in the novel's first chapter. It is also important at this point in the story, since it ensures that the workers' rebellion and the ensuing incidents are put into sharp relief and thereby magnified. Not surprisingly some aspects are given a symbolic value and impress Catherine deeply – the young worker who is shot still clutching his hammer (p. 168), or the eyes of the corpse which Catherine tends '[qui] ne voulaient absolument pas se fermer' (p. 184). Yet even though the experience of Cluses confirms the latent political sympathies in Catherine and her willingness to associate with working-class

people and their problems (a fact recognized by Jean in his reservation of separate hotel bedrooms (p. 184)), total assimilation is
impossible. To some extent her spirit of independence – 'cette
anarchie enfantine' (p. 139) – is responsible, but more so is her
inheritance. Whatever the conditions of her life in Paris, and
however much she may react against pressures to conform to her
mother's ideas of acceptable social behaviour, personal independence is assured by the money she receives from her father:
'L'argent tombait du ciel par la poste, venait de lointain, du
problématique M. Simonidzé, qui avait des puits de pétrole' (p.
135). At no point does it occur to her to refuse this 'mensualité
irrégulière' (p. 273), 'le petit mandat de Bakou' (p. 288). With it
she is able to live without working, to travel, and most
significantly of all, to pay for treatment in Switzerland when her
tuberculosis is diagnosed. This privilege is mentioned by Aragon
with increasing frequency in the third section of the novel, in
which Catherine's political involvement is also at its most
advanced, and in which she is associated with Victor ('pour elle
un type humain absolument nouveau' p. 288) for whom socialism
is, as Carré will say of Communism in *La Conspiration*, 'un style de
vie'. Once Victor disappears from her life, however, the
uncertainty and ambiguity reappear; as Aragon comments
towards the end of Part Three when Catherine enjoys London in
the company of Brunel:

> Elle n'était pas libérée des choses qu'avaient aimées sa mère et
> son père, le propriétaire de puits de Bakou. Elle se reprochait
> d'être là en décolleté, avec ce bandit en smoking dans un loge
> de Picadilly. [. . .] Mais qu'y faire? Elle aimait, à la fois, et
> haïssait le luxe. Elle voulait certains soirs oublier la misère. Son
> socialisme n'était pas encore de très bon teint. (p. 408)

This essential flaw in her character is also, and more subtly,
indicated by her illness. In a general way death and disease
feature prominently in *Les Cloches de Bâle* just as they do too in
Antoine Bloyé and *Le Cheval de Troie*. For Nizan in particular death
should be seen as the absolute form of the stifling, introverted
bourgeois world which he, like Aragon, attacks. Illness has much
the same significance, while abortion and miscarriages, combining both, allow for direct observations to be made on sexual
discrimination and on the differences between the bourgeois and

working-class societies. In *Les Cloches de Bâle* we need only compare Judith Romanet's abortion and Jeannette's miscarriage. Catherine's illness becomes apparent and develops during the period of her increasing political awareness at the same time as the marked increase in Aragon's repeated allusions to the money she receives from her father. The two are brought together in her being able to pay for treatment in the sanatorium at Berck and therefore appear to be *rejected* together when, having assaulted Baisedieu, she is expelled from Switzerland. Yet she will still succumb to the monied life style of Brunel, and only when she refuses his sexual advances – for which he betrays her to the police – is there a suggestion that she has finally changed: 'Elle est sortie du parasitisme et de la prostitution. Le monde du travail s'ouvre à elle' (p. 424).

Up to this point therefore Aragon has gone a long way in illustrating an important feature of socialist realist writing; what he himself defines as 'la rééducation de l'homme par l'homme, [. . .] la transformation du singe social de notre temps en l'homme socialiste de l'avenir'.[14] But he seems incapable of following this through completely and of presenting Catherine in a new, exemplary role – hence the introduction of Clara Zetkin. And despite the rhetoric of the closing pages, there is relatively little in *Les Cloches de Bâle* which a mid-1930s reader might interpret as a positive indication of how society should develop. Aragon works rather by implication and suggestion, best exemplified by his presentation of historical events. As we have already noted the opening section of the novel appears to be static, a further indication that the bourgeois society described in it is nonproductive and stagnant. Having moved back in time from the beginning of Part Two, however, Aragon is then able to shape history to suit his purpose. Thus the taxi driver's dispute (based on an actual event which he reported for *L'Humanité* in 1934) is presented in such a way that the strike appears to be justified. Manipulation of this kind (to be used extensively in *Les Communistes*) also allows Aragon to anticipate the approaching catastrophe of war: for example, just before the Cluses episode (p. 162 and p. 185) and through Bataille whose private obsession with death has a public significance: 'Nous sommes au bout d'une époque, au seuil d'un monde' (p. 238). And in view of the widely held belief that the working class was deliberately sacrificed by the bourgeoisie in the 1914–18 War, the various examples of its being exploited and attacked in peace time are also clearly intended as warning signs for the immediate future. This kind of control is also to be found in more particular aspects of style. Aragon adopts a position of omniscience which allows him to intervene and pass comment, to address the reader directly, commenting from his present (1930s) position on police activities for example, or turning to the future tense to offer interpretation or underline the inevitable progress which will be made.

Although in *J'abats mon jeu* (1959) Aragon subsequently acknowledged that *Les Cloches de Bâle* did have a number of quite serious structural defects, his remark four years later in an interview with Francis Crémieux, that writing had always been for him both the acquisition and communication of knowledge is more useful for a general assessment of his work.[15] But the question 'Communication to and with whom?' remains. For all its moments of brilliance *Les Cloches de Bâle* is essentially a negative work and, moreover, one which requires a highly developed degree of literary awareness on the part of the reader if Aragon's purpose in it is to be fully detected.

Paul Nizan: Antoine Bloyé *(1933);* Le Cheval de Troie *(1935)*

Although Aragon was perhaps the more notorious and colourful figure, Nizan had an equally important influence on the general intellectual climate of the late-twenties and early thirties. By the time he published his two essays *Aden Arabie* (1931) and *Les Chiens de garde* (1932) Nizan was already fully committed to the Communist cause, and was collaborating with a number of left-wing groups and reviews. However disillusioned a view he may present of these years in *La Conspiration*, there is no doubt that amongst French intellectuals Nizan was one of the more rigorous and orthodox in attitude. This becomes particularly clear when we examine his attitude to literature even though he did not focus his attention quite as narrowly on socialist realism as Aragon. In articles like 'La littérature révolutionnaire en France', 'Sur l'humanisme', 'L'ennemi public Nº 1', 'Une littérature responsable'[16] together with a large number of reviews in *Commune, L'Humanité, Monde* and *Europe*, he consistently returned to a number of themes. The early articles which can be read as a kind of manifesto, set these out clearly.[17] All literature for Nizan is propaganda: the idea of art for art's sake is false, simply one more fabrication of the political and economic system dominated by bourgeois capitalism. It is in other words an essential part of a self-perpetuating system and as such must be overthrown. Truly revolutionary literature will play its part in such a move: 'Une littérature révolutionnaire au sens réel et non plus au sens formel comprendra tous les écrits exaltant, préparant la révolution prolétarienne, puisant en elle tous ces thèmes et ses inspirations'.[18] Not surprisingly Nizan rejects Poulaille's theories and claims instead that proletarian literature can treat any subject as long as it is from a proletarian point of view with its 'plus spéciale conscience de classe. La littérature révolutionnaire décrira d'un point de vue révolutionnaire, tous les objets, y compris la bourgeoisie, y compris la nature'.[19] Like Serge, Fréville, Bloch and others, Nizan acknowledges that the situation prevailing in France is different from that in the Soviet Union. He also acknowledges, but dismisses, some of the attempts which have so far been made to move away from bourgeois escapist literature – populism ('un nouvel exotisme')[20] or the efforts of the *Monde* group. Others are granted grudging approval, though he regrets the absence of firm political direction. The *Europe* writers, for example, are described as 'ce groupe de bonnes volontés impuissantes'; Poulaille and Lucien Bourgeois are writers who '[font] entendre un certain nombre de protestations généreuses et vagues contre la guerre ou le colonialisme'.[21] Where he does see real hope is in the AEAR, 'un mouvement de masse fort précis et fort conscient', and in *Commune*, 'un organe assez violent de contre-attaque'.[22]

Like Aragon and Guéhenno Nizan believed that bourgeois culture exerted such a powerful influence that proletarian writers were in danger of betraying their class. Given this situation it would be quite normal that bourgeois writers, sympathetic to the cause of the working class, would undergo a form of political and intellectual retraining in order to give their sympathy greater ideological security. As he observed in 1935 (and in words which anticipated what Sartre would say over a decade later) the duty of such writers would then be to disclose as well as to direct:

L'écrivain est celui qui a pour fonction de définir et de révéler aux hommes leurs plus hautes valeurs et leurs plus vastes ambitions: il découvre les valeurs que leur vie implique et leur fournit des justifications qu'ils puissent tous accepter, parce qu'elles vont dans le sens de la grandeur et de l'accomplissement.[23]

Although in his reviews of the imaginative writings of others Nizan frequently deplored artistic weakness, there is in general in articles of this kind, the familiar concern for content and purpose rather than for style and form. On occasions he would even go further. As he wrote in a review of Malraux's *Le Temps du mépris*, in *Monde* (6 June 1935): 'La preuve exclut l'art [. . .]. La preuve relève de la science et s'administre par des techniques très précises dont les moyens ne sont pas ceux de l'art'. Yet in his own imaginative literature and with *Le Cheval de Troie* in particular Nizan succeeds in challenging such an extreme view.

As we have seen *Antoine Bloyé* was greeted enthusiastically by Aragon as an example of socialist realism, in which reality was not an end in itself but 'un moyen de transformation, sa propre transformation'. In other words, it is a revolutionary model, very much in line with the general proposals concerning literature which Nizan himself had been developing during the previous few years. (Nizan's own assessment of the novel in this respect is rather interesting: 'Je n'ai pas voulu faire de la politique dans mon roman. Mais s'il y a des conclusions politiques à en tirer, c'est le sujet qui le veut', *Le Rempart*, 16 November 1933.)

By comparison certainly with *Les Cloches de Bâle* the story of Antoine Bloyé is a simple one. Bloyé, a figure based, as Nizan admitted, directly on his father, gradually, by virtue of his intelligence and capacity for hard work, improves himself economically and socially. In the process, however, he becomes increasingly isolated and used by others until he is eventually discarded and left to die. In order to underscore the socio-political message of the book, Nizan shows that while Bloyé feels that he has betrayed his true origins, he never completely settles into his new class. His case is in fact rather like that of Catherine Simonidzé in reverse.

While *Antoine Bloyé* was hailed on publication as a socialist realist work it is so, as Susan Suleiman has argued,[24] only in a negative way, for at no stage does Antoine act in an exemplary or positive manner. In spite of several indications that he retains nostalgic memories of and sympathy for his humble origins, he remains too passive a figure, an unthinking victim of the pressures brought to bear upon him by the social class towards which he gradually moves and which he eventually joins. Furthermore he is almost permanently obsessed with thoughts of death, these too serving to turn him inwards upon himself. Although socialist realism, especially in France, was in its infancy, such limitations were serious, and that Nizan may have been aware of this is suggested by the amount of overt authorial interference in the novel. However, even when he concentrates in this rather narrow way on Bloyé as an individual, Nizan succeeds in offering a number of comments of some substance on society as a whole. Bourgeois society is shown to be made up of a series of isolated cells, each one existing according to certain preordained values. To accept such an existence – which Bloyé realizes he has done only when it is too late – is to accept a living death: 'il avait tout le temps vécu sa mort' (p. 310).[25]

Most critics agree that Nizan's achievement in *Antoine Bloyé* lies in his creation of an interior drama which is then successfully projected onto a larger public scale. Such a view, however, tends to disregard the extent to which the narrator also intervenes to observe, comment and judge, especially when such intervention is clearly an equally essential part of Nizan's method of directing our attention and of shaping our response. Indeed such techniques appear quite regularly and, notably in Chapter 13, are brought together in a way which suggests a considerable degree of conscious control.

The most obvious example of Nizan's concern for the need to create a specific context in which his characters will act, is in his Balzac-like provision of historical, geographical and sociological information: Finistère and its religious traditions (p. 41), the development of railways and of railway traffic (p. 121), the outbreak of war (Chapter 17), the evolution of provincial life (pp. 178–84) and marriage (pp. 144–6) which, seen as a replica in miniature of bourgeois society as a whole, anticipates the stereotyped union of Bloyé and Anne. Elsewhere he uses Bloyé as a filter for his own opinions (as he will use the younger Bloyé in *Le Cheval de Troie*). Thus when Bloyé, at the time of the strike (Chapter 14), recognizes the degree to which he has become isolated and alienated from the workers, Nizan intervenes to work into that awareness an explanation of it:

Ce soir-là, Antoine comprenait qu'il était un homme de la solitude, un homme sans communion. [. . .] Il éprouvait des sentiments difficiles et cruels. Il participait à la joie d'avoir remporté la victoire sur la grève, une joie de briseur de grève. Il était stupéfait de cette joie. Il détestait alors les ouvriers, parce qu'il les enviait en secret, parce qu'il savait au plus profond de lui-même qu'il y avait plus de vérité dans leur défaite que dans sa victoire de bourgeois. (p. 207)

Earlier in the novel when he is beginning to relate to the conditions of his work at Saint-Nazaire, Nizan 'explains' how he is beginning to develop: 'il commence à faire des rêves de grandeur, à se promettre un avenir important [. . .] Il aura peut-être du mal à y parvenir, mais il se connaît, il connaît sa dureté, sa résistance au travail, il se promène le soir en se disant qu'il arrivera . . .' (p. 55). And shortly after this when he enters the Ecole des Arts et Métiers we read: 'il ne savait pas qu'il faisait avec bien d'autres adolescents de son âge un des enjeux de la vaste partie que commençaient à engager les principaux maîtres de la bourgeoisie française' (p. 65).

While in terms of such authorial intrusion there is little in *Antoine Bloyé* to compare with the final section of *Les Cloches de Bâle*, Nizan appears to feel no more compunction than does Aragon at this kind of manipulation. On the contrary it seems that he uses it quite deliberately to provide a corrective to Bloyé's predominantly passive and negative attitude to life. And that Nizan was aware – perhaps too much so in fact – of the way in which various narrative techniques could be brought together in order to create a particular cumulative effect, is well illustrated in Chapter 13, 'Dans la vie des hommes'. In this chapter, which occurs almost exactly at the mid-point of the second section of the novel, the use of contrast, of movement from the general to the particular, of shifts of tense (a feature of the novel as a whole) and of words or phrases with a special reverberatory significance are all introduced as Nizan focuses on Bloyé's capitulation to the bourgeoisie.

In addition to a certain amount of historical and topographical information necessary for the development of the story, Nizan spends about three-quarters of the chapter offering an analysis of bourgeois existence and values. Initially this is of a general nature: 'dans ces années d'avant-guerre, la bourgeoisie française s'épanouit dans un grand calme et un grand contentement, elle est installée, il ne lui arrive pas de malheurs, les catastrophes ne sont pas suspendues au-dessus de sa tête, elle est étalée dans un pouvoir que nulle force ne semble menacer' (p. 173). The use of the present tense here, and in similar passages, predominates in the opening pages of the chapter and clearly indicates Nizan's aim to stress the permanent nature of a bourgeois ethos which (in a way which recalls Berl's essays) is ultimately encapsulated in the deification of 'Devoir' (p. 175). Within this opening section all references to Bloyé are of a kind which define him as a typical representative of this class, and the Balzacian formula 'Antoine est un de ces . . .' is particularly noticeable. Thereafter, having established a certain moral climate, Nizan concentrates on the particular area of the town to which the Bloyés move. Here society is divided between those of the working class and those 'dont le métier expire toutes les nuits' (p. 180), whose scorn for the workers and envy of the rich increase as does their means of self-importance and self-sufficiency. Nizan's description of their life, and of the Bloyés' as well, is full of expressions denoting superficiality, protection and delusion:

> ils avaient tous l'illusion de croire que les aventures du monde, les sursauts mêmes de leur planète ne les concernaient pas, ils se sentaient définitivement à l'écart, merveilleusement certains et protégés et toutes ces choses arrivaient pour leur servir de spectacle et de divertissement, pour servir de prétextes à leur jeu des commentaires et des jugements. [. . .] Ils se croyaient sages, ils se croyaient stables, ils se croyaient heureux. [. . .] Et Antoine vivait parmi eux, il était l'un d'eux; mois après mois, il s'enfonçait dans cette confiture douceâtre d'habitudes, il s'endormait' [. . .]. (pp. 186, 7)

The passivity of Antoine's attitude is symbolized by his ritualized life, and the faint stirrings in him, caused by visits to the work-shops and by his handling of tools, have no real effect. Like Marcelle, however meaningful they may be, they are firmly relegated to the past. Chapter 13 closes with the appearance of Bloyé's superior, Huet ('un grand bourgeois qui avait des traditions de famille', p. 194) who has been through the Ecole Polytechnique, knows Latin and quotes Barrès and Nietzsche. At present Bloyé is scornful, but Huet does represent the next rung on the social ladder. Nizan's irony is nicely muted: 'M. Huet baisait la main des provinciales nobles dans des salons où les Bloyé n'entraient pas. Mais l'ambition d'Antoine n'avait jamais visé si haut . . .' (p. 195).

By contrast with the dominant place it holds in the opening pages of the chapter, the present tense is used in the later section much more sparingly. Either it carries Nizan's 'moral' for him ('Tous les hommes regrettent les plaisirs des jeux collectifs' p. 188) or as before it underlines the present (1930s) relevance of his account: 'ils se livraient à des plaisirs aujourd'hui oubliés de leurs pareils, qui connaissent enfin, comme les ouvriers qu'ils méprisent encore, l'angoisse des semaines, des mois qui vont arriver . . .' (p. 184). Such comments together with his undisguised approval for the integrity of the working class are entirely in harmony with the composition of the novel as a whole. In *Antoine Bloyé* Nizan is not satisfied with a simple description of life in late nineteenth-century France. Yet in spite of various attempts to make it relevant for his contemporary audience ('un instrument de connaissance [. . .] un moyen de lutte contre la bourgeoisie')[26] *Antoine Bloyé* must still be considered to fall short of the idea of a revolutionary novel which he himself advocated, and which was central to the whole concept of socialist realism. Overall it remains a negative book. The faults of a certain kind of society may indeed have been exposed, but even less in *Les Cloches de Bâle*, there is neither a viable alternative proposed, nor even a moment of positive action, from which general theoretical points may be drawn or example taken. That Nizan himself recognized this is suggested by his second novel *Le Cheval de Troie* published in the autumn of 1935 nine months after his return from the Soviet Union where, in the previous August, he had attended the first Soviet Writers Congress.

According to Simone de Beauvoir, Brice Parain and Romain Rolland, Nizan returned from the Soviet Union considerably disillusioned, haunted by the spectre of death and of the utter loneliness of man in the face of it.[27] While this may have been true, and while death is given even greater prominence in *Le Cheval de Troie* than in *Antoine Bloyé*, there is little doubt that the overall tone of the second novel is more optimistic. It is also clear that Nizan was considerably influenced by the general intellectual and cultural climate which he had found in the Soviet Union. A foretaste of the kind of conflict to be treated in *Le Cheval de Troie* had been given in an essay 'Présentation d'une ville', published in the fourth issue of *La Littérature internationale* in 1934.[28] Heavily ironic in tone this essay continues the exposure of bourgeois standards and beliefs which we find in *Antoine Bloyé*. Again, however, there is the same imbalance. The workers described in a few pages in the penultimate section are shown to be too crushed, rendered impotent by the bourgeois machine which they serve. Only in the final section and in the capacity of an omniscient narrator who directs the wakening awareness of the workers, does Nizan point to a new, revolutionary future: 'C'était une ville où tout commençait: on se serait cru cent ans plus tôt, à l'origine même, aux premières sources de la colère et de la puissance ouvrières' (p. 194). But there is no demonstration of *how* bourgeois tyranny will be overthrown, of *what kind of action* the workers can best undertake in order to give themselves a sense of identity and mission. 'Présentation d'une ville', like *Antoine Bloyé*, is essentially negative.

The most significant differences between *Antoine Bloyé* and *Le Cheval de Troie* are first, that the real protagonist is a group of people rather than an individual; second, that these people have already reached a position of political conviction by which their lives are given direction. Furthermore as the title of the novel suggests the action – for all that it is local and limited in scope – is intended to have an epic ring to it. The events described last precisely for one week and take place in Villefranche, an amalgam of the provincial centres where Nizan has been politically active – Villefranche-sur-Saône, Bourg and Vienne. The Communists, a small, isolated group like those described in the essay, have for some time been trying to focus elements of political unrest more purposefully. Hitherto opportunities have come only through strikes or the distribution of their newspaper *Le Tréfileur rouge*. Now, however, the projected visit of a fascist speaker galvanises them into preparation and the novel describes the effect which this new political urgency has on public and private levels alike.

As Walter Redfern has observed, the opening scene of the novel is like 'a breathing space'.[29] Yet even though the group enjoys this brief country excursion, the signs of their normal, waking lives are always present. Like the pastoral interludes in works by Zola, the Goncourts or Philippe, this one is a deception, a false escape only. The women (with the exception of Marie-Louise) are prematurely old; the emblems of the society with which they are in permanent conflict remain visible even here – factory chimneys, church spires and the roof of the law courts. (Not insignificantly the direction in which they look in the first chapter is reversed in the final paragraph of the novel which, like the ending of *Le Feu*, is heavy with the symbols of freedom.) Parallel to this concentration on the place of action is a manipulation of time: Part One lasts for six days; Part Two for one only. Nizan also creates a sense of *actualité* by alluding to real events and people.[30] By these means *Le Cheval de Troie* has an immediacy lacking in *Antoine Bloyé*, and demonstrates that the kind of activity in which Bloyé and his associates indulge is not merely speculative. What the reader witnesses in the novel is an attempt, however small, to make history: 'changer le monde' (p. 53).[31] Unlike *Antoine Bloyé, Le Cheval de Troie* is a positive book.

In spite of this new certainty and of some of the technical and stylistic devices prompted by it, *Le Cheval de Troie* still follows a hesitant line between imaginative literature and propaganda. Where Nizan is especially successful in combining these is in the way he relates private dilemmas to public issues. Thus while Catherine is clearly seen to be a victim of an unjust social and political system, Albert, in some ways helpless too, is guilty for his passive, naïve (p. 80) acceptance of it: 'il fermait les yeux, il n'y avait plus qu'à se laisser emporter par le mouvement de la machine: à partir de cette minute, il n'avait plus d'initiative à prendre' (p. 83). For him to participate actively in the struggle against the system requires something as tragic as Catherine's death. In a different, but equally instructive way, we have Lange who represents the opposite position to that held by Bloyé (who, we are told, once resembled him, p. 117).[32] By contrast with Bloyé, who has deliberately modified his personality to suit that of the group, Lange has become increasingly uncommitted and isolated. When he first appears he is described by Bloyé as 'un mort', in Nizan's terminology a complete denunciation of someone who has accepted a life of passive self-indulgence. This is underlined by the descriptions at the end of Chapter 5 of his relationships with women, and, more particularly, by those of his involvement with the political manifestations in Chapter 9. In the latter he is shown at first to be an observer, but gradually he is drawn into the fascist crowd whose exaltation he finally shares: 'Lange fut entraîné dans le mouvement du monde, il vivait, il refaisait partie comme les autres de la machine, des batailles, il ne contemplait plus, il connaissait la passion. [. . .] son exaltation était aussi forte qu'une satisfaction sexuelle' (pp. 174, 5). (The reference to the machine here should of course be linked with that contained in Albert's acceptance of events.) In Lange's case isolation, cynicism and passivity are shown to lead to an *unthinking* acceptance of the values and repressive measures of those in authority. The contrast between this position and those of Bloyé's group is unambiguous.

Nizan also draws attention to the difference in values between the two sides through the images he uses in his descriptions of their meetings. Thus the fascist rally:

> Ils venaient d'être enfermés dans le puits noir du théâtre: la salle était obscure et froide et la réunion avait d'abord ressemblé à une descente dans un monde sous-marin avec toutes ces sirènes peintes qui enroulaient leurs queues d'aronde sous la rampe du balcon, un monde sous-marin au sommet duquel une verrière bleue laissait tomber une lumière avortée comme celle de la lune sous la mer. (p. 139)

But this atmosphere of a sinister, murky underwater world is not limited to the final pages: it appears regularly, though not always with quite the same emphasis, throughout the book, thereby directing our emotional response to the final events in a particular way. In Chapter 1 Bloyé arrives at the top of the hill out of breath 'comme un nageur sorti de l'eau' (p. 27); the bourgeois inhabitants of Villefranche are described as 'des crustacés ou des poissons s'agitant lentement dans l'eau et les algues d'un vivarium' (p. 40). The description of the passage where Lange goes after the dinner party in Chapter V is also coloured in a similar, though more subtle and incidental way, and specifically prepares us for Lange's evolution at the end of the novel. As in *Antoine Bloyé* images which denote superficiality are also prevalent in descriptions of the bougeoisie and its political activities. The visiting speaker is 'un acteur célèbre' (p. 130), the riot squad has officers 'avec des décorations' (p. 131), the young fascist supporters 'portaient des bérets basques, des insignes, des cannes' (p. 135) and so on. Not surprisingly Nizan's need to stress the alternative, positive values of the Left is conveyed in a similar way: the workers' rally is greeted by the sun and by the warm red of the unfurled flags (p. 136). A lack of organization is compensated by a sense of warmth and life, conveyed by the image of fire (p. 137), and a shared identity of feeling is shown to be of greater significance than that of superficial dress. And when the riot squad (armed with guns and protected by armoured clothing) drives the workers (who have no protection and only stones as weapons) back to their part of the town, it is met by total resistance (pp. 194–6). It is a final demonstration of where true values and fraternity are to be found.

While, especially in the last quarter of the novel, Nizan's use of image and contrast may appear rather obvious and schematized, we should not forget his own criteria by which form is of necessity simply a means of conveying content, even though it should be in itself artistically acceptable. In *Antoine Bloyé* Nizan explains how Antoine's death, which is a 'fact' from the opening of the novel, has occurred: alternatives are alluded to but cannot, by virtue of the retrospective nature of the account, be developed other than by authorial intervention. The contrastive use of image in *Le Cheval de Troie*, together with the developed relationship between private and public issues, all the while underpinned by a faith in a revolutionary future, mark a considerable advance in technique therefore.

Originally Nizan had planned to write *Le Cheval de Troie* as a first person narrative. Whether he abandoned the plan because he sensed it would result in that person's enjoying a superior and privileged position is not certain. Whatever the reason, there is no doubt that while Bloyé sinks his identity with that of the group as a whole, he is the one singled out on several occasions to be Nizan's *alter ego* voicing much of his political philosophy in pithy epigrammatic phrases: 'Changer le monde' (p. 53); 'Après la patience et l'espoir, la violence viendra' (p. 211). But it is less in examples like these than in Nizan's inability to do without what Adèle King has defined as 'une perspective supérieure qui juge l'action'[33] that problems emerge. In terms of the novel's political message the narrator, as in *Antoine Bloyé*, benefits from a superior collective knowledge, regularly taking over and developing ideas or interpreting situations and events. This is particularly noticeable in the final chapters. For example:

> Le sens politique de la journée, ils le dégageraient plus tard, ils pensaient premièrement à leur nombre, à leur dignité et à la fin de leur solitude. Et le sens politique de la journée, c'était peut-être simplement que des milliers d'hommes avaient été capables de colère, après tout. (p. 189)

Or:

> Ils pensaient aux temps qui viendraient. C'était ainsi. [. . .]
> Pendant des années cette explosion de l'histoire avait paru un
> songe et une légende qui ne concernaient pas plus les provinces
> françaises distraites et dormantes dans une terre de catas-
> trophes que les typhons des mers de Chine. [. . .] Un monde
> naissait. La France entrait dans le jeu des nations, pour elle
> aussi la violence qui refait l'histoire commençait. Plus de
> projets, d'attentes dans cet avenir incroyable où on ne comp-
> terait un jour les victimes qu'en gros, où personne n'aurait le
> temps de remarquer spécialement telle ou telle mort: ce serait
> comme un cataclysme naturel, un cyclone, un raz de marée.
> (p. 203)

Elsewhere he enjoys an omniscience which enables him, both to
observe Catherine and to register her emotions as she lies dying,
or to slip momentarily from an objective *il*, when describing
Lange's attitude to the demonstrations, to a subjective *je* (p. 167).
Again – and in a manner which recalls Barbusse – when describing the workers' reactions after they have prevented the fascist
rally from taking place, Nizan describes, speaks for them and
finally analyzes:

> Les ouvriers regardaient les gardes qui formaient une épaisse
> bande noire à l'entrée du boulevard où s'était aligné au début
> de l'après-midi le mince barrage de gendarmes. Ils se deman-
> daient le sens de la journée. Nous avons empêché les fascistes
> de défiler, nous les avons chassés, c'est une victoire, mais nous
> avons reculé devant les gardes, c'est peut-être une défaite qui
> annule la première victoire. Ils se demandaient ce qu'ils
> allaient faire: se disperser, rentrer chez eux? Mais ils avaient
> du mal à accepter que la journée finît après tout par avorter. La
> colère n'était pas épuisée; la colère qui s'est nourrie pendant
> des années ne s'épuise pas comme la faim, la colère est plus
> exigeante que la soif et la faim; elle n'était pas assouvie et elle
> les retentait encore dans l'attente jusqu'au dernier moment
> d'une seconde victoire; la colère les avait soulevés et elle ne les
> laissait pas retomber, elle n'était pas comme une vague qui
> soupire et s'abaisse mais comme la loi la plus profonde de leur
> vie. Ils ne se savaient pas tant de réserves de colère. (p. 179)

In this passage as elsewhere, not only the shifting narrative view-point, but also the developed image in the second half all too readily suggest that the need to proselytize could not be entrusted to the description of events alone.

It is here perhaps that we have a clue to one way of attempting to arrive at an evaluation of such socialist realist works. For all that they claimed that the stylistic and formal qualities of imaginative writing should not be neglected, the main concern of Aragon and Nizan was unambiguously didactic. By any standards which argue that the use of art for any purposes other than aesthetic ones will necessarily result in its impoverishment, these novels will automatically be considered flawed. Accusations will be freely made of schematization, of the undisguised manipulation of characters, events, and symbols, of the use made of an omniscient author and above all of the introduction of undigested abstractions. Furthermore in terms of the criteria by which such accusations are made there can be no real counter argument. By the same token, however, merely to dismiss such criteria (as indeed many including Nizan and Aragon did) as being narrow and conservative, intent on preserving one (bourgeois) kind of literature only, is, it could be argued, equally narrow and unproductive. In order to attempt to arrive at a more balanced, albeit naïve assessment of socialist realist works, we can only relate them to the principles by which the authors were guided, and which were developed in a very specific intellectual and political climate. Whatever doubts Aragon may have expressed in later years, or however uncertain Nizan may have suggested he was by *La Conspiration*, there is no doubt that during this period – and Aragon for considerably longer – they both unquestioningly accepted that literature was an important element in the education of the general public's social and political thinking. To this end socialist realism was not intended to be merely a fictive representation, however accurate, of the real world. Instead it was to be one which offered an analysis of that world and of the fundamental social and political forces at work within it.

Part III

6 The New Left

From the outbreak of the Second World War in 1939 and in particular from the German invasion in May and June 1940 up to the Liberation of Paris in August 1944, France underwent an experience without precedent in the modern history of any of the other major nations in Western Europe. During the First World War French soil had been the battle-ground on which millions had died, the country's own male population had been decimated to such an extent that all subsequent developments – sociological, political, religious and cultural alike – were radically altered. Victory had been won at an incalculable price, and peace had at best never been more than insecure. From the early thirties the threat of fascism had loomed increasingly large and for many further conflict on a world-wide scale appeared to be an unavoidable reality. Giraudoux's message had indeed been prophetic. But unlike the earlier conflict, the Second World War and especially the reality of occupation by an enemy force brought new problems and dilemmas. Not only was France initially defeated physically, she was also for the most part spiritually and morally broken. The French nation had – to use a popular image of the day – been raped by an aggressor with the tacit approval of many and the active, willing cooperation of more than a few; friendships and families had been destroyed from the inside and in spite of ultimate resurgence and victory the damage inflicted during these few years would never be completely repaired.

Although there is certainly still much information after forty years which has yet to be made public (and indeed much that will never be so) the roles played by those on the Left during this period have been extensively analysed.[1] The vigorous anti-fascist and anti-Nazi feelings expressed during the 1930s, and not least by members of the PCF were, of course, severely tested by the Nazi-Soviet pact of August 1939. For some, like Nizan, the pact was a betrayal and would only be countered in terms of personal conscience by resignation. For others it could be justified in terms both of the International Party line and also as a positive contribution to world peace. Active opposition to the government's policies caused the PCF to be outlawed; *L'Humanité* was published clandestinely; *Commune* was banned and ceased publication altogether; arrest, trial and imprisonment threatened many. During the early months of the Occupation the communists maintained their pacifist position, though there were early signs of a hardening of attitudes. In December 1940 on the twentieth anniversary of the foundation of the PCF, a pamphlet entitled 'Le Parti communiste à vingt ans' attributed to Gabriel Péri contained a marked anti-fascist tone. By the middle of 1941 following the German invasions of Greece, Bulgaria and Yugoslavia, the Party's attitude had become even more hostile; and with the invasion of the Soviet Union in June all necessity to remain faithful, however reluctantly, to the official Party line was removed.

The history of the Resistance and of the role played by the PCF in it has been charted at length by a number of commentators. In the end the Party emerged with distinction and more importantly with credibility. In 1946/47 it could boast 800,000 members and seemed ready to assume a position of power and influence. A mixture of euphoria, indecision and firm political opposition proved too strong, however, and in 1947 Ramadier dismissed the communist ministers in his government. Yet in spite of this political failure, the moral and intellectual influence of the PCF remained vigorous. Much was made both during and immediately after the war of the virtues of those like Jacques Decour, Georges Politzer, Gabriel Péri and Danielle Casanova (frequently compared to St Joan) who had been tortured and killed by the Gestapo; emphasis was placed on the values of respectability, of family and of spiritual life – a fact reflected, as Aragon approvingly notes in *L'Homme communiste*, in the 'natural' language of party members.[2] While the reasons for it may have been quite different, the sense of sharing and collectivity was pronounced, and many (especially amongst the young who had been influenced by the heroism of works like Malraux's *La Condition humaine*) found in Communism a new and hopeful solution to their personal dilemmas. Edgar Morin in his *Autocritique* expresses the attitude of many when he writes: 'j'étais un de ces adolescents pour qui devenir communiste signifie en même temps devenir homme. L'entrée au parti se confondait pour moi avec l'initiation virile, le risque de mort, l'engagement dans la vie authentique'.[3] The Resistance was, to use Caute's phrase a 'fertile recruiting period'.[4] Within the narrower confines of internal responsibility and action an important lead was also given by various groups, the majority of whose members were communist. In 1941 the Front national pour la Libération et l'Indépendance de la France was established, largely the result of the activity of Jacques Decour former *rédacteur en chef* of *Commune*. He also planned to establish a *Comité d'Ecrivains* and on Aragon's advice made contact with Jean Paulhan. These two, together with Jacques Debû-Bridel, were quickly joined by Charles Vildrac, Jean Guéhenno, Jean Blanzat and a cleric A.-J. Maydieu, and planned the first issue of *Les Lettres françaises*. In February 1942 Decour was arrested (and later shot on 30 May) and the issue was abandoned, Decour's sister destroying the articles which had already been prepared. In July, Claude Morgan was partly successful in regrouping those interested in the scheme but, faced with difficulties of communication, went ahead alone. In September 1942 *Les Lettres françaises* made its first appearance, roneotyped on poor quality paper and circulated in secret. Its manifesto, originally written by Decour, was a call to people of all persuasions to resist; the literary tradition of France was under attack: 'LES LETTRES FRANÇAISES sera notre instrument de combat et par sa publication, nous entendons nous intégrer, à notre place d'écrivains, dans la lutte à mort engagée par la Nation française pour se délivrer de ses oppresseurs'.

During the following months the *Comité national* grew in size, notable newcomers being Eluard and Sartre by February 1943, and Mauriac in August of the same year. Contributions by these and by Aragon, who was still in the southern zone, were received, but for the most part the first nine issues of the paper (the tenth in September 1943 was the first to be properly printed) were the results of the efforts of Claude Morgan. During these early months the militant and patriotic tone of the paper never varied: 'Il ne suffit pas d'être un patriote. Encore faut-il être un patriote agissant' (July 1943). Writers should publish 'des œuvres exaltant l'amour de la patrie et de la liberté, rendant hommages aux Francs-Tireurs et Partisans qui luttent courageusement pour bouter hors de la France les hordes nazies et leurs valets

Kollaborateurs' (October 1942). In terms of the true nature and role of literature, however, the most far-reaching statement came from Sartre in his second article 'La littérature, cette liberté!' (April 1944). In this, anticipating much of the general thesis to appear later in *Qu'est-ce que la littérature?* he moves – if only by implication – the act of writing from a political context to a philosophical one:

> On n'écrit pas en l'air et pour soi seul; la littérature est un acte de communication: le lecteur est aussi indispensable que l'auteur à la réalisation d'un livre. C'est *pour lui* et *par lui* finalement que le livre existe. [. . .] la littérature n'est pas un chant innocent et facile qui s'accomoderait de tous les régimes: mais elle pose d'elle-même la question politique; écrire, c'est réclamer la liberté pour tous les hommes; si l'œuvre ne doit pas être l'acte d'une liberté qui veut se faire reconnaître par d'autres libertés, elle n'est qu'un infâme bavardage.

Such a statement as this, heavily existentialist in tone, was not one which *Les Lettres françaises* was to adopt as its own, however. With the Liberation and the official recognition of the paper, it became, in spite of its genuinely wide coverage of cultural affairs, increasingly dogmatic especially over literature. Sartre, who by October 1945 had launched *Les Temps modernes*, was branded by Roger Garaudy (*Les Lettres françaises*, 29 December 1945) as a 'false prophet'. Literature and in particular the novel were discussed in terms strongly reminiscent of the socialist realist debate of the 1930s. Elsa Triolet in an article 'L'écrivain public' (23 June 1947) produced what could virtually be taken as an editorial statement:

> Aujourd'hui l'artiste d'avant-garde a le bonheur d'être une sorte d'*écrivain public*. *L'écrivain public*, celui qui exprime ceux qui ne savent pas écrire, l'écrivain public, celui, qui, comme le magicien d'autrefois, exorcise la foule, qui, comme le psychanalyste d'aujourd'hui, cherche à la libérer en nommant les maux qu'elle ne sait pas préciser. L'écrivain public, celui qui épouse et devance l'événement, qui l'exprime et le commente, le devine et l'éclaire socialement et poétiquement parlant.

Overtly Communist – and later Stalinist – in sympathy, the

paper increasingly gave space to theories of art and literature propounded by such hard-liners as Pierre-Daix ('le réalisme socialiste est l'expression esthétique de cette force politique' 25 August 1949), René Lacote and Laurent Casanova. The last of these emerged during the late 1940s as the Party's principal theoretician in intellectual and cultural matters, and was responsible for the appearance in 1949 of *La Nouvelle Critique*.

By late 1947 the PCF, which, in spite of various differences of opinion with the government, had hitherto none the less remained generally supportive, moved clearly into opposition and isolation. Stalin, who saw the Marshall Plan to be a threat to Soviet influence in Western Europe, accused the French Party of being too conciliatory. Led by Thorez, it consequently submitted itself to an *autocritique*, recognised its past errors (including that of the Front populaire), became openly hostile to government policy and unquestionably admired all that was Soviet. In *L'Humanité* on 26 April 1949, a poem by Eluard both reflected this new state of affairs and more importantly demonstrated how even the most talented of writers could be persuaded to sell their souls:

Frères l'URSS est le seul chemin libre
Par où nous passerons pour atteindre la paix
Une paix favorable au doux désir de vivre
La nuit se fait toute petite
Et la terre reflète un avenir sans tâche.

For anyone who had witnessed the shifting positions of the PCF during the late 1920s and 1930s, such intransigence and unquestioning acceptance was not perhaps all that surprising. For many writers and intellectuals whose sympathy for the Left and even for Communism did not, however, find a counterpart in actual political allegiance, matters were not to be so simply resolved. While they may have found a common purpose in the Resistance – witness the mixed political nature of the Front national – the dilemmas which developed out of the now fashionable, but well-tried notion of commitment were not so easily resolved by all.

Amongst writers on the left there was a fundamental and widely shared belief that literature should in some way play a responsible role in the struggle against oppression of whatever kind. The idea that responsibility should in turn necessitate blind acceptance of values dictated not by immediate circumstances but by a remote central committee was another matter entirely, however, and gave rise to considerable and often bitter debate. It was, for example, an issue which tormented Camus whose work particularly during the last fifteen years of his life returned constantly to the dilemma so tellingly illustrated in the short story 'Jonas ou l'artiste au travail' (*L'Exil et le Royaume*), namely that of commitment at the expense of artistic and personal integrity. Ultimately for Camus there could only be an unhappy compromise, a grudging acceptance of the artist's new role, and of the fact that art could still serve a valuable purpose. By 1953 he would write:

> le temps des artistes est fini. Mais nous devons refuser l'amertume. L'une des tentations de l'artiste est de se croire solidaire et il arrive en vérité qu'on le lui crie avec une assez ignoble joie. Mail il n'en est rien. Il se tient au milieu de tous, au niveau exact, ni plus haut ni plus bas, de tous ceux qui travaillent et qui luttent. Sa vocation même, devant l'oppression, est d'ouvrir les prisons et de faire parler le malheur et le bonheur de tous. [. . .] Sans la culture, et la liberté relative qu'elle suppose, la société, même parfaite, n'est qu'une jungle. C'est pourquoi toute création authentique est un don à l'avenir.[5]

The idea that circumstances were now different from what they had been before the war (though much of this debate sounds surprisingly similar to the ones developed in the late 1920s by Benda, Nizan, Berl and others), was also central to the position adopted by *Les Temps modernes*, which was to become the most influential non-communist periodical of the post-war years, and by one of its founder members, Sartre, in his essay, *Qu'est-ce que la littérature?* All literature, argued *Les Temps modernes* in its initial editorial statement, in some way relates to the socio-political circumstances of its period: 'Tout écrit possède un sens, même si ce sens est fort loin de celui que l'auteur avait rêvé d'y mettre. [. . .] L'écrivain est *en situation* dans son époque' (October 1945). This theory together with that of literature having necessarily to be free, which Sartre had already outlined in his article in *Les Lettres françaises*, are both central to his longer essay.

The general thesis of this is sufficiently well known for there to be any need to examine it in detail here. But in addition to the central concepts of freedom, responsibility, demystification and literature as a form of witness and conscience ('la littérature est, par essence, la subjectivité d'une société en révolution permanente' p. 195),[6] Sartre does discuss in the final section the dangers of controlled writing, referring specifically to both Catholic and Communist works. The sharpness of some of his comments can no doubt be in part attributed to his personal quarrel with Garaudy (p. 317), but his general view that Communism as currently preached (and the religious analogy is a particularly apt one), is politically conservative and artistically stultifying, leading as it does to stereotypes and propaganda, is expressed with considerable passion and conviction. Literature becomes merely one more means of achieving a political end already clearly defined and sanctified: 'l'œuvre d'art devient moyen à son tour, elle entre dans la chaîne, ses fins et ses principes lui deviennent extérieurs, elle est gouvernée du dehors' (p. 317). Camus too, in spite of his quarrel with Sartre in the early 1950s over the whole issue of the intellectual's responsibility and action, sees art and literature in particular as having a unique guiding influence, and in turn he dismisses all forms of controlled writing. In *L'Homme révolté* (1952) discussing the function of the imagination in realistic writing he explicitly rejects socialist realism on the grounds that it is preselective, limited and distorting, even though he acknowledges that all such writing implies choice of some kind:

Réduire l'unité du monde romanesque à la totalité du réel ne peut se faire qu'à la faveur d'un jugement *a priori* qui élimine du réel ce qui ne convient pas à la doctrine. Le réalisme dit socialiste est alors voué, par la logique même de son nihilisme, à cumuler les avantages du roman édifiant et de la littérature de propagande.[7]

Whatever the force and currency of such views – and a novel like Simone de Beauvoir's *Les Mandarins* (1954) suggests that behind them a great deal of uncertainty and unease remained – the French Communist Left was in no doubt as to what its aims and priorities should be. In 1945 at the tenth congress of the Party, Thorez's call for an intellectual renaissance in France had attracted many. Before long, its broad appeal was tempered by intransigence. Pierre Hervé who in *Action* (6 December 1946) had

argued that art should occupy a protected 'zone libre' was
severely rebuked by Aragon in *Les Lettres françaises* for neglecting
his political responsibility. In 1947, at the following congress held
in Strasbourg, directives which were to infuse all Party thinking
on cultural matters well into the next decade were already making
a first appearance. As Fauvet has pointed out, such a policy was
in a way a counterreaction to enforced political isolation. An
unswerving orthodoxy was as marked in discussions and recommendations about art and literature as it was in reactions to such
political issues as the labour camps, the trials of Rajk and Kostov,
the policies of Tito in Yugoslavia or, later, the Kruschev
revelations about Stalin, and the invasion of Hungary. Certainly
there were, amongst writers and intellectuals, some defections,
notably those of Vercors, Claude Roy and Roger Vailland, but in
general the influence of the Cold War, already marked by 1949,
continued to have its effect and led to a clearly definable artistic
and literary style. As in the mid-1930s Moscow became the source
of all wisdom; Stalin, his minister of culture Zdhanov and Thorez
became cult figures whose authority and judgement were beyond
dispute. Casanova and Kanapa emerged as the leading intellectual spokesman for the party, their views expressed not only in
works like *Le Parti communiste, les intellectuels et la nation* (1949) or
Situation de l'intellectuel (1957), but in reviews like *Pensée*, the *Cahiers
du Communisme, Europe* (which became communist dominated),
and above all *La Nouvelle Critique*, newly founded in 1948. Aragon
remained as ever the leading party writer and cultural father
figure, Pierre Courtade, André Stil and Roger Vailland produced
novels certainly written 'to order' but not, on occasions, without
some skill. Stil and Vailland wrote essays concerning the theory of
literature, the latter in particular producing an interesting
variation on the by now well worn theme of socialist realism.
Indeed, whatever Sartre, Camus, Merleau-Ponty and others may
have thought about it, and however limited it may have ultimately proved to be, the impact made by communist writers and
intellectuals was stronger than ever before.

Of the principal reviews in which the new orthodoxy was
expressed, *La Nouvelle Critique*, explicitly designed for the purpose,
holds pride of place. Already anticipated by Aragon in a speech,
'La Culture et sa diffusion' delivered in April 1947 at the Maison
de la Pensée in Paris, the review was published in December 1948

one hundred years after the Communist Manifesto. At once clear advance warning of its editorial position was given: 'La Nouvelle Critique démasquera vigoureusement tous les mensonges, toutes les falsifications, toutes les manœuvres idéologiques des fossoyeurs de la culture, de l'indépendance nationale et du progrès. Elle sera impitoyablement et profondément critique' (No. 1, p. 18). If the language of this statement with its insistence on demystification and exposure sounded not all that unfamiliar, its uncompromising message was in distinct contrast both to the conciliatory attitude of a few years earlier and even to the manifestos of the communist dominated reviews of the 1920s and 1930s. To read *La Nouvelle Critique* now with hindsight is a trying, if not painful experience. So rigorously does its team of regular contributors apply current orthodox criteria to a variety of subjects from American influence in Europe, the Korean and Algerian wars on the one hand, to reviews of films, books and art exhibitions on the other, that interpretation and assessment are both predictable and repetitive. So too is the language in which much of the review is written. When André Stil was awarded the Prix Staline in 1952, *La Nouvelle Critique* carried an article by Victor Joannès; its eulogistic, not to say sycophantic style is typical of many:

Le Prix Staline de littérature décerné à André Stil, c'est pour nous, pour notre peuple comme un salut fraternel de combat des peuples soviétiques adressé à notre lutte nationale pour la paix et la démocratie, pour la liberté et l'indépendance, évoquée par le livre.

La classe ouvrière de France, notre peuple, notre Parti y voient, nous en avons la certitude, une raison supplémentaire d'attachement et d'amour inébranlables envers l'Union soviétique, envers le grand Staline.

Oui, nous aimons le pays de Staline, et la récompense accordée à André Stil qui a su mettre sa plume et son talent à la disposition des exigences populaires et nationales nous est allée droit au cœur. [. . .]

Que l'Union soviétique, pays du socialisme, pays de la véritable démocratie, pays de la collaboration entre les peuples et rempart de la paix, n'est pas un pays "étranger" pour les peuples, l'attribution du Prix Staline à notre camarade André Stil en est une preuve supplémentaire. (April 1952, xxxv, p. 9)

Whatever our reactions to language and sentiments of this kind, the fact remains that *La Nouvelle Critique*, like *Commune* nearly two decades earlier does, by virtue of its range of interests, provide an invaluable source of information concerning left-wing thinking on the role and purpose of literature. In addition, the Editions de la Nouvelle Critique also published separate volumes (often collections of articles and essays which had already appeared in the review itself) by its leading spokesmen, Aragon, Casanova, Kanapa and, importantly for the debate around literature, by Stil. In 1948 with an introduction by Jacques Duclos they also published a translation of three talks by Zdhanov on the arts, *Sur la littérature, la philosophie et la musique* which acquired the status of dogma.[8]

The general line of argument of these pieces strongly recalls that of the Soviet Writers Congress in 1934: decadence, evident in a variety of ways in Western civilization, must be eradicated and replaced by sound socialist values. In his first speech Zdhanov attacks two journals, *Zvezda* and *Leningrad* for having published works by Zostchenko and Akhmatova, based on the theories of art for art's sake and directed, he claims, at the privileged class of pre-Revolutionary Russia. Zdhanov argues that instead such journals should see it their duty to provide a lead for the public at large. He offers a *résumé* of earlier thinking on socialist art citing writers like Tchernychevski, Dobrolioubov ('le champion de l'art réaliste et socialement orienté' p. 27) and Plekhanov, as well as Lenin and Stalin. Only by following their lead can writers provide the kind of literature which will fully satisfy the increasing expectations of the Soviet people. No matter how fine the *forms* of Western bourgeois literature may be, its moral basis is rotten. By contrast Soviet literature must be patriotic and unashamedly didactic, preaching present virtues and indicating an even better future.

L'écrivain ne peut rester à la traîne des événements, il doit marcher à l'avant-garde du peuple en lui désignant la voie de son évolution. Se guidant sur la méthode du réalisme socialiste, étudiant consciencieusement et attentivement notre réalité, s'efforçant de pénétrer plus profondément la nature du processus de notre évolution, l'écrivain doit éduquer le peuple et l'armer idéologiquement. (p. 36)

Given the undisputed social and political superiority of the Soviet Union it must be possible to create 'la littérature la plus avancée du monde' (p. 36).

The same presupposition and dogmatism characterise the two other speeches. Too much contemporary philosophy is idealistic – that is, independent of historical development – and without direction or purpose. Once again Zdhanov attacks the decadence and depravity of the Western bourgeoisie, citing *Les Temps modernes* as being symptomatic by its championing of Jean Genet and his *Journal d'un voleur*. Much music too is characterized he claims by formalist trends, the taste of a small elite, and must be revised. Bourgeois music, like philosophy and art, is 'en pleine décadence et dégradation' (p. 78); true classical music should unite 'une forme éclatante à un contenu profond' (p. 75) and find its inspiration in popular music. Here Zdhanov appears to be on much shakier ground than in his statements about literature, employing only the vaguest of terms and finally taking refuge once again behind the theory that, for it to be truly accessible, music too must adopt socialist realism as its guide.

Such views, welcomed with unqualified praise by Pierre Hentges in *Pensée* (no. 21, 1948), are important, since they provide the theoretical basis for most of those expressed during the next fifteen years or so in the pages of the party journals in France. Thus Pierre Daix in the second of two articles in *La Nouvelle Critique* on Balzac and realism writes: 'Le réalisme socialiste, c'est d'abord désormais une conception du monde qui se fonde sur le mouvement réel de l'histoire. C'est d'abord l'action politique militante. Il faut que l'artiste participe à la lutte réelle des hommes pour changer le monde, pour être capable d'exprimer la vérité du monde' (May 1949, VI, p. 65). Jean Larnac writing in more general terms in *Pensée* (No. 30, 1950) expresses a similar view: 'Il faut que l'écrivain socialiste prenne conscience du devenir des hommes, de leur effort vers le mieux être, de leur développement révolutionnaire. Historien scrupuleux, il doit aussi se montrer moraliste' (p. 115).

The idea of the artist as a militant figure and of socialist realism as a direct reflection of the revolutionary development of society is again expounded by Daix, this time in a lengthy reply (later published separately as a book) to Maurice Nadeau. Nadeau had suggested (not unreasonably) that the wording of an *enquête* launched by *La Nouvelle Critique*, 'A quoi servez-vous?' anticipated certain answers. Daix responded:

> le réalisme socialiste part du nouveau contenu de la réalité, conséquence du triomphe de la révolution socialiste. [. . .] Il implique un comportement social nouveau de l'artiste, sa liaison avec le mouvement révolutionnaire, sa responsabilité devant celui-ci. C'est donc au sens strict du mot une méthode de connaissance, d'activité et de travail. (*La Nouvelle Critique*, April 1957, LXXXIV, p. 69)

André Stil wrote in a similar vein: 'Faire connaître, comprendre, aimer ce type d'homme, cette classe, pour ce qu'ils portent en eux de l'avenir, aide cet avenir à naître, comme cela peut se faire par l'art et au profit de l'art' (November 1960, CXX, p. 96).[9]

Unashamedly tendentious, comments of this kind are, of course, substantially little different from those made by Aragon and others twenty years earlier. So too are the views that such writing can only be fully achieved within the context of the Communist Party, that the world described by it is not only a socialist one but a peaceful one, and that above all (echoing Zdhanov), bourgeois art and literature must be shown to be decadent and depraved fit only for 'des vieilles sociétés conservatrices, réactionnaires' with which they deal (*La Nouvelle Critique*, April 1951, XXV, p. 87). Yet within such often uncompromising statements we do find a hint of a renewed concern for the relationship between what is being described (*contenu*) and the methods used for that description (*forme*). Indeed by the mid-1960s a striking and important change in thinking on this whole matter was to evolve.

Given the currency of *autocritique* amongst Party members during the post-war years, concern for the accessibility of socialist realist art is perhaps not surprising. Very much within the tradition of the Universités populaires, study groups and the *Musée du soir*, the Batailles du Livre were established, gatherings where attempts were made to bring working-class people into direct contact with writers and books, to promote sales of books at reasonable prices and to encourage reading and discussion. As André Wurmser observed, however, such an undertaking could not be expected to effect any radical changes overnight.[10] Moreover it was in danger of being too intellectual: 'Il faut parler pour être entendu et il faut parler pour servir' (*La Nouvelle Critique*, March 1951, XXIV, p. 79). Daix, again in his reply to Nadeau, is more specific still, and anticipates the later development of the concern for a book's reception: 'Un roman, un poème, toutes les choses écrites n'existent qu'à partir du moment où elles vivent dans ceux qui les reçoivent' (April 1957, LXXXIV, p. 172). One immediate possible solution to this potential problem is to be found in the role of the critic who can interpret 'difficult' works for the uneducated consumer. (It is worth reminding ourselves in passing that Sartre considers this issue at some length in *Qu'est-ce que la littérature?* and dismisses 'Party' critics for being conservative.) Already in 1950 Aragon and Elsa Triolet had discussed this issue: 'Que tous les livres progressistes ne soient pas également faciles à lire pour un lecteur non éduqué, c'est exact, mais n'avons-nous pas la critique qui est là pour organiser la compréhension d'un livre, lorsque ce livre est digne d'intérêt?' (*La Nouvelle Critique*, July–August 1950, XVIII, p. 74). With specific references to Aragon's *Les Communistes*, Stil makes exactly the same point in the *Cahiers du Communisme* (August 1951, no. 8, p. 989).

While on one level such statements raise the question not only of the critic's role, but of the accessibility of his interpretation and language, on another they contain an implicit defence of the novelist's freedom. There is, to be sure, no more of an attempt to counter the kinds of objection to controlled or directed writing made in the 1930s by Bloch, Gide and Malraux than there was then, but the whole issue of the appropriateness of form and style is one which is given increasing attention. Thus in May 1951, Pierre Abraham, then chief Editor of *Europe*, writing in *La Nouvelle Critique* on Balzac and Proust, interestingly suggests that the former's work is more accessible to working-class people largely due to the fact that he draws many of his analogies and images from the world of plants and animals. Proust, with his frequent use of the world of art and especially of painting necessarily appeals, Abraham argues, to a quite different public. Rather more traditionally Jean Varloot in 'Le Roman français en 1951' (*Pensée*, no. 39, 1951) acknowledges that the 'new' realist writer must both select and link 'l'aventure individuelle et l'aventure collective [. . .] Ainsi sont évités les deux défauts: la schématisation du roman à thèse ou de propagande, et la mutilation du populisme, du roman ''prolétarien''' (p. 110). Even so, concern for form is not any more easily translated into positive recommendations than it was twenty years earlier; the conviction that 'correct' content will inevitably inspire an appropriate form still tends to be widely shared. Typical is François Billoux in *La Nouvelle Critique*, June 1951: 'Nous ne sommes pas des esthètes et nous savons que la forme est d'autant plus facile à trouver et facile à bien réaliser que l'on est convaincu sur le fond' (XXVII, p. 102). Three years later Daix extends such a view, and claims that since socialist realism as already defined by Zdhanov is now accepted, and by definition implies a fusion of content and form, inappropriate style can only indicate a failing in content: 'un contenu typique, exprimé dans une forme qui ne serait pas typique et donc adéquate à ce contenu, ne serait plus un contenu typique' (*La Nouvelle Critique*, March 1954, LII, p. 278). For Daix as for so many others the formula was without flaw. The Second Congress of Soviet Writers held in Moscow in December 1954 and which Aragon attended also helped to ensure that orthodoxy was maintained.

Within a decade however, there were distinct signs of change. In June–June 1964, *La Nouvelle Critique* published a special issue entitled 'Esthétique et littérature' in which an introductory article 'Questions posées', André Gisselbrecht makes what only a few years earlier would have been an heretical statement. The practice of *autocritique* was once again about to lead to a complete *volte face*. Gisselbrecht claims that it has become increasingly apparent that 'la conscience socialiste la plus haute n'est pas nécessairement supérieure du point de vue artistique au déchirement bourgeois. Il n'y a pas une ligne ascendante, continue, en art, de la moindre à la plus grande lucidité idéologique et morale' (CLVI-VII, p. 12). There are, he continues, two kinds of revolutionary writing: one which portrays the society of the future (still, presumably, socialist realist art though he does not define it as such), the other which disturbs and questions, '[qui] vise moins à dénoncer ou exalter qu'inquiéter et troubler' (p. 13) – what Malraux in the 1930s and Camus in the 1950s had defined as belonging to the long established tradition of negative writing. Within this second category there is also room, he claims, for works hitherto condemned as decadent, precisely because their form, reflecting their content, can be seen to be illustrative of the bourgeois world which it is still necessary to expose and eventually destroy. This particular interpretation of art and especially of writing is extensively developed a few years later within the context of the debate surrounding new criticism. By the mid 1960s two factors are particularly important. The first is the recognition that writers can no longer realistically be expected to produce their works according to specific directives; the second is that the kind of normative criticism favoured by the proponents of socialist realism is severely limited, if not worthless, when an attempt to evaluate a work as literature has to be made. Several months later Claude Prévost also argues that while it is possible to respond in one (limited) way to the ideas or the values expressed in the work of Kafka, 'on n'a pas encore *compris* ni *expliqué* vraiment le secret de son art' (*La Nouvelle Critique*, February 1965, CLXIII, p. 82). Indeed when he now suggests that attention should be paid primarily to form and not to content, Prévost essentially challenges a long tradition of marxist criticism.[11]

Such developments were given more 'formal' recognition at a meeting of the Central Committee of the PCF at Argenteuil, 11–13 March 1966. At this Garaudy, whose book *D'un réalisme sans rivage* (1963) showed how far his own thinking had evolved since his earlier *Une littérature de fossoyeurs* (1947), delivered a major speech primarily concerned with religion, but in which he also commented significantly on literature and art. Art, Garaudy argues, is not simply the projection of ideas in images. Even though it is linked to social class and forms part of the superstructure of society, it also has its own *spécificité*: 'réduire l'œuvre d'art à ses "ingrédients idéologiques", c'est non seulement perdre de vue sa spécificité, mais aussi ne pas tenir compte de son autonomie relative et du développement inégal de la société et de l'art' (*Cahiers du Communisme*, nos. 5–6, May–June 1966, pp. 17, 18). Moreover since art has to be recognized as being itself part of that reality which in its realism it reflects, and since that reality is constantly changing and evolving, so must we be prepared to recognize and admit to a variety of styles and form:

> un *pluralisme* fécond de styles, des écoles [. . .] Le réalisme c'est donc une *attitude* à l'égard de la réalité et non pas une méthode. La méthode depend, à chaque époque, du pouvoir de l'homme sur la nature, du niveau des techniques et des rapports sociaux, et il appartient à l'artiste et à l'artiste seul d'en découvrir le mode d'expression littéraire ou plastique. (p. 19)

Following on from this, André Stil, in a contribution entitled 'Le Parti et la création littéraire et artistique', claims – even if he seems reluctant to go quite as far as Garaudy – that the creative process 'n'accepte jamais de rendre tous ses comptes à la seule raison, encore moins de se plier à ses ordres et défenses' (p. 59). Individuality in art is no longer considered to be mere opportunism, anarchic irresponsibility or bourgeois self-indulgence, but rather a vital and non-reducible factor. This kind of statement from a writer who only just over a decade earlier had produced one of the most emphatic defences of the normative principles of socialist realist art as defined by Zdhanov, is a measure (once again) of the Party's, or its intellectuals' ability to modify, if not to reverse, decisions in order to justify hitherto apparently unacceptable positions.

When the conference closed, a general resolution was passed which contained, amongst other matters, a summary of the Party's new attitude to literary and artistic creation:

> Qu'est-ce qu'un créateur? Qu'il s'agisse par exemple de la musique, de la poésie, du roman, du théâtre, du cinéma, de l'architecture, de la peinture ou de la sculpture, le créateur n'est pas un simple fabricant de produits desquels les éléments sont donnés, un arrangeur. Il y a dans toute œuvre d'art une part irréductible aux données et cette part, c'est l'homme même. Tel écrivain, tel artiste était seul capable de produire l'œuvre créée.[12]

Although not as potentially radical in its implications as Garaudy's remarks had been, there was enough in this statement to ensure that the Argenteuil conference would have an important influence for years to come.

Before we examine some of the more characteristic examples of writing to come from this period, two further attempts to formulate a theory of literature deserve brief attention. The first, and not surprisingly more orthodox of these, is a collection of articles – all of which had already been published elsewhere – by André Stil entitled *Vers le réalisme socialiste* (1952).[13] The second is a more original and somewhat idiosyncratic essay by Roger Vailland, *L'Expérience du drame* (1953).[14]

Stil's complete acceptance of the Party line on all matters had been apparent from the Liberation, and by 1952 he had risen to the position of editor in chief of *L'Humanité*. He had already published a number of short stories, and in 1952 was, as we have noted, awarded the Prix Staline for the first volume of his trilogy *Le Premier Choc*. In May of the same year he was arrested and, like Jacques Duclos, was sent to the Santé prison for having encouraged, through the columns of *L'Humanité*, demonstrations against Colonel Ridgway, who had been appointed allied commander in Europe. With the possible exception of Aragon, Stil was therefore both the most promoted of the PCF's writers and in a position of some public notoriety.

In his article on Aragon's *Les Communistes*, published in the *Cahiers du Communisme*, Stil had given an unhesitatingly orthodox evaluation of the book, justifying what he claimed were its literary qualities, in terms of its militancy, historical accuracy and optimistic message. In the same year he had also championed the work of Fougeron whose paintings of mining communities in the north of France were proclaimed as masterpieces of human insight and artistic skill.[15] Both of these articles are contained in *Vers le réalisme socialiste* as is the text of the speech he gave on being awarded the Prix Staline, 'Militant et Ouvrier'. That there is nothing innovatory or extraordinary in these essays should not be surprising. Communism as the guiding spirit of all aspects of existence extends its influence to literary creation (pp. 84–88). As in the case of Aragon, 'correct' values and interpretation of events will automatically produce an appropriate style. Once again we have a contribution to the discussion surrounding content and form: 'la qualité n'est pas seulement une question de forme, mais d'abord de contenu [. . .] la qualité de la forme elle-même n'est pas seulement une question de métier et de travail, mais est fonction directe du contenu et de la réaction de l'artiste devant ce contenu' (p. 89). Accuracy in historical detail (p. 65), in language (p. 67), optimism (p. 70) and the educative role of the novel – 'une forme d'art qui s'inspire de l'efficacité supérieure de la critique et de l'autocritique' (p. 93) – are all equally familiar themes. And like so many who believed in the efficacy of literature and especially of the novel as a political weapon, Stil scorns the idea that militancy must necessarily result in schematization. Aragon has avoided this, he argues, by having facts carry his argument for him, though he conveniently overlooks Aragon's initial selection, alignment and interpretation of those facts. Like the older novelist Stil appears to believe that from the very fact of militancy a new, advanced style of writing will emerge to replace the worn out, decadent forms of the past.

> Sous l'effet du travail de militant peut se créer, doit se créer et se crée effectivement un type nouveau de travail d'écrivain, où l'écriture s'apparente de plus en plus à l'action. Entre ce contenu et ces méthodes nouvelles d'écriture et l'action du militant il n'y a bientôt plus contradiction, mais un échange et une aide réciproque. [. . .] c'est alors que ces moyens nouveaux qu'il a acquis se trouveraient en rupture avec une vie qui ne serait plus à leur niveau, et qu'il éprouverait la contradiction entre cette vie et les œuvres plus avancées qu'il voudrait écrire. (pp. 84, 5)

Just what form these new works will have is a question which Stil leaves unanswered. Like Aragon's *Pour un réalisme socialiste* published nearly twenty years earlier, Stil's essays are no more than a convenient summary of current orthodox views, with little chance of appeal to any other than the converted. As Stil himself acknowledged much later, if it were to be successful this kind of writing required the 'connivence entre celui qui écrit dans cette direction et un public. [. . .] Ces conditions ont existé pendant quelques années. Puis elles se sont dégradées'.[16]

By comparison Vailland's essay may at first seem almost irrelevant. Essentially it deals with a variety of matters related specifically to the theatre – the development of tragedy, the art of acting, the relationship between actor and audience, for example – some of them closely linked by Vailland to his personal obsessions concerning seasonal development and intelligent self-control. There is too a passing reference to 'les exigences du "réalisme" qu'exige aujourd'hui le public d'Union soviétique et des démocraties populaires' (p. 151) which perhaps suggests a mild impatience with the preoccupations of some current theoretical writing about literature.[17] Vailland's position (unlike Stil's) vis-à-vis the PCF was, even by this date, less than central. Certainly through his activities during the Resistance, his attitude towards the Korean War or to the American presence in Europe, Vailland has shown himself to be close to the orthodox Party position and thinking. In May 1950 he wrote in his diary that he was 'plus décidé que jamais à ne plus travailler qu'avec le peuple organisé dans le P.C.',[18] and in a letter to Pierre Berger in November

1951, that he whole-heartedly supported Party policies.[19] But it was not until June 1952 that Vailland sent a formal application for membership to Jacques Duclos (then in prison) on a copy of his banned play *Le Colonel Foster plaidera coupable*.

However convinced Vailland may have been about his intentions, and however committed he may have shown himself to be as an active member of the PCF during the next four years, his intellectual position always retained a strong individualist element which, whatever its origins, was ultimately to contribute to his defection. It may have been this element which in part at least, prompted him to produce *L'Expérience du drame* and to disclaim any attempt to formulate rules (p. 151). It may also have been at least in part responsible for the essay's having been virtually ignored as a theoretical text by the Party's major reviews. For those to whom Vailland's novels before 1953 were familiar, such an interest in the theatre could not have been surprising, however since each has a basic five-part (act) structure which closely follows that of a classical tragedy. The early part of *L'Expérience du drame* considers this structure and its inherent dynamic movement in which a single event may modify 'la situation initiale de telle manière que ses contradictions latentes se transforment en conflits manifestes' (p. 133). This understanding of tragedy which, Vailland claims he acquired at an early age was a perfect introduction to and preparation for a marxist interpretation of reality:

> Une éducation fondée tout entière sur l'étude de la tragédie classique m'inclina tout naturellement à ne pas envisager la vie ou l'histoire comme une addition de faits, comme un déroulement continu et inorganisé, mais comme un développement d'événements simultanément indépendants dans la mesure où chaque événement se constitue, comme une tragédie bien faite, en unité de temps, de lieu et d'action; liés dans la mesure où les événements s'enchaînement nécessairement comme l'acte à l'acte, la scène à la scène.
>
> C'est la tragédie qui m'a fourni ma première méthode d'analyse de la réalité. [. . .] une action dramatique, une et multiple dans ses conflits successifs, toujours divers et nécessairement enchaînés. (pp. 144, 5)

The equation which Vailland establishes here is a neat one, and his suggestion, however naïve, that it would be extendable to the novel, at least has the merit of concentrating on the literary aspects of the issue rather than on the need for ideologically correct content:

> pourquoi [. . .] ne pas écrire des romans dont la lecture se précipite comme une action et qui provoque à l'action? Les lecteurs habituels de romans policiers sont facilement tentés de jouer les policiers dans la vie, mais un autre genre d'intrigue, bâtie selon les mêmes lois dramatiques, pourrait les inciter à un autre genre d'action. (pp. 190, 1)

In spite of a number of features, and in particular his portrayal of the 'bolchevik hero', which suggest that he was rather more influenced in his imaginative writing by contemporary Party ideas than he cared to admit, Vailland did succeed in producing a number of novels in which form and content are successfully integrated. But he was the exception rather than the rule. In general, the militant writers of the left in the 1950s conform more readily to the precepts of socialist realism, with even greater emphasis on the ideological correctness of their works, than their predecessors of the 1930s had done.

7 Three Party Writers: André Stil, Roger Vailland, Pierre Courtade

1 ANDRÉ STIL

The reception given to André Stil's writing and especially to *Au château d'eau* (1951), the first volume of his trilogy *Le Premier Choc*, illustrates the range of response which all three of these authors experienced. Kanapa praised him for having taken the current political situation in France, and for having transformed it into an original subject for his novels;[1] Joannès claimed an international significance for his work, praised its uplifting qualities and the accuracy with which he had depicted the real world;[2] Anissimov, director of the Gorki Institute, regarded *Le Premier Choc* as 'une œuvre optimiste, toute pénétrée d'une foi indestructible dans la victoire du peuple français'.[3] In contrast Nadeau, writing in *Les Temps modernes* at a time when that journal was largely in sympathy with Party policies, dismissed Stil's work as two dimensional, exaggerated and, in terms of plot, a copy of the bourgeois novel. Stil himself was dismissed as 'un porte-parole qui clame une vérité formée à l'avance [. . .] l'officiant d'un culte'.[4]

Stil spent his formative years in the industrial areas and docks in the north of France, a region which has remained the setting for nearly all his imaginative writing. At school his academic ability already created, at an early age, problems of class betrayal, and over the years he felt increasingly that his roles as a Party committee member, journalist and novelist threatened to sever his contacts with his origins and what he liked to think of as his true self. Although he had always been a compulsive writer, it was not until 1946, when he first met Aragon, that Stil became convinced that his writing would have a purpose. Yet the question 'une littérature de la classe ouvrière ou la classe ouvrière dans la littérature'[5] remained unresolved. Like Vailland he found populism unattractive. (Ironically he was awarded the Prix Populiste in 1967.) He also disliked the attitude adopted towards the working class by someone like Zola in *Germinal* on the grounds that it was one devoid of real knowledge: 'cette vue extérieure me paraissait ce qu'il fallait le plus éviter dès le début'.[6] Through his treatment of the working class in his own work he hoped to create something new: 'Du point de vues des formes, notamment, il y a là des richesses qui n'ont pas été explorées. La voix de la classe ouvrière, ses gestes, sa respiration presque incitent à des modifications de l'écriture littéraire'.[7] Language – especially the vocabulary of certain trades and occupations,[8] and syntactical formations – in particular interested him, though he has admitted that the degree to which local dialect can be used without modification is a problem which he has never happily resolved. From his earliest published writing, the *nouvelles* in *Le Mot 'mineur', camarades* (1949) the idea of militancy in literature was allied to his concern for realism: 'La préoccupation de la réalité me pousse, pour commencer, à écrire presque des reportages, de caractère littéraire ou philosophique, à partir directement de ces réalités. [. . .] c'est vrai qu'alors [. . .] une préoccupation de combat n'essayait pas de se dissimuler'.[3] Stil has admitted subsequently, that during the years immediately following the Liberation the time was ripe for such a literature, even though it was of limited duration. Rather more interesting, given his own complete orthodoxy during these years, is his belief that while a similar politically inspired literature could reappear in the future, it would have to be as the result of 'un élan réel, spontané, il ne faut pas que ce soit réponse à une commande extérieure, serait-ce une informelle "commande sociale"'.[10]

Stil was mainly launched on his career as a militant Party writer by the success of 'La Fleur d'acier', one of the short stories in his second collection *La Seine a pris la mer* (1950) which, recommended to Thorez by Aragon, was printed in *'L'Humanité-Dimanche*. Within months the first volume of *Le Premier Choc* had been published and Stil remained for more than a decade both prolific and uncompromisingly orthodox. During these years two major themes dominate his work: the threat of American influence in French affairs and the Algerian war. Each is treated as it directly affects working-class people; each is interpreted strictly within the perspectives of the policies of the PCF.

The three volumes of *Le Premier Choc*[11] describe the resistance of the workers in 1950/51, in a port somewhere on the south-west coast of France, to the arrival of an American arms ship. Stil takes an overall view of their attitudes and shapes his material in such a way that Communism is shown ultimately to offer the only viable alternative. As befits a work of socialist realism the situation depicted is historically accurate (if selective) and the work has a clear movement forward. Stil also strives – and sometimes succeeds – to combine personal and domestic elements with public ones. This is particularly so in the first volume which opens with a description of the appalling housing conditions of several of the novel's principal families, and closes with the security of the *blockhaus* into which they eventually move.

Given Stil's aim to reflect the reality of working-class life as a whole, many of the 'domestic' sections of the novel are concerned with the elderly, children and women, even though the political point of such sections is rarely missed. Thus Léon is gratuitously killed by an American lorry as he escorts school children across a dangerously busy road (vol. i, Chapter 16); the seventy year old Andréanie couple (vol. ii, Chapter 27) whose lives have already once been destroyed by the Germans are driven to suicide by the thought that it could happen again; Francine's baby, expected in the first volume, is born in the third but lives only after a struggle (vol. iii, p. 304); and of all the women Paulette Leroy (wife of the local Communist leader) grows in stature, not only being an exemplary mother and wife but becoming, by virtue of her own political activity, an equal in her own right. As in a novel by Poulaille very little concession is made to the bourgeois world unless its representatives can be shown to recognize the justness of the workers' cause. Three examples in particular are worth comment. The first is that of the Duquesne couple who during the war had housed a German officer. The wife is shown to have erred through ignorance ('Elevée dans l'ignorance et le mépris de la masse qui travaille, elle avait accepté sans même y réfléchir les idées qu'il (son mari) lui offrait', vol. ii, p. 199). Gradually she 'educates' herself into an understanding of the situation and the return of the officer as an agent for the Americans precipitates a crisis. She signs a petition calling for action to be taken against the Americans, leaves and is eventually divorced by her husband who

remains unthinkingly embedded in a concern for his reputation
and self-esteem. The second is that of Gisèle whose 'collaboration' extends to her having an affair with an American, and
whose life is shown to be uttely without purpose. Unlike Mme
Duquesne she experiences shame too late and her attempts to
blame her isolated bourgeois childhood (vol. ii, p. 145) are
without weight. Hers is the perfect case of unthinking irresponsibility, a betrayal of both nation and basic human values. In
contrast we have the case of the local doctor Degand and his wife
who throughout are shown to be both sympathetic (they openly
support the Mouvement de la Paix) and actively helpful to (if not
ideologically convinced by) the Communists' cause. Unlike the
Duquesne couple or Gisèle who are eventually lost from the story,
Degand remains to the end at which point he is about to be caught
up in the demonstration. Indeed the whole of Chapter 26 in the
third volume, 'La Promenade du Docteur Degand' is a
metaphorical journey which takes us through his life. He
represents the uncommitted liberal conscience whose true
conviction has not been fully recognized; at the end it comes to
him like religious faith: 'il se sent lié à eux par quelque chose de
plus fort que les idées' (vol. iii, p. 270).

In his accounts of cases of this kind Stil strongly implies that
political success or personal integrity can only be realized through
collective action and mutual support. On both the large scale of
the community life in the *blockhaus*, and in his treatment of
individual family cases, Stil can be convincing and shows certain
similarities to Zola, Barbusse or Poulaille. Once we consider his
political motives and the effect which these have on the novel's
style and structure, however, we immediately encounter those
characteristics which opponents of socialist realism single out for
criticism. Thus it is the case that even amongst the workers, those
like Papillon, who has temporarily left the Party, or like Robert,
who gives priority to union activities, are shown to have weaknesses. Papillon is a loud-mouthed blusterer; Robert is
unreliable. But this simplistic link between political soundness
and character is more readily used in descriptions of those classed
as bourgeois or fascist. Those of Gisèle and her father with their
isolated, cluttered house, hypocrisy, 'allures de nouveau riche'
(vol. i, p. 117) and fantasy world (vol. ii, p. 68); of the prefect
(vol. iii, Chapter 27) who with his officials is shown to be weak
and untrustworthy; of the CRS (vol. iii, Chapter 22) who are

cynical, drunk on duty and brutal. And above all of the Americans who are seen not simply as mindless, arrogant, gum-chewing beings interested only in money or sex and quite incapable of assimilating the slightest amount of French culture, but as a new occupying force. Indeed throughout the novel the theme of occupation and resistance is ever-present (strengthened by the actual arrival of some Germans as in the Duquesne episode) and in this respect faithfully echoes attitudes towards American influence in Europe prevalent in the Communist press of the late forties and early fifties.[12]

There are ways, too, in which Stil's intrusion and control are equally hard to justify. Unlike Barbusse in *Le Feu*, or Vailland in *Beau Masque* or *325,000 francs*, who openly acknowledge their presence in their novels, but like Nizan in *Le Cheval de Troie* or Courtade in *La Place rouge* who do not, Stil frequently implies by the incidence of *moi* and *nous* that he is, on occasions, both a participant in and recorder of the action. He also remains omniscient as narrator and, more importantly, guide and interpreter for the reader. In this respect Stil is some way from the claim he makes in his essay on Aragon that facts and events should speak for themselves. Nowhere does he hesitate to explain or comment. In the chapter 'L'Encre renversée' (vol. ii, Chapter 18) in which school children are used as a model of the adult world about them, he introduces a paragraph not only to show how politics infuse all levels of society, but how much in need children are of guidance:

> Dans ces conditions, pas de politique dans les classes, c'est parler dans les nuages. Dans la vie, les enfants sont dans la politique jusqu'au cou. Les questions auxquelles le maître ne répond pas, ils les posent aux parents. Et c'est parfois une grande expérience pour un enfant que le plus pauvre docker soit plus capable de lui montrer le fond des choses que les distributeurs officiels de la science. Cela peut mener loin, et pas forcément dans la bonne direction. (p. 166)

Or, commenting on Leroy's enthusiasm for his political activities in 'Les Gens au fond des lits' (vol. i, Chapter 10) – a chapter which also ends with a vision of domestic bliss in the ideal Soviet society (pp. 135, 6) – and generalising through the use of the pronoun *on*, he offers a typical 'moral': 'Quand on est ainsi, enthousiaste, on resterait éveillé toute la vie. On a la tête claire.

Combien on se sent différent, la nuit. . . . Sans doute est-ce encore un vice du monde de maintenant, qu'on ait besoin d'être derrière ce rideau de nuit et de silence pour laisser aller son cœur . . .' (p. 134).

Intrusions of this kind are largely responsible for two fundamental flaws in the novel. The first is that, as at the end of *Le Feu*, the register of language changes. Stil (like Poulaille) believed that dialect and the idiom of working-class speech could bring to the novel a new and vital dimension, and much of the novel is written in this way. But with each intrusion, whether interpretative, descriptive or moralising ('La liberté, c'est seulement ce qu'on a le courage de faire', vol. I, p. 182), the total impression is broken, and Stil appears almost as much an outsider as he accuses Zola of having been. The second affects the overall structure which is essentially a series of individual episodes irregularly linked across the three volumes. This has the advantage of keeping a number of themes alive, and thereby of creating the impression of a more complex texture, than the essentially linear sequence of events might otherwise allow.[13] Volume I is in fact quite successful in this respect, though this is possibly explained by the speed with which Stil claims it was written – 'jeté sur le papier en quatre-vingts heures'.[14] Thereafter we find signs that he was probably trying to structure the work rather more consciously. The chapters essential to political debate (Chapters 13–15) are central in volume II; the opening eleven chapters in volume III deal with political activity leading directly to the first demonstration and confrontation with the CRS: Chapter 26, describing Degand's walk, is placed immediately before the final triumphant march and occupation of the Préfecture. And the most glaring example of Stil's control is the climactic ending in the two final chapters with a vision of the future and of a new society: 'Demain aussi viendra plus vite qu'on ne le croit, et demain à notre époque, c'est la vie, la vraie' (vol. III, p. 299). All those elements so essential to the didactic purpose of the book are here gathered together and triumphantly reiterated for the last time – the unquestionable rightness of Party policy, the need for unity, patriotism, *autocritique* and the willingness to learn from experience, the guiding influence of Thorez (familiarly referred to as Maurice throughout) and the central committee, and, above all, the rejuvenating effect of collective involvement. In particular they are expressed in and by Léon, a Party delegate from Paris, who arrives messiah-like bringing not only hope but approval, and is a model for Leroy and others to follow. The tone of these final pages shows that any pretence at objectivity, however precariously maintained earlier, is now completely abandoned:

> Léon, comme homme, c'est vraiment malgré lui qu'on le trouve exceptionnel, qu'on l'admire. [. . .] Il a dans les quarante ans et a milité un peu dans toutes les régions. Il en rapporte, avec une mémoire extraordinaire et qui se déclenche avec un à-propos stupéfiant, des milliers d'anecdotes. Il fait ainsi l'effet de porter un peu de toute la France dans les plis de ses habits. [. . .] On dit quelquefois qu'un militant doit s'effacer devant le Parti. Lui, ne s'efface pas, reste tout entier, mais sa force est toute entière celle du Parti [. . .] impregné du Parti comme il est de la vie, de la Pensée du Parti, il sait dire les choses importantes, nouvelles, que personne ne voyait. Mieux, il sait les faire dire aux autres, par des questions, sans montrer que lui les voyait avant. [. . .] On croit sentir là comme le reflet à travers lui d'une façon d'être de Maurice. (pp. 309–14)

Militancy and the rhetoric of political conviction are here undisguised, and what few merits *Le Premier Choc* may have as a piece of imaginative writing are eclipsed as it lapses into something more akin to a political tract or manifesto, a fact which Stil has subsequently acknowledged.[15]

Three years after the publication of the final volume of *Le Premier Choc*, Stil conceived the idea of a new novel *La Question du Bonheur est posée*, originally intended as a massive work of more than five thousand pages.[16] Given the conceptual and practical problems of such a venture, however, this was abandoned and Stil embarked instead on what amounts to a series of volumes of short stories linked to one another by characters and themes, but none the less autonomous. Some, like *Nous nous aimerons demain* (1957) or *Le Foudroyage* (1960) are defined as novels, but what is important is Stil's increased awareness of the problem presented by political literature of the kind he aimed to write: 'La politique, dans le roman, devient le sucre dans l'eau. Si le sucre n'est pas bien fondu, quand on vous offre un verre d'eau sucrée, c'est qu'il n'est pas bien préparé'.[17] It soon became apparent that the short story which, because of its highly concentrated nature, left much unsaid or implied, was the most appropriate form for Stil's purpose.

In works other than those dealing with the Algerian problem in the *Question du Bonheur est posée* series, we rediscover those issues which Stil had treated in his earlier volumes of short stories and in *Le Premier Choc*. In *Le Blé égyptien* (1956), for example, we have the plight of the elderly and retired worker, the ignorance about contraception, the effect of capitalist enterprises on workers' living conditions, inadequate protection against machinery and chemicals, the problem of fatigue, the sense of the workers' solidarity or the rejection of anyone concerned solely with personal gain. We also find the same atmosphere of a closely knit working-class world ('une presqu' île de la ville dans l'usine', p. 14) separated, like the *blockhaus*, from the oppressive world of management and officialdom. Despite recurring characters and themes each story is essentially a unit in its own right. The role of the reader is also seen to be vital: 'La nouvelle c'est un peu une cuillerée de réel soluble, dans laquelle chaque lecteur met l'eau qu'il veut mettre'.[18] This does not mean that Stil is reluctant to intervene. He does so in various ways some of which are just as self-evident as that in *Le Premier Choc*. In 'La montre' the watch, always fast by ten minutes, is used to symbolize the workers' revolution which will take ten years to implement; in 'Chanter' the spring sun heralds the elderly's determination not to surrender to oppressive circumstances; in 'Si le coeur t'en dit' Stil draws a simple comparison between Léonce's ambitions to better himself materially (and hence socially) and Aimé's commitment to his fellow workers; correct French and *patois* are contrasted throughout to make a distinct social point. Elsewhere Stil continues to resort to such techniques as direct address, and in particular to open or thinly disguised authorial comment. In 'Un coup à se tuer' (pp. 65–7) we find an outright description of attempts by the bourgeoisie to undermine and destroy the workers' movements and ambitions; in the same story Aimé's sister Christiane, already a Party member and secretary of their local cell, gently offers him a political lesson: 'Mais ce n'est pas la question de tel ou tel travail. Tu changeras dix fois de métier, tu ne changeras pas de vie. C'est bien autre chose qu'il faut changer' (p. 25); in 'Le Blé égyptien' Stil includes two undisguised commentaries (*plongées*) – albeit written in the same style as the rest of the story and ostensibly Aimé's reflections – on aspects of factory work and motivation. Yet however obvious such examples as these are, at no point does Stil resort to the kind of extensive didacticism of *Le Premier Choc*. Indeed in late volumes, his accounts of events and situations carry his argument for him with many, as in *La Douleur* (1961) or *Pignon sur ciel* (1967), having an almost parable-like quality.[19]

This gradual substitution of illustration for explanation is particularly effective in *Nous nous aimerons demain* and *Le Foudroyage*, both strong indictments of the Algerian war.[20] Certainly there are moments when Stil's voice is heard as when Raymond remarks in the first novel: 'Mais tant que cette guerre existe nous en sommes tous responsables' (p. 215); or when Bernard reflects in the second: 'La guerre, c'est pourriture et compagnie. Les gens y deviennent leur contraire' (p. 194). But such moments are relatively scarce. More effective is the manner in which the structures of the two works are used to interrelate the war with working-class society in France. Two aspects of this technique deserve attention.

The first is what Stil defines as 'écrire en creux'. By this he intends that the novel should illustrate a character's self-discovery, and by this means also invite the reader to arrive at an understanding of, say, the war. In this Stil adapts the socialist realist technique of the educative journey. Unlike other writers, however, Stil does not move forwards towards an anticipated future, but backwards, gradually laying bare a truth which is present from the beginning, but hidden or repressed. The first two chapters of *Nous nous aimerons demain* describe Raymond's mobilisation and later return from Algeria: the rest of the book gradually reveals the truth about his experiences which he himself tries unsuccessfully to erase from his memory. In Part II this process partly takes the form of a straightforward account of a breakdown which involves a form of pre-echo. Objects (a cigarette lighter) or incidents (killing rabbits, watching workers pruning vines) evoke in Raymond's mind memories of torture and oppression, though this is not made explicit until the final section of the novel. At that point more overt accounts of Raymond's war experiences prompt the reader to reconsider the implications of earlier sections with new understanding.

The second aspect of this structural control is the constant interplay between Raymond's 'normal', life, especially his relationship with Annie, and the war. In the opening section nature provides an escape for them from, and almost an idealized alternative to, the harsh world of their working lives dominated by the foundry. On his return Raymond discovers that even this has been destroyed by modern machinery, just as the wild beauty of Algeria has been destroyed by the war. More importantly, just as nature cannot be restored neither can their love, and the novel closes with a sense of sadness at the irreparable damage that has been done. In *Le Foudroyage* the same techniques reappear. Here the link between the two worlds is maintained by the alternating sections describing two brothers' lives in the mining community (Albert) or in Algeria (Bernard). Again events unfold. Bernard moves towards his moment of truth as he is drawn increasingly into the war, finally executing an Arab prisoner and becoming involved in torture; Albert's 'journey' takes him into the mines when a collapsed gallery causes all miners to work together in a rescue operation, and to ignore the personal animosity which exists between them as individuals. Two worlds again echo one another: memories of Algerian workmen from Bernard's childhood are set against exploited farm workers in modern Algeria; of cats' urine which used to seep under the coal-house door and that of prisoners herded together in a tent; of the brutal trapping of lizards and torture.

Whereas in *Nous nous aimerons demain* the whole question of the effect of war on people is left basically unresolved, in *Le Foudroyage* it is much more brutally treated. Bernard loses Colette, and it is not even certain that he is morally redeemed by the heroic actions (he saves a convoy from ambush) which result in his death. Daffenies writes that 'Il n'était plus le même [. . .] Et il voulait se racheter' (p. 258), but Albert's doubts in the closing lines have more force: 'quand ils nous auront retourné le corps, la question se posera: Est-ce qu'ils viendront, le Parti, les jeunes, est-ce qu'ils viendront à l'enterrement, comme pour les autres soldats? Avec leurs drapeaux . . . La question se posera' (p. 271).

In view of the way in which it is linked with Stil's observations about working-class life, the war is presented in these two books virtually as an allegory of capitalist society as a whole rife with indoctrination and control. Both also close superficially at least on a note of pessimism, but the implication that a solution can be reached, and that personal integrity can be maintained through a sharing of responsibility is strong. While direct references to politics are few, positive attitudes are seen to result from Party membership: problems can be shared and analyzed, and decisions taken in the light of collective experience. Communism as such is no longer stridently proclaimed as it is in *Le Premier Choc*, rather its influence, like a religious faith, is simply assumed.[21]

Both in content and form writing of this kind is far removed from the socialist realism which Stil supported so vigorously in the early 1950s. Nearly thirty years after *Le Premier Choc*, Stil accepts the proposition that such writing is limited both by its concern for accurate representation and by 'l'indication d'un devoir formateur du réalisme auprès des lecteurs par les exemples et les héros positifs'.[22] He also implies that *as a writer* he himself was never at ease with the idea: 'On a pu, comme critique, comme théoricien, faire de cette formule un instrument de travail. Mais au moment de l'écriture, on apprend que toute formule emprisonne plus qu'elle ne libère'.[23] Such an acknowledgement of the irreducibility of literary creation to preconceived norms should not, however, be taken to imply that Stil abandoned his views on the necessary interdependence of form and content. Throughout the 1960s and 1970s his preferred form of writing even in books like *André* (1965) or *Beau comme un homme* (1968) which he describes as novels, remains that of the short story. Episodes – reflections, descriptions, technical passages, even, in *André*, diagrams and photographs – are held together by the constant preoccupation with the problems of oppression and injustice, and with the search for fulfilment and happiness. Stil appears to have had little interest in the theoretical debates surrounding language and writing as a political activity beyond maintaining his belief in the necessary presence and participation of the reader for the complete realization of a work's significance. Writing remains for him an important and responsible activity, but political convictions are muted, and the need to prove or to proselytize, so keenly felt in the early 1950s, is tempered by what he calls 'cette spécificité du travail romanesque'.[24]

2 ROGER VAILLAND

Given the facts of his upbringing and of the first thirty years of his life Vailland, unlike Stil, would hardly seem to have been a potential convert to Communism. Born into a conservative, middle-class family he followed a traditionally academic school career in Reims and Paris. Friendship with René Daumal and Roger Gilbert-Lecomte led to the formation of the Grand Jeu group (outlawed by Breton in 1929), though in the main Vailland remained very much a fringe figure. During the 1930s he earned a precarious living from journalism (with *Paris-Midi* later *Paris-Soir*), incurred substantial debts, broke with his parents and turned increasingly to drugs. The Popular Front, the Spanish Civil War, the Nazi-Soviet pact appear to have prompted little or no reaction in him, nor did the cultural and literary debates of the 1930s.

Although initially indifferent to French defeat and to the Occupation,[25] he was drawn to the Resistance and sometime early in 1943 joined a Gaullist network. Through his friend Jacques-Francis Rolland he applied in late 1942 or early 1943 to join the PCF but was, not surprisingly, refused. Between then and 1952 when he joined the Party, Vailland demonstrated his commitment to Communism in his journalism for *Libération* and *Action*, and in two novels, *Bon Pied Bon Œil* (1950), ('mes adieux à la culture bourgeoisie')[26] and *Un Jeune Homme seul* (1951). At the same time his predilection for independence and individualism remained strong, as did his interest in the amateur ('celui qui ne fait pas profession, (qui) n'est pas contraint par la nécessité').[27] These two forces – discipline and individualism – highlight his work and finally contributed to his break with the PCF.

Initially, and not altogether unjustifiably, Vailland was considered by leading Party intellectuals to be a somewhat doubtful ally. He had little to do with the Communist dominated *Lettres Françaises* or with *La Nouvelle Critique* in its early years. Unlike Stil, or his friend Courtade, he continued to carry the stigma of having been (and possibly of having remained) a 'petit intellectuel bourgeois'. But his perseverence eventually persuaded the PCF of his good faith and for several years he held a position of some eminence, especially as an imaginative writer. He offered with *L'Expérience du drame* in 1954 an interesting if personalized variation on the socialist realist theme and in his novels, and especially in *Beau Masque* and *325,000 francs*, he demonstrated how his ideas could be put into practice.

On 9 August 1950 in a letter to Courtade, Vailland claimed that henceforth it would be impossible for him to write 'autrement que dans une perspective totalement communiste';[28] Courtade's reply (22 August) was cautious, clearly aware of the strong element of non-conformism in his friend. His assessment was accurate, and both *Bon Pied Bon Œil* and *Un Jeunne Homme seul* in different ways, justify this caution. In the first Rodrigue though a member of the Party has still to reach full political maturity; in the second Eugène-Marie Favart (clearly an autobiographical figure) moves from the enclosed world of his bourgeois upbringing to work and share responsibility in the Resistance. Each novel depicts, in its own way, a journey of self-discovery and liberation. Politically, however, the books are interesting not so much for what is achieved (which is litle), but by the ways in which the protagonists are 'educated' by others. While he is in prison, for example, Rodrigue studies the works of Saint-Just, is defended by Jeanne Gris – a simple girl, of working-class origins but intellectually and politically certain – and admires his fellow political prisoner Albéran – 'le combattant communiste, le bolchevik, un type d'homme absolument nouveau'.[29] But Albéran never appears in the novel and this, together with his name which derives from *alba* (Latin: white) which gives *aube* (French: dawn), obliges us to see him as a symbol only. In *Un Jeune Homme seul* Madru, the railway worker, fills much the same role for Eugène-Marie. His Resistance activities are exemplary, and after he has been killed the *éloge du mort* is a recognition of his completeness as a man; he too is the 'vrai bolchevik'. In some respects Albéran and Madru are like Leroy in *Le Premier Choc*, creations of the Stalinist cult, though Vailland avoids Stil's excessive admiration and eulogistic tone. Significantly Vailland's interest in such a character relates as much to their qualities as individuals as to their status as political models.[30] In a letter to the critic Pierre Berger he wrote: 'je n'entends pas bien sûr par ce mot bolchevik une référence nationale, mais une distinction précisément entre les héros et ceux qui ne sont pas moins bons ''en soi'', mais qui les reconnaissent comme modèles, entraîneurs, et meilleurs dans le moment'.[31]

Whatever the qualities of these characters, however, there is a distinct difference in emphasis between the two books. In the former, Rodrigue, though ideologically more secure at the end, is never seen to achieve anything: his rumoured activities remain (as Marat cynically reflects) self-indulgent. In the latter, Eugène-Marie finally takes his place in the ranks of Resistance workers, but also acts positively when he helps Jacques Madru escape from the police. By the end of 1951 Vailland too had moved to a position from which he was ready to embark on six years of intense political activity which included the writing of *Beau Masque* and *325,000 francs*. [32]

The first of these novels was greeted by the Communist press as an unqualified success: 'Peu de livres aussi pleins sont aussi exempts de schématisme' wrote André Wurmser in *Les Lettres Françaises* (11 November 1954), for example. The basic theme of the novel is exploitation and the principal action the threat to job security posed by American financial involvement in a silk-making concern, the *Filatures et Tissages Anonymes* (FETA). The workers are led by Pierrette Amable who finally draws them together in the organisation of a strike and a massive demonstration which is ultimately dispersed only by force. Caught between the two sides is Beau Masque, an Italian immigrant worker (Vailland originally considered portraying him as a North African), a Communist sympathizer with a record of political action behind him. When at the end he is shot, he is the symbolic victim of the capitalist system and of CRS aggression. Vailland also interconnects these three elements through personal relationships: Beau Masque becomes Pierrette's lover and fathers her second child; Philippe Letourneau, step-son of the present owner of FETA, Valerie Empoli, falls in love with her and leaks information concerning the company's plans. While therefore Vailland's principal concerns and targets are similar to those of Stil, his plot is much tighter. He analyses both sides of the conflict and thereby largely avoids much of the caricature and two-dimensional description of *Le Premier Choc*, though the bourgeoisie as represented by the Empoli empire is shown to be essentially fragmented and decadent, wracked by dissension, rivalry, jealousy and irresponsibility. Furthermore Nathalie, whose six per cent of the company's shares is enough to provide total power for one faction or the other, is dying from tuberculosis. Like her class as a whole she is internally rotten. As Philippe remarks to Mignot: 'Vous ne pouvez pas savoir à quel point ma classe est déjà décomposée' (p. 101). Philippe himself, while neither sick nor weak, lacks the commercial ruthlessness of his step-father; at the same time he is socially barred from joining the workers. While therefore Vailland does give us greater insight into the bourgeoisie – even to the extent of expressing grudging admiration for the skill with which Empoli manages his affairs – the overall picture is one we would expect.

In contrast working-class society, whatever its internal divisions is essentially healthy and vigorous. Pierrette, by her integrity and political assiduousness, has won the respect of employers and fellow workers alike. She is clearly distinguishable from those around her who, for all their political good faith, tend to be dull and stereotyped in comparison. Mignot, serious and unimaginative, is the secretary of the local cell; Cuvrot leader of the Communist minority on the town council, but living in the past; Louise, the delegate of the Force Ouvrière ever willing to compromise with the management; Marguerite, sentimental and politically naïve 'qui ne pensait qu'à s'évader de Clusot' (p. 87). Yet Pierrette, though in a different way from Leroy, is almost too exemplary. A lone figure, her self-imposed solitude may have made her political role easier, but it also endangers her personal relations. Her affair with Beau Masque to some extent rescues her from this but, as Mignot comments, it also undermines her political stature: 'les camarades t'accordent moins de confiance depuis que tu t'es mise avec Beau Masque [. . .] les camarades responsables se doivent d'avoir une vie privée irréprochable' (p. 352). Ultimately she successfully organizes strike action and the anti-American demonstration, but her achievements are limited. The whole affair is finally settled, not on account of the workers' pressure but because the fear that family scandal will become public is too strong. Pierrette's closing words – 'Nous sommes vainqueurs. Nous sommes les plus forts' (p. 458) – have a slightly hollow ring, and the ending of *Beau Masque* is far more muted – but perhaps more realistic – than that of *Le Premier Choc*.

Clearly, however, the novel bears many of the features required by socialist realism in the 1950s. In terms of content, local and national issues are carefully interlinked: American involvement in French affairs is openly attacked, bourgeois capitalism is exposed as decadent and immoral, and individual attempts at rebellion are shown to be of little value. Communism and working-class unity are portrayed as holding the key to the future. On occasions, in order to present as complete a picture as possible, Vailland resorts, like Nizan in *Le Cheval de Troie*, to some schematization, though with the exception of the Epilogue he generally avoids the blatant proselytizing of Stil. His acknowledged role as journalist-observer does allow him a degree of freedom in the way he presents his material. He is *confidant* to various characters in turn, he has access to the correspondence between Philippe and Nathalie (Part III), he reproduces sections of his private diary, offers us a family tree and a map by which we can follow the demonstration more easily. And Part V is written like a piece of day-to-day *reportage*. At the same time because he is omniscient Vailland can intervene to comment or to interpret – on the rhetoric of political speeches (p. 332), on Pierette's development as 'une révolutionnaire professionnelle' (p. 95), on the limited effect of passion on the mind (p. 437). He also resorts on occasions to naïve symbolism or to stereotypes: the workers (like Nizan's) have no proper weapons, the CRS forces are armed and attack defenceless women (p. 442).

Beau Masque, however, has two essential qualities. First in its structure which, as an exposition of the theory advanced in *Expérience du drame*, ensures that there are no loose ends; second in the manner in which Vailland succeeds in giving almost equal weight to the personal dimension of Pierrette's activities as to their political significance. Yet in these very qualities we can find the potential danger for much socialist realist writing. While the main body of the novel closes with words anticipating a future which will develop from present circumstances, this future is not demonstrable. So the Epilogue must be read as an attempt by Vailland to ensure that the full import of what has gone before is grasped. Stylistically it is justifiable as the final piece in a journalistic report. It also gives the book a temporal unity of a complete year and by describing events in the spring holds the promise of new developments. But the need to underline the novel's political meaning for once causes Vailland to lapse into a language more suited to the manifesto or essay: 'Dans le monde entier simultanément une nouvelle classe d'hommes était en train de prendre conscience de ses intérêts, de sa force d'atteindre à la maturité. [. . .] L'histoire de l'homme était ainsi en train de prendre son "tournant décisif" ' (p. 461).

Despite its warm reception *Beau Masque* left Vailland dissatisfied particularly over the portrayal of the exemplary revolutionary figure. Even after the completion of *325,000 francs* he wrote to Sylvestre Bonnard: 'Je m'embarque dans une grande entreprise romanesque; au centre un révolutionnaire professionel, ce que je n'ai pas réussi avec Pierrette Amable, la solitude du communiste quand il est vraiment à l'avant-garde.'[33] This ambition was to remain unrealized, but the problem of individual or collective action was to be explored again and with a different emphasis in *325,000 francs*.

This novel developed out of visits which Vailland made in 1955 as a journalist for *L'Humanité* to Oyannax, the centre of the French plastics industry. So deep was the impression which the experience made on him, however, that he decided to write a novel instead: 'Ce ne sont pas des articles que j'écrirai mais un livre, car la portée sera plus grande. C'est trop important.'[34]

The novel is more local than *Beau Masque*, relating the attempt of a young worker Bernard Busard to realise his ambition of marrying Marie-Jeanne Lemercier and of leaving his native town of Bionnas. An opportunity appears in the form of a snack bar on the N.7 for which a deposit of 700,000 francs is required. His family's saving and Marie-Jeanne's dowry make up slightly more than half the amount, and he sets out to earn the rest manning full-time a machine in one of the factories, sharing the work in eight-hourly shifts with Le Bressan, a local peasant. During the final shift his hand is smashed and while he has earned his money – and hence Marie-Jeanne – he is no longer acceptable as a manager for the snack-bar. Instead he becomes the owner of the local café and, after a rapid decline in trade, has to consider returning to the factory where, because of his disability, he will be obliged to accept a lower than average wage.

As a critique of bourgeois capitalism *325,000 francs* is clearly closely related to *Beau Masque*. There is, however, a new element in this novel in the form of Vailland's implied criticism of the workers as represented by Busard. Unlike the bird after which he is (surely ironically) named, Busard is quite incapable of rising above the conditioning factors of his social and economic background, so blinkered and trapped is he by his personal dilemma.

While to focus in such a way on a personal and local issue may reduce the wider political significance of the novel, it allows for a more intense and controlled work than *Beau Masque*. Characters are fewer in number and defined with an economy of detail. Even Chatelard, the local union leader, whose role might well have been developed, appears only briefly and essentially in contrast to the unheroic Busard. Of the four major characters Le Bressan and Juliette Doucet are frequently used as *confidants* and are depicted as free and generous in contrast to Marie-Jeanne and Busard. From the beginning Marie-Jeanne is shown to have a number of dominant characteristics which relate in a very precise way to the development of the plot. She is neat (*poncée*) and severe with a 'singulière unité de style' (p. 342), and is often described in a way which draws on images of mutilation (her link with the machine) and medieval ritual.[35] The latter, relating particularly to courtly love, dictate the pattern of her relationship with Busard. Strict control of this kind is also apparent (as in *Beau Masque*) in the novel's structure. The time span is exactly one year, the place of action remains Bionnas and there are no extraneous plots. The eight chapters too can be rearranged into five sections – like the five acts of tragedy. The description of the cycle race (Chapter/Act I) has the function of a predictive Prologue; the final chapter that of a *dénouement*. These features, with a number of carefully placed omens and echoes which, like a series of cross references, draw the text closely together, ensure that the action of the novel emerges almost as a specific case history. In his role as participant observer Vailland is again able to comment or interpret at will. Thus he interrupts a conversation between his wife Cordelia and Marie-Jeanne (Chapter II) with statements about the situation of women generally in Bionnas, the dangerous side-effects of certain adhesives or the ignorance of the working class about contraception. In Chapter IV he deplores society's priorities ('Les affaires du cœur n'ont plus de rapport avec la grandeur d'âme', p. 137); in Chapter III he describes the presses, the dulling effect they have on the workers and resulting accidents.

In January 1963 Vailland claimed that *325,000 francs* was 'le meilleur de mes romans, vrai rêve, rêve vrai, une vraie histoire qui peut être interprétée totalement par Freud, par Marx et par bien d'autres, elle a toutes les faces possibles de la réalité'.[36] Critical reactions to this statement have tended to isolate the Freudian element and have concentrated on the sexual inferences contained in Vailland's descriptions both of the machines and of Marie-Jeanne. Busard's injury too is generally interpreted as a symbolic castration, a final and absolute punishment for his having failed to act heroically. As a political or left-wing novel, produced in the mid–1950s *325,000 francs* gives little immediate impression of being very positive. Like the 'circuit de Bionnas' the pattern of life in the town is both repetitive and potentially unending ('en huit'). Nor is there a Leroy or even a Pierrette Amable to lead others to an improved future. Busard and Marie-Jeanne are, like so many of their class, largely unaware of their environment or of the forces which control their lives.[37] Escape may be glimpsed, but they have been conditioned into imagining it only in clichés or stereotypes – *un vrai métier, un snack-bar, une Cadillac*, for example – most of which, in practical terms, are quite unattainable. The social system of which they are part seems for the present (1954–5) at least largely impregnable. Possibly Vailland is implying that for the existing capitalist system to be overthrown more initiative and vigorous action than has been the case in the past is necessary. Busard, who recalls that both Chatelard and his father have bemoaned the opportunities missed in 1936 and 1944 for the Left to assert itself, is determined not to sacrifice himself 'pour une révolution dont la date est toujours remise' (p. 162). But by pursuing his own plan for escape Busard is guilty not only, as Chatelard reminds him, of acting against union regulations, but individually. Moreover there is no intervention by Vailland in the novel to suggest that Busard's failure is a necessary stage in a historical process which will eventually lead to better things. Instead what seems to emerge is that Busard, as a representative of his class, lacks or at best surrenders the qualities to help effect such a change. While he may be tempted to blame fate for having caused him to fall in the cycle race or to lose his hand in the machine, Vailland strongly implies that the real reason lies in his being qualitatively deficient.

Unlike *Beau Masque* which examines the workers' conditions together with a specific issue from a variety of angles, *325,000 francs* explores an individual's plight from the inside. But Busard is neither Henri Leroy nor Pierrette Amable; nor is he Simon Bordes in *La Place rouge* whose ultimate certainty is as much born of experience as of any intrinsic virtues he may have. He is more complex, less easily categorized and certainly not exemplary. Whatever suggestions may have been advanced for Vailland's depiction of him, the novel is successful in its exposure of capitalist exploitation and of indoctrination. But the inherent conflict between *individual* self-fulfilment – possible only for those defined by Vailland as heroes – and *collective* action remained unresolved.

Stalin's fall from grace in 1956 was more than a political shock to Vailland, though he remained a Party member until 1959 when he left 'sur la pointe des pieds'. Some of his subsequent writing continued to touch on social issues. *La Loi* in part deals with the impact of modern civilization; *La Truite* with the impersonality of large commercial enterprises. And Vailland continued to hope

that he would one day write the political novel which he had failed
to produce in the mid-1950s. But in vain. In an interview with
Francis Jeanson recorded shortly before his death Vailland
repeatedly returned to the paradox which had always obsessed
him – 'l'impossibilité de faire un'[38] – and which had essentially
prevented him from arriving at the neat conjunction of the
exemplary individual and the group seemingly required by
socialist realism.

3   PIERRE COURTADE

In Part Four of Courtade's last novel *La Place rouge* (1961), Simon
Bordes arrives in occupied Paris from the southern zone. He is
stopped by the German police who discover various books,
including Malraux's *La Lutte avec l'ange*, (which was, of course,
never completed) in his luggage. An officer remarks: '-Entre
nous, je me demande pourquoi on interdit des livres? Vous
connaissez quelqu'un qui a changé d'avis à cause d'un livre,
vous? C'est pas ça qui fait que les gens changent d'idées' (p.
165).[39]

For Courtade whose early death curtailed a promising and
interesting literary career this issue had always been an important
one. He believed that his imaginative writing should not only
reflect his own political engagement, but should engage others as
well. Yet according to his friend and fellow journalist Jean
Recanati and others he also complained that his activities as a
political correspondent consumed time which he could otherwise
have devoted to literature.[40]

The son of a post-office employee Courtade successfully followed a conventional educational programme, obtaining both a
licence and a *diplôme d'études supérieures*. After a short career as a
teacher of English at the Collège de Nantua, he joined the *Progrès
de Lyon* towards the end of the 1930s. He also visited the Soviet
Union for the first time during these years. With the Occupation
Courtade soon became involved in the Resistance. Already left-
wing in sympathy (though not yet a member of the PCF) he was
responsible for the 'Bulletin d'information' of the Conseil
National de la Résistance. In 1942 at Lyon he met Aragon who
persuaded René Tavernier to publish, in November of the following year, Courtade's first short story 'La Salamandre' in his

review *Confluences*. With the Liberation Courtade joined the Communist dominated Agence France Presse and Action where he formed part of a talented team of journalists containing Vailland, Claude Roy and Jean Pronteau. In July 1946 at the invitation of Thorez he left *Action* for *L'Humanité* joining the PCF at the same time.

As a journalist and ultimately as editor, Courtade became one of *L'Humanité*'s leading contributors specialising in foreign – notably American – affairs, always following a strictly orthodox party line. In 1954 he was elected to the Central Committee of the PCF, though like Aragon he was never given any specific political responsibility. In 1960 he became *L'Humanité*'s Moscow correspondent. Without ever expressing admiration for Stalin in quite the same fulsome terms as many, he none the less remained convinced of the Soviet leader's greatness and at least in public showed himself to be loyal even after 1956. Whether in the end with the changing climate he would either, like Vailland, have suffered some personal crisis or, like Hervé, have left or have been excluded from the Party is impossible to say. In 1962 he lost both his father and his son and himself first experienced the heart trouble from which he was to die a year later.

From obituaries, recollections and the occasional article in which he is mentioned since 1963, a number of characteristics regularly emerge: his intelligence, his humour, his bouts of melancholy (especially in later years and perhaps occasioned by illness), his intensity and his humanity. For some, like Françoise Giroud, he was 'le symbôle même des contradictions déchirantes qu'un communiste français de sa génération a eu à assumer pour tenter demeurer d'accord avec lui-même, en même temps qu'avec le parti'.[41] Similarly Vailland saw in him 'un des hommes qui incarnent le plus vivement les contradictions de notre temps.'[42] Edgar Morin believed him to have been genuinely self-deceived over communist policies to the extent that he eventually allowed the role required of him to absorb his true nature entirely.[43]

If we are to judge by his letter to Vailland (11 April 1962) Courtade was aware of the problems which his position within the Party created for him as an imaginative writer:

je me demande si un romancier communiste peut écrire des romans sur le communisme. Là était mon erreur sans doute. Dans le meilleur des cas je ne pourrai jamais être qu'une espèce de Bernanos dans mon Eglise. Ça ne va pas très bien. . . . Je vois bien que comme romancier je me suis engagé dans une voie sans issue, et en même temps *je n'en puis pas sortir*, car au fond le seul sujet qui m'intéresse c'est la politique et, très précisément, le communisme.[44]

His own imaginative writing is limited: four novels and two volumes of short stories. The problem to which he refers in this letter is only treated in the last novel, *La Place rouge*, a 'confession romanesque' as Charles Haroche called it in *France Nouvelle* (22–8 November 1961).

Much of Courtade's work relates to specific circumstances – the Resistance or the Korean war for example, and contains many of the themes treated by Vailland and Stil. In spite of his complete orthodoxy in strictly political matters, Courtade always resisted the canons of socialist realism, though *La Place rouge* shows some evidence of Zdhanov's influence at a time, ironically, when it was beginning to decline. There is in fact some reason to suppose that Courtade's interest in and analysis of the predicaments and psychology of individuals would have provoked considerable criticism from many of his militant left-wing colleagues, had it not been for his public position. Whether he reflects through the narrator on captivity and torture in 'Occupations', or on the mentality of collaboration in 'La Carpe', or 'Les idées et les tanks' (surely based on Drieu la Rochelle: 'J'étais un acteur, Messieurs, dans cette comédie nécessaire' *Les Animaux supérieurs*, p. 73),[45] he never loses sight of the individuals involved whatever their position. Far removed too from any preconceived ideas based on socialist realism are his nostalgic explorations of the past ('Vingt ans après') or his obsession with illness and death, in the case of 'Une Affaire de cœur' no doubt provoked by his own experience: 'Il a dû se crever, vous savez, entre son boulot et la politique, et en plus il devait mener une vie de patachon, et manger n'importe comment' (*Les Animaux supérieurs*, p. 236).[46] In *Les Circonstances* Courtade's analysis of what André Gisselbrecht has described as 'des qualités ou des tares, des ressources ou des défaillances d'un homme à la limite du privé et du public'[47] and, above all, the concise way in which he deals with them, far outweighs the occasional lapse into caricature (especially of the Nazis) and amply refute Etiemble's accusation of 'doctrinal interference'.[48]

In his novels, however, Courtade shows rather less security. While he certainly shared none of Stil's enthusiasm for Zdhanov's directives he produced works which were clearly 'of their period'. In essence all four are accounts of a series of self-explorations. In *Elseneur*[49] (a loose adaptation of the Hamlet story), Haeling (Horatio/Courtade himself) moves through and emerges from the Resistance having learned that collective involvement is to be preferred to intellectual detachment. In some ways Haeling's final rejection of individual action ('On m'a toujours appris qu'un homme seul pouvait tout résoudre', p. 265) sounds like an echo of the attacks made on the existentialists by *La Nouvelle Critique*. From the closing paragraphs, however, it is clear that Courtade is considering matters in more personal terms. Like Vailland's *Un Jeune Homme seul, Elseneur* demonstrates that while the ways to Communism are various, what is important is finally to have arrived: 'C'est vainement qu'il eût espéré les trouver dans les mêmes dispositions d'esprit que lui-même. Ils n'avaient pas suivi le même chemin. Ils ne se comprendraient toujours. Mais l'essentiel n'est pas là' (p. 266). Closely related to this theme of exploration and discovery is that of mask. In *Elseneur* the use of allegory is particularly apt, each character playing a role demanded of him by circumstances often to the point of total absorption. Thus Horn (Polonius/Claudius and Pétain): 'L'habitude politicienne de présenter aux photographes un sourire confiant destiné à rassurer les admirables populations d'Elseneur avait fait de sa bonne humeur un masque inséparable de l'habit de cérémonie, du piquet d'honneur et de l'hymne national' (p. 9). Only when he is asleep does the mask dissolve and his true face appear.

These two themes reappear in Courtade's next two and most narrowly political novels, *Jimmy* (1951) and *La Rivière noire* (1953),[50] the first based on his experiences in America, the second on the Korean war. Unlike Stil who in *Le Premier Choc* isolates his Americans within a French context and resorts to caricature, Courtade attempts to analyse them from within. The emphasis is much the same, however, and the stereotyped and anonymous nature of American society is heavily underlined. From the beginning Jimmy and Lucy Reeds are presented as an unthinking, conventional couple: 'Elle ne s'occupait de politique. Dans sa famille on avait toujours voté pour les républicains, et, Jimmy, qui venait du Sud était démocrate, mais ça n'avait pas d'importance' (p. 18). A series of consciously neat paragraphs charts their life together, punctuated by a number of 'instant' definitions. Lucy, for example, is 'la-femme-qui-vous-aide-dans-la-vie-et-partage-vos-soucis-et-vos-joies' (p. 26). Advertising and the cinema, both fundamentally erotic, are singled out as the principal contributory factors in the creation of this society: 'Il [Jimmy] avait vécu au milieu des sollicitations, d'une publicité sexuelle qui envahissait toute la vie, par les journaux, par le cinéma, par la rue. Un entremêlement fantastique de cuisses, de poitrines, de sourires, de combinaisons, de bas. Rien qui ne fût rapporté au sexe' (p. 74). In his work or in his attitudes towards women, Europeans and Blacks, Jimmy is presented in most respects as a typical representative of American society. But he is also 'un type qui cherche' (p. 40) who is occasionally uncertain of himself. His political education begins when he becomes involved with the organisation of an open-air concert given by the black Communist singer Paul Robeson which is brutally broken up by the local authorities with the full connivance of the police. This causes Jimmy, especially when he is suddenly reminded that Lucy's maiden name is Goldman and possibly Jewish, to question the values by which he has hitherto lived. He leaves America and his family to spend a year on a G.I. scholarship in Paris.

In Part Two Jimmy matures both politically and emotionally. Yet there is no instant conversion and Courtade not unsuccessfully explores his (Jimmy's) inner debate especially as he discovers that certain deep-rooted attitudes (his disgust when Françoise dances with a negro in a night club) are not easily lost. Whereas in Part One, however, in which the sometimes naïve and transparent style is often the ideal medium for the impression Courtade wishes to convey about American society, in Part Two the public dimension to Jimmy's experiences is rather too obviously set out. Thus the American attitude to political events, which includes an absolute belief in the need to destroy all things Soviet, is represented by James H. Dingy. But Dingy is allowed no role in the novel other than that of being a standard against which Jimmy's progress can be measured. Bill Williams, an American journalist, is equally marginal, even though his articles about dockers or about the Korean War are 'exemplary' in their truthfulness, and his presence has an extra formative influence on Jimmy.

Like Haeling, Jimmy gradually comes to realize that he cannot live either in distraction or by proxy; nor can he for ever be running away from responsibility as he has done by going to France. Evidence that he is changing comes when he finally agrees to sign an anti-atomic bomb petition and when he testifies on behalf of a Parisian worker who has been wrongly arrested after a Communist demonstration. These acts, for which he is reported to the FBI in Paris, result in his being sent back to America. In Part Three he now sees events with new eyes. He refuses to play the part required of him by the authorities in the inquest on the Robeson concert, and is immediately regarded as a dangerous and subversive element in society with Communist sympathies. In the closing paragraphs Courtade intervenes once again to draw the moral of the book for us:

> Il savait qu'une vie tout à fait différente commençait pour lui. Qu'il serait désormais un homme profondément différent. Que ni le bonheur, ni la vie quotidienne n'auraient le même goût.
> Il ne savait pas encore à quel point il serait exigé de lui, ou comme il serait difficile de garder vive dans la tempête la petite flamme qu'il avait allumée . . . . (p. 358)

Jimmy is a long novel, and such a scant summary is necessarily inadequate, but it is evident that it is not, like *Le Premier Choc*, a book of blatant Communist propaganda. Communism is certainly the shared political creed of those both in America and Paris who believe in freedom and pacifism, but it is not exclusive. Nor do we find in *Jimmy* the ideal Communist worker in the mould of Leroy or Amable. Roger the Parisian worker is sincere and hard-working, but he is in no way idealized as a model for Jimmy to follow. None the less it would be absurd to deny that Courtade's aim is to present Communism as the sole worthwhile political system, the only one which can give meaning to collective action without the loss of individual conscience or identity. It is significant that all responsible for Robeson's visit to Albany should be quite different from one another in character and temperament, but united in intention. By contrast others, like Jimmy's boss James White, not only conform to the conventional image of American types (White is white-haired, wears gold-rimmed spectacles and smokes cigars), but are shown to have allowed their roles to usurp their true selves. Thus even though he is ravaged by his son's death in the war, White continues to talk of the justness and worthiness of the American cause.

The same themes are to be found in *La Rivière noire* in which a young lieutenant Larillière having been wounded in a Korean attack on his defence post and having been treated in a Korean hospital, realises, shortly before his death that America is at fault. Like Jimmy, Larillière – interestingly described as looking like a missionary (p. 15) – is shown to be less manic in his attitude to the war than many of his fellow soldiers, especially the ex-Nazi Werner whose pathological delight in killing is meant to be more than just a personal characteristic. With the exception of Larillière, French soldiers in general are guilty of brutality, rape and murder, and the novel is one of the most outspoken indictments of France's role in the war. At the same time *La Rivière noire* is far more overtly a work of propaganda than *Jimmy* and one in which Courtade has clearly surrendered literary considerations for the sake of propaganda.

In an interview in *Les Lettres Françaises* (2–8 April 1959) Courtade remarked: 'Les soldats sont trop *intéressants* du point de vue littéraire, c'est-à-dire complexes, pleins de contradictions, trop humains.' For someone who had already dismissed socialist realism as constricting and artificial, such a statement is at best naïve. Only Larillière, whose growing doubts about the role he is obliged to play, shows any depth of personality. Elsewhere characters are entirely one-dimensional: Pommardier the political opportunist; Griffiths the obtuse and stupid American advisor; Li Ki To the representative of local authority's indifference; Tran van Dan the ideal heroic Communist fighter who, having lost an arm, will devote his life to the Party's glory. Structurally too the book suffers. While characters are introduced and dismissed at random set pieces are given deliberate prominence and quickly lose any literary value as essential elements in the construction of the plot: the descriptions of the worst atrocities exactly half-way through (pp. 95–102), of the Savel dinner party (pp. 164–73) or of the hospital scene at the end when it is revealed that the name of the nurse and local town means 'Paix Sereine' (p. 204).

Whatever Party critics claimed to the contrary, with *La Rivière noire*, Courtade's imaginative writing reached its lowest point; it is what Caute calls 'creative writing reduced to the level of thinly fictionalized journalism'.[51] With *La Place rouge*, however, Courtade did much to redress the balance. In spite of his doubts expressed to Vailland, this final novel offers some evidence that

Courtade had finally discovered a formula by which personal conviction – and the aim to convince others – could be carried by a piece of imaginative writing.

Courtade's novel is the account of the political education of Simon Bordes, and is written in the form of a metaphorical journey of self-discovery from a starting position of teenage romantic idealism, through scepticism to unquestioning (and uncritical) certainty or faith. The novel begins in France in 1935, and ends in Russia in the post-Stalin atmosphere of 1958. It is divided into eight parts of different lengths each relating to a crucial period or incident in Simon's life. It becomes evident early in the book (p. 42), that even if Courtade and his hero are not precisely synonymous, they are at least to be closely identified with one another; indeed by the last two sections of the book, Courtade alternates quite regularly between the third and first person singular pronouns for his narrative voice.

La Place rouge begins promisingly. The opening section is an account of a showing of Eisenstein's *The Battleship Potemkin* at which Simon meets a number of friends who are to reappear in the rest of the novel as representatives of different points of view. In the cinema too is Gide who, praised here for his recent support for Communism, will subsequently be violently attacked for what is considered to be a turn-coat attitude. Even though he falls well short of Nizan's achievements, Courtade has some success in this section in mixing the political with the personal. Yet as soon as he begins to describe Simon's relationship with Camille (whom he will eventually marry), or Paul Grange's with Paulette, sentimentality is never far below the surface. Because, it is implied, of their social position, their love for one another can find an outlet only in a series of nights spent together in various sordid hotel bedrooms; they belong to a depressed class from which escape can only come ultimately in death. In a way there is a resignation in their attitude at this stage which reminds us of Albert's in *Le Cheval de Troie*. Against this, however, Courtade describes Simon's sense of comradeship which Paul and Cazaux (here a member of the Jeunesse Communiste but later to become disillusioned with Communism) enjoy. After the performance they go to the somewhat obviously named café *L'Avenir*, and Courtade cannot refrain from pointing the moral: 'Cependant les jeunes gens d'aujourd'hui debout devant le zinc de *l'Avenir* continuaient le voyage du *Potemkine*' (p. 47). Here the sense of comradeship develops as they talk into the night. They are joined by Sacha who is to emigrate to Russia, his papers holding for them an almost religious fascination. At this point one of the novel's central flaws begins to appear. Already in the descriptions of Eisenstein's film Courtade's *own* enthusiasm for its political impact has emerged in spite of a token 'pense Simon Bordes' (e.g., p. 42). Now in the café, the same hiatus exists between the profundity of the *unvoiced* thoughts of the young men, and the way in which when expressed they are full of jargon, repetitive and poorly articulated (pp. 60–70).

As a beginning, however, the first section, for all its weaknesses, does have some positive qualities. Simon's political and emotional uncertainty are made clear and, even though we are never left in any doubt as to what values Courtade himself believes in, an illusion of freedom is partly retained. Thereafter as the novel develops Simon is placed into situations which, in true socialist realist fashion, are clearly intended to have an instructive effect on him. As a result, much of the internal debate of the kind we meet in *Jimmy*, and which could have added considerable psychological depth and interest to Courtade's depiction of him, is lost. Thus in Part II he is faced with the view, expressed by Prévôt, that the Nazi-Soviet pact will ultimately be seen to be justified. For Simon who has already visited Russia the choice is between personal intuitive response and the optimism born of total faith. ('Je te parle de choses que j'ai senties . . . enfin . . . humainement, et tu me réponds par des abstractions' p. 119). His romanticism continues; he is unwilling to commit himself to the Party's discipline ('J'aime mieux [. . .] être un bon sympathisant qu'un communiste médiocre' p. 194). Gradually a change occurs, neatly corresponding with his meeting Justine, a resistance worker, whom he marries after Camille's death. By 1954 and now a member of the Party, we find him justifying (in words which could have been Vailland's) his earlier procrastination, by reference to his 'esprit petit bourgeois dont j'avais bien du mal à me défaire à cause de mes origines' (p. 261). From now on Courtade is able to show how Simon has reached full political maturity. Like Prévôt he too has faith and the Stalin trials, while they cause Cazaux to leave the party 'sur la pointe des pieds' (p. 270), are accepted as a necessary link in the chain of historical progress. Finally in the last part of the novel Simon visits Sacha in Moscow. Everywhere he sees evidence of a new prosperity;

Sacha's earlier hardships (which he believes he must have exaggerated) are now seen to have been worthwhile. The promise of the Potemkin mutiny has begun to be realized; progress is inevitable. As Sacha remarks in the closing pages: 'Nous construisons le xxie siècle dans un décor du xixe siècle. . . . Tandis que vous . . . , vous êtes une société du xixe siècle dans un décor du xxe·' (p. 311).

In many respects, thematic and stylistic alike, *La Place rouge* clearly resembles Courtade's earlier novels, but there are a number of important distinctions all clearly interlinked: the period of time covered, the use of history (events, debates and people) and the confessional-autobiographical nature of the book. With the first two Courtade is following recommendations of (though not exclusively used by) socialist realist theoreticians. The period of time covered is longer than in his previous novels, and the selection of key years, creates a rigid and recognizable framework within which people are seen to play their authentic roles: Gide who moves from sympathy for to rejection of Communism; Le Bras (Guéhenno) who remains beset by doubts and anguish; Grande (Péri) the militant who dies at the hands of the Gestapo and becomes a national hero; Busard (Vailland) who works in the Resistance, fascinates women and remains enigmatic; Cazaux (Hervé) who loses his early militant enthusiasm[52] and eventually leaves the Party, no longer intellectually or emotionally at one with its narrow orthodoxy. Whereas in the earlier novels, historical models had been introduced to give authenticity and point to the plot, in *La Place rouge* they are also part of a general context from and in which the narrator sets himself and learns. (In this sense *La Place rouge* is closer to *Elseneur* than to the other novels.) Thus Bordes's personal conviction at the end has to be measured against that of others, especially Cazaux, and has to be seen to be not only stronger, but the only one possible. Carré's 'style de vie' applies here too, a point underlined throughout the book by the parallels made between political and religious faith. Towards the end of 'Cazaux et l'histoire' in Part VII the message is clear:

(Simon) ne doutait pas qu'un changement s'était produit en lui qui se préparait depuis des années. Il y avait de l'allégresse là-dedans, et comme une lumière qu'il se proposait de diriger désormais sur les hommes et sur les choses et non pas

seulement sur lui-même. [. . .] 'savoir reconnaître l'essentiel.
Cazaux ne savait pas ce qu'il faisait. Il se croyait communiste,
il se comportait comme un communiste et même très bien dans
le détail, mais il lui manquait l'essentiel: il ne croyait pas à la
nécessité historique du communisme'. (p. 284)

Significant too is the fact that the following section of the novel
should contain the account of Simon's father's death, since the
whole of Part VII can then be read as Simon's total break with the
formative influence of the past. In terms of structure as well as of
content therefore, Part VII, like Part IV in which Simon meets
Justine/Laurence, is important in that it marks the end of one
situation and prepares a new one. In Vailland's terms 'le passage
dramatique d'une situation à une nouvelle situation, radicale-
ment, qualitativement nouvelle'.[53]

In the final analysis, Courtade's own objection that he was
rather like a Catholic writer proclaiming his personal faith, is at
least in part valid. But like a good Catholic novel, *La Place rouge*
largely succeeds in presenting the narrator's ideological conviction not as 'god-given', but as something reached through
experience and essential to the book's unity. If we compare *La
Place rouge* to *Clarté*, we find less authorial interference. Debate is
conducted and affirmations of ideological positions are made in
Courtade's work by characters in their own language. In this
respect Courtade's confusion of his own voice as narrator with
that of Simon is more acceptable than, say, Barbusse's with
Paulin's. (Had Nizan persevered with his intention of writing *Le
Cheval de Troie* as a first person narrative, a comparison between it
and *La Place rouge* might have been fruitful.)

In terms of content all the works discussed in this chapter are
demonstrably those of politically motivated writers, reflecting the
attitude of the PCF to various issues of national importance
during a specific period in French history. They also treat a
number of common themes all of which relate to a greater or
lesser degree to the precepts of socialist realism: the use of history,
the exposure of capitalism and of bourgeois society, the presentation of exemplary figures, the idea of an educative 'journey'
through life, and so on. Furthermore, and in spite of what individual authors may have said, these works show stylistic similarities which equally stem from the prescriptive nature of socialist
realism, and from the attitudes and expectations of the authors.

In this respect there are, as we have seen, inevitable qualitative differences. Schematization, much apparent in the later volumes of *Le Premier Choc* or *La Rivière noire*, is successfully avoided (or at least well disguised) in *325,000 francs* or *La Place rouge*; caricature overused again by Stil in places is relatively controlled by Courtade in *Jimmy* or by Vailland in *Beau Masque*; authorial presence and involvement, openly acknowledged by Vailland, feature without comment in works by Stil and Courtade; structural control and the balance of episodes are more successfully achieved in *325,000 francs* and some of the volumes in *La Question du Bonheur est posée* than in *La Rivière noire* or *Le Premier Choc*.

In themselves variations of this kind are hardly surprising and are by no means limited to these few examples. But as in earlier cases of militant writing they are infused by the authors' conviction and faith. Without exception they are all attempts to shape the reader's response, to demonstrate to him the incontrovertible validity of certain attitudes and positions. Except unconsciously there is no room for ambiguity in this writing: socialist realism taken to this degree is unashamedly and openly didactic.

Conclusion

While in many ways the Argenteuil conference helped to effect the release of tension which had been overdue for several years, an immediate and total change in Party attitudes to art and literature was not likely. As Claude Prévost has acutely observed, whatever was issued as a final declaration of policy, 'on était toujours dans la théologie'.[1] Especially amongst those close to the centre of the PCF it was inevitable that the resolution should be viewed with reservation. One example of this can be found in an interview given by Roland Leroy, published in the *Cahiers d'histoire* in 1976. While reiterating the themes of 'la liberté de création pour l'artiste' and of 'la spécificité de la création artistique', Leroy also stresses the need for developments in art and science always to be 'conciliables avec la politique générale du Parti'.[2] To some extent remarks of this kind must be seen to be prompted by the fact that it was Garaudy (expelled from the Party in 1970), who had made, in 1966, what were perhaps the most striking claims for greater artistic freedom. In 1968 Garaudy had been one of the Party's strongest critics of the Soviet Union's intervention in Czechoslovakia. His protests continued and when in 1970 he argued that the PCF was once again submitting too readily to Soviet authority, he suffered the inevitable consequences. It is distinctly possible that Garaudy's own private philosophical debate may well have led him eventually to leave the Party, but he became instead the convenient (for the Party) victim of circumstances. When Garaudy's own attacks on Sartre and the existentialists during the post-war years are recalled, as well as his dismissal of bourgeois literature in *Une littérature de fossoyeurs* (1947), the irony is obvious. For Leroy and those of similar opinions 'le réalisme sans rivage' became a kind of slogan for all that was potentially dangerous in the Argenteuil debate.

The recognition that there had been a need for a new direction in the cultural policy of the PCF did, however, have very considerable repercussions. In literature these affected two related areas. The first, already a matter for debate before 1966 was the 'specificity' of a work, not only the question of its inherent qualities and uniqueness, but its internal fluidity and the fact that it can not be seen to obey and to fit preconceived criteria. Aragon, who thirty years earlier had so vigorously argued the case for socialist realism and whose own imaginative writing had become increasingly 'orthodox', now emerged again, this time voicing a new or at least modified 'truth'. Already before Argenteuil he had certain reservations about the question of politically directed literature.[3] His own *Les Communistes*, in its first version, was now behind him. In 'Il faut appeler les choses par leur nom', an article published in *Les Lettres françaises* in April 1959, we read:

Celui qui, par exemple, puisque je suis communiste, écrirait un livre qui supposerait la difficulté déjà résolue, ou qui croirait la résoudre par son livre . . . je veux dire qui fabriquerait dans son livre un monde communiste ne soulevant point d'objection, qui écrirait pour les convaincus le livre de *ma* conviction, celui-là, je dois le dire, serait pour moi purement et simplement illisible.

And even more significantly: 'Il n'y a pas de lumière sans ombre. Un livre sans ombre est un non-sens, et ne mérite pas d'être ouvert'. It was this permanent ambiguity of the written word, its refusal to be fixed by any one interpretation, realized in and through the act of reading which was in part responsible for his 're-writing' *Les Communistes*. Realism, and especially socialist realism, had, he claimed, 'le caractère expérimental' and should be 'un art de perpétuel dépassement. Rien ne lui est plus opposé que la formule, la recette, la répétition. Et qu'il s'agisse de la peinture ou de l'écriture, l'art, c'est toujours la remise en question de l'acquis, c'est le mouvement, le devenir'.[4] What is crucial is the potential which language has to lead the reader into an unsuspected area of experience: 'Le roman est à mon sens un langage qui ne dit pas seulement ce qu'il dit mais autre chose encore, *au-delà*. C'est cet au-delà qui m'est précieux'.[5]

Such acknowledgement on the part of one who had remained for so long the PCF's principal creative writer, also has its parallel in much of the work of Communist and pro-Communist critics. It has, as we noted earlier, resulted in a reassessment of Kafka's work. But the situation is not the same as the one which developed in the mid-1930s, when writers hitherto designated as bourgeois and decadent suddenly, and for what Caute would term 'reasons of utility', became acceptable. What we have instead is a much more complex view, not just of literature or even of literature as an art form which offers a 'realistic' representation of society, but of literature and language as particular manifestations of what structuralists term surface features of society as a whole. One instance of this expanded view is Claude Prévost's call, in a series of articles published in *La Nouvelle critique* in 1970–71, for a re-examination of Lenin's criticism of Tolstoy. Lenin, Prévost claims, has been misrepresented; he is neither narrowly ideological nor reductive in his assessment. But he does use the language of his day – in this sense it is historically fixed – and only by recognizing this fact can we penetrate beyond it and into a fuller understanding of the formative social, economic and political forces at work at that time: 'dans la mesure où tout texte plonge dans un hors-texte, il a préparé le terrain pour l'étude de ce hors-texte historique'.[6]

Such extra-literary considerations as these were already well advanced and widely debated. New criticism as it was known, in all its various forms – semiotics, linguistics, structuralism, psychocriticism and so on – was and continued to be eagerly adopted by Marxist critics since it provided them with ways of linking the analysis of a literary text with more fundamental analyses of society as a whole. Thus Georges Mounin in 'Linguistique, structuralisme et marxisme' (*La Nouvelle Critique*, nouvelle série, VIII, October 1967), an article inspired by Barthes's work, sees language as a system of communication linked to certain forms of socio-economic organisations. Julia Kristeva in 'Littérature, sémiotique, marxisme' (*La Nouvelle Critique*, XXXVIII, November 1970) argues that a text should offer not merely a passive record of whatever it sets out to represent, but a critical analysis of it as well. For her much new criticism has been over-concerned with 'une désarticulation du signifiant seul'. While this is a valuable starting point, it must be developed so that such analysis is linked with the philosophical perspectives from which a text has emerged. In addition issues which could broadly be placed under the heading of the sociology of literature were also extensively debated—readership and the distribution of books, the social status of the writer, the influence of the educational system, the role of publishing houses, the impact of the mass media to name but some.

In April 1968 at Cluny *La Nouvelle Critique* organised a 'colloque' around the theme 'Linguistique et littérature'; two years later a second one, 'Littérature et idéologies', followed. Taken together with work regularly published in reviews like *Tel Quel*, in its new post-1960 style, and in the PCF's intellectual and cultural 'house journals', *Pensée* and *La Nouvelle Critique*, the transactions of these conferences amply illustrate the way in which the post-Argenteuil climate developed. Although clearly a more complex one, this decade is just another period in the history of the relationship between the PCF, literature and criticism, which, like that of the early 1930s or the post-Second World War years, has produced its own directives, values and language.

The relationship between 'literature and the left' is not to be confined solely to this relatively narrow context, however. Certainly there have been no attempts during the last thirty or forty years to launch movements of the populist or proletarian kind – even though the Prix Populiste continues to be awarded. But novels which treat specific aspects of working-class life continue to be written. Some remain essentially descriptive, others are more strident in tone and, without perhaps prompting Zola's 'frisson de terreur', none the less challenge readers' attitudes. A representative list of such works would certainly include the following: Christiane Rochefort: *Les Petits Enfants du siècle* (1961); Bernard Clavel's series *La Grande Patience* (1962–1968); Georges Perec: *Les Choses* (1965); André Stil: *André* (1965) and *Beau comme un homme* (1968); Claire Etcherelli: *Elise ou la vraie vie* (1967); Pascal Lainé: *L'Irrévolution* (1971); Emile Ajar: *La Vie devant soi* (1975). Amongst the principal issues and themes dealt with in these works we would find the monotonous nature of various kinds of working-class existence, the pressures created by an increasingly technological and materialistic society, prostitution, the problems of overcrowded living conditions and of inadequate parental care, alcoholism, the role of women in society and the problems of class betrayal and of communication.

That such works should have been written and presumably will continue to be so, is no more extraordinary than the fact that they were already well in evidence before the publication of *Germinie Lacerteux*. As I stated in the Introduction, a Part Four in a book such as this which sought to single out the most characteristic and important aspect of this relationship between literature and the left since the mid-1960s would have to concentrate less on imaginative writing as such and more on the changing and complex critical debate of which some brief indication has been given above. While the ambitions and objectives of many French writers and intellectuals who openly sympathise with the working class, or who express allegiance to left-wing political groups may not have changed fundamentally, the means by which they may be achieved have. Indeed for many, literature – and certainly the novel – is no longer regarded as being either an effective or even relevant factor in matters of social and political concern. In whatever way we interpret it, Sartre's much repeated remark originally made in 1946 in 'Ecrire pour son époque' captures and sums up the more recent attitude of many: 'Le plus beau livre ne sauvera pas les douleurs d'un enfant: on ne sauve pas le mal, on le combat'.[7] Once again, however, this places the emphasis on the *conscious* use of literature as a vehicle for social or political comment. As we have seen, many of the works to which reference has been made in the preceding chapters, were written by authors with less than militant intentions; some have provoked unexpected reactions; others have either been forgotten altogether or are of little more than historical interest. To what extent therefore is it either possible or indeed useful to consider them as belonging in some way to a common tradition?

In his recent book *Abroad*,[8] Paul Fussell makes the point that to talk of 'travel books' at once takes us into 'complicated territory, where description, let alone definition is hazardous'. One reason for this is that the adjective 'travel' does not simply qualify the book in question, but results in any assessment of it being at least in part dependent on criteria which are not strictly literary. The same problem, as Fussell rightly states, arises as well with 'war memoir' or 'first novel' or 'picture book'. And to these we could add 'religious poem' or 'political play' or 'social novel'. Indeed once we begin to move in this direction Orwell's warning words and objections may not be far away.

What therefore of the novels discussed in this book? In terms of subject there is little doubt that they are related. All deal with working-class people, most of them single out their suffering and their exploitation at the hands of people, institutions or events over which they ultimately have no control. Their reactions, which clearly reflect the attitude of the author himself, are shown to vary – resignation, anger and/or revolt for example. And closely linked to this and due almost entirely to the influence of the Soviet Union and to the role of the PCF is an increasing element in much of this writing of politicization. But again we must ask whether beyond subject and theme is it possible to claim that these books belong, recognizably, to the same category or tradition? Some features of style and structure do recur, especially in those works which are intended by their authors to go beyond mere description and to express a particular (personal or party) point of view or to provoke reaction. We find for example, direct authorial presence, the presentation of one or more characters either to make statements of a didactic or corrective kind, or to act in an exemplary manner, the use of contrasting episodes, and characters, sometimes resulting in rigidity and schematization, or the addition of an interpretative chapter or epilogue. Rather less obvious are the use of certain images to convey either a sense of oppression (usually based on towns or machines) or of victimization (animals and birds), the contrast between the enclosed quality of town (and often tenement) life and the countryside, or the idea of life as a journey on which various experiences are encountered. Examples of local dialect, of working-class speech and the use of simple, often repetitive syntactical structures are also typical of much of this writing.

In some cases, of course, repeated characteristics of this kind are simply the result of influence, conscious or not, from one author to another (Zola and Barbusse, Mirbeau and Philippe or Aragon and Stil). In others the 'requirements' of a movement or group can have their effect; many populist, proletarian and socialist realist works are all, to some degree at least, recognizable. But beyond this it is difficult if not impossible to be categorical. Literature *of* the left, even if we consider only the novel, clearly has a number of different guises. Its status too, especially in its more militant forms, will be regularly and not unreasonably challenged on grounds of its being two dimensional, apologetic in tone, schematic and of verging on propaganda or documentary journalism. To this there can be no reply other than that of claiming the need for a different *lecture* and the application of criteria different from those used in the assessment of works which are not committed or ideologically motivated – or at least not apparently so. And though less contentious an issue, the appeal of plots involving those designated by the Goncourts as 'des petits et des pauvres' will inevitably arouse more interest in some than in others. We can, however, even within the relatively limited context of France during the last hundred years or so, consider such literature as forming part of a cultural, social and political interchange in which the parameters have rarely been fixed for long. The relationship between literature *and* the left is a complex one. I have attempted in the foregoing chapters and in the space available to give some indication of a number of the more identifiable aspects of it – but there is a great deal more to be explored.

Appendix

TRANSLATIONS

(a) *Titles*

Included below is a list of translations of the titles of all imaginative works and of a number of essays which I have used or to which there is reference in the text. Where published translations exist I have provided the date of the standard or most recent editions. Undated titles are mine. I have not included translations of the titles of critical or historical works (whose content is obvious from the original title) nor of journals and articles. In the case of the last the context or selected quotations provide sufficient information for titles to be understood.

(b) *Quotations*

All translations are my own. Where the sense seems to me to demand it I have arrived at a compromise between translation and paraphrase. I have not translated phrases whose meaning is clear (e.g. 'ignorance bestiale'); nor have I translated a phrase on more than one occasion. *Peuple* and *bourgeois* present problems. Normally I have left the latter but where necessary I have translated *peuple* as, for example, 'working-class people', 'the lower classes' or 'ordinary people'.

Agar, Emile	*La vie devant soi* (*Everything to Play For*)
Aragon, Louis	*J'abats mon jeu* (*Open Hand*)
	Les Cloches de Bâle (*The Bells of Bâle*, 1937)
	Les Communistes (*The Communists*)
	'Front rouge' ('The Red Front', 1933)
	L'Homme communiste (*The Communist Man*)
	Pour un réalisme socialiste (*Towards Socialist Realism*)
Artaud, Antonin	*Le Printemps 71* (*Spring '71*)
Barbusse, Henri	*Carnet de guerre* (*War Note-book*)
	Clarté (*Light*, 1919)
	Les Enchaînements (*Chains*, 1925)
	L'Enfer (*Inferno*, 1932)
	Faits divers (*Thus and Thus*, 1928)
	Le Feu (*Under Fire*, 1955)

189

La Lueur dans l'abîme (*Light in the Darkness*)
Manifeste aux Intellectuels (*Manifesto for Intellectuals*)
Les Pleureuses (*Mourners*)
Russie (*One looks at Russia*, 1931)
Les Suppliants (*Supplicants*)

Beauvoir, Simone de   *Les Mandarins* (*The Mandarins*, 1956)
Benda, Julien   *La Trahaison des clercs* (*The Betrayal of the
                        Intellectuals*, 1955)
Breton, André   *Second Manifeste du surréalisme* (in *Manifestos of
                        surrealism*, 1969)
Camus, Albert   *L'Exil et le Royaume* (*Exile and the Kingdom*, 1958)
                       L'Homme révolté (*The Rebel*, 1953)
Clavel, Bernard   *La Grande Patience* (*Patience*)
Courtade, Pierre   *Les Animaux supérieurs* (*Superior Animals*)
                       'Vingt ans après' ('Twenty years afterwards')
                       'Une affaire de cœur' ('An affair of the heart')
                       Les Circonstances (*Circumstances*)
                       'Occupations' ('Occupations')
                       'La Carpe' ('The carp')
                       'L'Idée et les tanks' ('Ideas and tanks')
                       Elseneur (*Elseneur*)
                       Jimmy (*Jimmy*)
                       La Place rouge (*Red Square*)
                       La Rivière noire (*The Black River*)
Dabit, Louis   *Hôtel du Nord* (*Hôtel du Nord*, 1931)
                       L'Ile (*The Island*)
                       Petit Louis (*Young Louis*)
                       Villa-Oasis ou les faux bourgeois (*Villa 'Oasis'*)
                       La Zone verte (*The Green Area*)
Dorgelès, Roland   *Les Croix de bois* (*Wooden Crosses*, 1920)
Douart, Georges   *Opération amitié* (*Operation Friendship*)
Garaudy, Roger   *Une Littérature de fossoyeurs* (*Literature of the graveyard*,
                        1948)
                       D'un réalisme sans rivages (*No Limits to Realism*)
Genet, Jean   *Journal d'un voleur* (*The Thief's Journal*, 1965)
Giono, Jean   *Le Grand Troupeau* (*To the Slaughterhouse*, 1969)
Goncourt, Jules et
  Edmond de   *Germinie Lacerteux* (*Germinie*, 1955)
Guéhenno, Jean   *Caliban parle* (*Caliban speaks*)
Guilloux, Louis   *Angélina* (*Angélina*)
                       Jeu de patience (*Game of Patience*)
                       La Maison du peuple (*Home for the people*)
                       Le Pain des rêves (*The Bread of dreams*)
                       Le Song noir (*Bitter victory*, 1936)
Hamp, Pierre   *La Peine des Hommes* (*Man's Burden*)
                       Le Lin (*Flax*)
                       Le Rail (*The Railroad*)
                       Vin de Champagne (*Wine from Champagne*)
Hugo, Victor   *Les Misérables* (*Les Misérables*, 1933)

Lainé, Pascal	*L'Irrévolution* (*The Impossible Revolution*)
Lemmonnier, Louis	*La Femme sans péché* (*The Virtuous Woman*)
Malraux, André	*La Condition humaine* (*Man's Estate,* 1948)
	La Lutte avec l'ange (*The Struggle with the Angel*)
	Le Temps du mépris (*Days of Wrath,* 1936)
Mirbeau, Octave	*Le Calvaire* (*Calvary*)
	L'Abbé Jules (*Father Jules*)
Nizan, Paul	*Aden Arabie* (*Aden Arabia,* 1968)
	Antoine Bloyé (*Antoine Bloyé,* 1973)
	Le Cheval de Troie (*The Trojan Horse,* 1937)
	Les Chiens de garde (*The Watchdogs,* 1972)
	La Conspiration (*Conspiracies*)
Panferov, Fedor	*La Communauté des gueux* (*Botherhood of Beggars*)
Perec, Georges	*Les Choses* (*Things*)
Philippe, André	*L'Acier* (*Steel*)
Philippe, Charles-Louis	*La Bonne Madeleine et la Pauvre Marie* (*Good Madeleine and Poor Marie*)
	Bubu de Montparnasse (*Bubu de Montparnasse,* 1952)
	Charles Blanchard (*Charles Blanchard*)
	Croquignole (*Croquignole*)
	Le Père Perdrix (*Old man Perdrix*)
	Quatre Histoires de pauvre amour (*Four Stories of Poor Love*)
Poulaille, Henry	*Les Damnés de la terre* (*The Damned*)
	L'Enfantement de la Paix (*The Birth of Peace*)
	Pain de Soldat (*Soldiers' Bread*)
	Le Pain quotidien (*Daily Bread*)
	Les Rescapés (*The Survivors*)
Rochefort, Christiane	*Les Petits Enfants du siècle* (*Children of Today*)
Rolland, Romain	*Danton* and *Le 14 Juillet* (both in *The Fourteenth of July,* 1928)
Stil, André	*André* (*André*)
	Beau comme un homme (*Handsome Like a Man*)
	Le Blé egyptien (*Egyptian Corn*)
	La Douleur (*Pain*)
	Le Foudroyage (*The Collapse*)
	Le Mot 'mineur', camarades, (*The Word 'Miner', Comrades*)
	Nous nous aimerons demain (*Tomorrow, All Will Be Well*)
	Pignon sur ciel (*The Sky Was their Doorstep*)
	Le Premier Choc, 3 vols
	I *Au Château d'eau* (*The Water Tower*)
	II *Le Coup du canon* (*Gunshots*)
	III *Paris avec nous* (*Together with Paris*)
	La Question du bonheur est posée (*A Question of Happiness*)
	La Seine a pris la mer (*The Seine has reached the sea*)
	('*La Fleur d'acier*', '*The Flower of steel*')
	Vers le réalisme socialiste (*Towards Socialist Realism*)
Thérive, André	*Le Charbon ardent* (*Live Coals*)

Valéry, Paul	'Crise de l'esprit' ('Crisis of the Mind') (in *Collected Works*, vol. X, 1963)
Vallès, Jules	*Le Bachelier* (*The Schoolboy*)
	L'Enfant (*The Child*)
	L'Insurgé (*The Rebel*)
Vailland, Roger	*Beau Masque* (*Beau Masque*)
	Bon Pied, Bon Oeil (*Just Fine*)
	Le Colonel Foster plaidera coupable (*Colonel Foster Will Plead Guilty*)
	Expérience du drame (*Experimentation in the Theatre*)
	Un Jeune Homme seul (*A Lonely Young Man*)
	La Loi (*The Law*, 1958)
	325.000 francs (*325,000 francs*)
	La Truite (*A Young Trout*, 1966)
Vincennes, Jean de	*De Pauvres Vies* (*Sketches of Poor Life*)
Zola, Emile	*L'Assommoir* (*Drunkard*, 1958)
	Au Bonheur des dames (*Ladies' Paradise*, 1957)
	Germinal (*Germinal*, 1964)
	Quatre Evangiles (*Truth*, 1903)
	La Terre (*Earth*, 1962)
	Thérèse Raquin (*Thérèse Raquin*, 1962)
	Trois Villes (*Lourdes*, 1894)

(b) QUOTATIONS

Page   *Foreword*

xi   a revolutionary or a revolutionised country.

xii   For *whom* are you writing.

xii   The theatre must be resurrected by and for the people. A new art for a
         new world must be established.

xv   subject matter and form/structure.

Introduction

3   The sincerity, emotion and reality of the story.

         working-class authors.

         self-taught one-time members of the working class who have become
         proletarian intellectuals.

4   'Here begins the story of the dockers of the Place de Grève'.

5   But the art of writing would be a weapon as well, words would be
         actions.

         they (the naturalists) extract partial truths, material by which the
         organisation of a more equal, less imperfect society rebuilt from top to
         bottom will be made easier.

         rotten and cracking open everywhere.

         a new society built on the real foundations of Freedom and Justice.

         if art wishes to be great it must be socialist in inspiration.

         the æsthetic independence of our literature.

         an iconographer of decadence

         this Napoleon of filth.

Chapter 1   'Un roman qui aura pour cadre le monde ouvrier'

7   A novel which will take the working-class world for its setting.

         The public likes novels which do not tell the truth: this novel is a truthful
         one.

         The public doesn't like the truth, it prefers to have lies for its money.

         prostitutes' memoirs, bedroom confessions, adventures which end
         happily.

         We were curious to know [. . .] whether, in a country without social hierarchy and a recognized aristocracy, the misery of the poor and wretched would provoke as much interest, emotion and pity as the misery of the great and wealthy. In a word, whether tears shed in the lower ranks of society would cause as much sympathy as those shed in the higher ones.

8   the stench of the people.

the major serious, passionate and living form of literary study and social inquiry.

8,9   A novel which will take the working-class world as its setting [. . .] The depiction of a working-class household of our time. The intimate and profound drama of the decline of the Parisian worker under the deplorable influence of the world of the toll-gates and cafés. The authenticity of such descriptions will add greatly to this novel. Up till now people have shown us workers in the same way as they describe soldiers – completely falsely. It would be a courageous deed to tell the truth and to claim light, air and education for the lower classes by an open exposition of the facts.

9   the first novel about working-class people which doesn't lie and which bears their stench.

they are kept in ignorance and are ruined by the world of need and misery in which they live.

It's simply a question of context. Workers are suffocating in the cramped, filthy areas where they are obliged to live on top of one another.

10   The advent of democracy has revitalized our politics, our literature, our customs and our ideas. I'm simply making a point, nothing else.

I do not want to set up or defend a religious or political creed. My study is simply a particular analysis of society as it is. I merely record. [. . .] People will look in vain for a conclusion, a moral, any sort of lesson based on the facts. I have simply displayed facts, nothing but facts whether they are to be praised or deplored.

11   Poor girl, we forgive her. And yet, having had a glimpse of what she must have suffered at the hands of those who exploit working-class people, we pity her. We have a lot of sympathy for her, but bitterness as well at this overwhelming discovery. Our thoughts went back to Rose whom we thought was devoted to us, and we were greatly disappointed to see that there was a whole area where we had no part. All our lives we felt mistrustful about the entire female sex.

12   this underworld, the people.

communal grave.

I'm plastered! All these bottles have had it.

Page

12   the novel today is based on documentation which is reported or based on real life in the way that history is based on written documents.

All the time she had to put up with cowardly and cruel jokes, the nastiness of these men content to have this ignorant and wild little girl as a martyr with her sickly, oppressed appearance, her thin and pitiful country dresses.

13   From this ugly woman there emanated a mysterious, acrid air of seduction. [. . .] Everything about her, her mouth, her eyes even her ugliness provoked and solicited. She possessed a sex appeal which attacked and held on to the other sex. She incited lust and caused people to be disturbed.

with a sort of animal devotion and [. . .] with the gentleness of a dog.

struck with the terror of a lost animal which looks for somewhere to hide.

a bestial joy.

she came back to him like an animal brought back by hand and from which the rope has been removed.

this almost animal feeling at the approach of a master.

with the eyes of a dog

she went wandering through the streets at night with the suspicious and furtive appearance of an animal who digs around in the dark pushed on by appetite.

14   In the distance the countryside stretched away, shining and vague, its greenness lost in the golden haze left behind by the day which blots it out and which turns the houses pink.

15   Germinie grabbed Gautruche's glass, drank half of it in one go and gave it back to him by the side where she had drunk.

The poor person is just as much your citizen as the rich one.

16   In a word, a very precise picture of the life of working-class people with its filth, its sloppy ways, its crude language, etc . . . A frightful picture which will carry its own moral.

the novel about Gervaise is not the political novel.

17   And once he got the use of his legs back he harboured a bitterness against work. It was a miserable job spending days, going along gutters, like a cat. Bourgeois people are not stupid. They send you to your death; much too cunning to risk themselves on a ladder they settle themselves comfortably by their fires and couldn't care less about poor people.

In twelve hours this blasted machine would make hundreds of kilos of them. Goujet wasn't spiteful, but at certain moments he would have happily picked up Fifine to smash all this iron work out of anger at seeing arms that were stronger than his. It made him very sad even when he was being reasonable to say that flesh couldn't struggle against metal. One day, certainly, the machine would kill off the worker; already their day's pay had dropped from twelve francs to nine and they were talking of reducing it again.

18   People were crying on every floor, the sound of misery echoed along the corridors and stairs. Even if someone had had a dead person in their room that wouldn't have produced such an awful sound. A real last judgement day, the end of everything, an impossible existence, the crushing of the poor. A woman on the third floor was going to do a week on the pavements on the corner of the rue Belhomme. A worker, a mason from the fifth floor, had stolen from his boss.

People were there on top of one another, rotting together; exactly like apples in a basket where there are some that are ruined.

You have no idea how getting away from the streets of Paris, where there is a real smoke of brandy and wine, sobers up the drunkards.

19   the novel remains full of despair, without any outlet, totally negative and, in spite of initial appearances, of limited social bearing. Against a harmful system there is only the undercurrent of indirect virtue which all works of truth possess. But when the truth which is demonstrated is not firmly attached to a fundamental reality, this element relies too much on individual appreciation.

a second working-class novel . . . particularly political.

it is only at the time of writing *L'Assommoir* that, having been unable to put into it a study of the political and, above all, social role of the worker, I decided to reserve this for another novel.

the introduction of a serious and in depth investigation of the social question.

20   When I wanted to project socialists into my novel, to concern myself with modern socialism, I came up against a difficulty which was greater than all the others. There are so many sects, so many different schools.

I don't think that the revolutionary socialist movement will begin in France, our nation is too soft. It's even because of that in my novel that I have personified violent socialism in a Russian.

Naturalism doesn't make pronouncements. It examines. It describes. It states: this is. It's up to the public to draw conclusions.

a work of pity, nothing else . . .

a shudder of terror.

21   an ogre [. . .] which nothing can satisfy.

she had a superb skin, fresh as milk, with chestnut hair, and a round face with a tiny nose nestling between the cheeks. The blanket had slipped and she was breathing so gently that her breast, which was already heavy, hardly stirred.

21, 22   it was Catherine who got up. As normal she had, in her exhaustion, counted the four chimes of the clock from the room below without finding the strength to wake up completely. Then, her legs thrown out of the blankets, she felt around, lit a match and a candle. But she stayed sitting down, her head so heavy that it hung back between her shoulders giving in to the irresistible need to fall back onto the boulster.

Now the candle lit up the square room with two windows and filled by two beds. There was a cupboard, a table, two chairs in old walnut whose smoky colour cast shadows on the pale yellow walls. Nothing else, rags hanging on nails, a jug on the tiles near an earthenware bowl used as a washbasin.

[. . .]

Yet Catherine made a despairing effort. She stretched, ran her hands through her reddish hair, which hung over her forehead and neck. Slight for her fifteen years, only her delicate arms could be seen outside the narrow nightdress: they were white like milk and clashed with her colourless complexion already ruined by constant washing with coarse soap.

22   And so Maheude and her children went in, frozen, famished, frightened out of their wits when they saw this room where it was so hot and where the smell of brioches was so good.

23   You load of bandits, you'll see what will happen when we're back in control!

the bourgeois organised visits at such a rate the the Grégoire family decided to follow suit. [. . .] When, about three o'clock, they and Cécile, their daughter, arrived at the collapsed mine they found Madame Hennebeau there who had arrived first, dressed in sea blue and protecting herself against the pale February sun with a sunshade.

24   Now the April sun shone fully and gloriously in the sky warming the teeming earth.

25   he hadn't yet got to the point where he had created a system for himself.

From then on Etienne was the undisputed leader.

His growing popularity made him more excited every day [. . .] to become the focus of attention, to feel that the world revolved around him – the one time mechanic and face worker with black greasy hands – increased his vanity. He was moving up a rung, he was joining the detested bourgeoisie with intellectual satisfaction and a feeling of well-being which he did not acknowledge.

was drunk with popularity.

25   his ambition (was) to give up manual work, to devote himself entirely to politics, but to do so alone, in a clean room, on the pretext that intellectual work is all-absorbing and requires a great deal of peace.

26   her shoulders sagged as if weighed down by fate.

trotting lines of men, their heads down, just like animals being led to the slaughter-house.

but there will always be bosses, of course. There's no point giving yourself a headache worrying about that.

26, 27   Now the April sun shining gloriously in the open sky warmed the teeming soil. Life came forth from her fertile womb, buds burst into green leaves, the fields trembled with the movement of the grass. Everywhere seeds were swelling, lengthening, cracking the surface of the land, encouraged by a need for warmth and light. The sap was rising in abundance with whispering voices, germs of life spread with the sound of a kiss. On and on, more and more clearly his comrades were tapping as though they were drawing near the surface of the ground. On this youthful morning in the fiery rays of the sun this noise announced that the countryside was expectant. Men were springing up, a massive, black, avenging army, slowly germinating in the furrows, growing for the harvests of future years. Soon their germination would burst the earth open.

27   No dawn lit up the dead sky.

29   Barbusse has clearly understood that artistic creation has to be used to serve working-class people struggling for their freedom from the capitalist yoke. The true artist can not stand aside from this great struggle.

particularly persuasive confirmations of the development of the revolutionary awareness which is everywhere to be seen.

thanks to Barbusse's efforts [. . .] it is possible to depict the proletariat in books and for it to recognise itself in them.

29, 30   The writer, the thinker, the guide must see beyond what are thought to be the immediate advantages and beyond the present moment.

30   As far as he is able and given the path he has chosen for himself the writer's duty is to encourage progress and improvements in the lives of that mass of people with whom he is involved.

to introduce the notion of collectivity into art.

The Dreyfus case [. . .] forced me out of my individualist apathy.

31   a need for national glory.

a social war which will take what is perhaps the decisive step forward for our cause.

32   insipid descriptions.

harnessed in mud

a snail walking on its hands.

33   A charge must be magnificent. All those men marching as if on parade. And the bugle sounding in the countryside.

I wouldn't have thought that there would be so many men sitting on chairs during the war.

I saw his body go up, straight, black, the two arms fully stretched out and where his head had been a flame.

34   The desert starts to disappear.

I can see shadows beginning to appear. Gradually men come out of the background. In odd corners something more substantial is taking shape, then these human shadows begin to move and to become distinguishable.

the great drama which we are acting.

the impression of a splendid opera set, both magical and sinister.

a terrible curtain cutting us off from the world, from the past and the future.

enormous and misshapen lumps: kinds of bears.

34, 35   sinister troglodytes coming half out of their mud caves

35   Basically they are real soldiers. 'Us, we're not soldiers, we're men', said Lamuse [. . .]. They are men, ordinary men, suddenly snatched from life [. . .] simple men who have been made even more simple and whose basic instincts have been strengthened by circumstances – self-preservation, and self-centredness, a tenacious hope that they will survive, the pleasure of eating, drinking and sleeping.

They are not soldiers: they are men. They are not adventurers, warriors destined for human slaughter – butchers or cattle. They are labourers and workers who are recognised by what they wear. They are civilians who have been torn up by the roots. [. . .] They are simply men.

36   hell on earth

an unnatural resting place.

The wind gets up. It is icy and it cuts right through to our bones. On the wretched, devastated plain with bodies scattered between its seething, watery craters, between motionless heaps of men stuck together like reptiles, on this flat, foundering chaos, slight movements can be made out.

38   You'll never hear two soldiers open their mouths for a minute without
          saying or repeating things which printers don't like printing very much.
          So what do you do then? If you don't say it your picture won't be an
          accurate one.

          I'll put bad language where it should be.

          So you want my opinion? Although I don't know much about
          books – that's brave, because it doesn't get done and it'd be good if you
          dare do it but you'll find it hard because you're too polite.

39   the solid mass of men who for months have been gathering in the north-
          east and emptying the rest of France. Workers mostly [. . .] no
          professional people in those I find around me.

          a bit withdrawn, quiet, correct.

          We are fighting soldiers and there are almost no intellectuals, artists or
          wealthy people who would risk their heads in the trench slits during this
          war except as they went by or as officers.

40   When the country, justice and freedom are in danger it's not by taking
          shelter that we can defend them.

          The future! The work of the future will be to wipe out the present – and
          more completely than people imagine, like something awful and
          shameful. And yet what is happening now had to happen. Shame on
          military glory, on armies, on the job of being a soldier which turns men
          first into stupid victims and then into disgusting killers.

          Once again I watch these creatures who have gone by here . . .

          'Yes, that's war that is', he repeats in a faint voice. Nothing else.
          What he means and I understand it too is: More than those assaults
          which are like parades . . .

41   Liberty, fraternity are words; equality is something.

          Their eyes have been opened. They start to notice the infinite simplicity
          of things.

          what has always been starts again but with a different name.

          I want to draw attention to the way historical situations recur with
          frightening regularity – the similarity in the great crises of humanity, the
          similarity or the monotony of the way men have always exploited each
          other ever since societies existed.

          The novel is the modern version of the epic. [. . .] The novelist–poet
          must think about truth, about the stirring issues of past and future, and
          he must not retreat from describing how things are.

42   Every day of the week is the same from beginning to end. [. . .] I simply
          go along with everyone else.

42   The same complicated and dull existence carries me along like everyone else.

I find that I am earmarked to follow Crillon on the town council. I expect I'll get there one day. I go on becoming somebody simply by the force of circumstances without bothering. Without anyone else taking any interest in me. [. . .] My future will be just like my past; it's already like it.

I am going towards enlightenment.

43   The animal was on the ground on its knees, crushed, cut down.

I get back to the house excited by the way I have acted, still quivering, still proud and full of joy. I have answered the call of blood. It's the great instinct from the past which made me clench my fist and threw me like a weapon against the enemy of everyone.

the black hoards, the crowd.

the vast expanse of men sets off, shouting, moving in the same direction along the street. An unending echo of noise surrounds us; it's like being in hell surrounded by bronze walls.

he makes me think of a fleeing animal hopping through the half-light.

the wretched brotherhood of the streets.

We are all dressed alike.

People know for you!

44   the soldier was carried away by the wind in enormous pieces, buried in the sky.

A flash of light filled my eyes, everything was light. I am lifted up, shaken by an unknown blade surrounded by extraordinary brightness [. . .] I fall, fantastically, out of the world having had the time in this flash of light to see myself, to think about my insides and my heart thrown to the wind and to hear faint, low voices saying: Simon Paulin died aged thirty-six.

44, 45   I wake up uttering a cry like a new born child.

I went to sleep amid chaos and awoke like the first man.

to gather together in order to be stronger, at peace and even to live.

modern slave

the magic of the past and the poisoning influence of tradition.

the man of light and simplicity.

46   It's marvellous how warlike people are.

brightness, light, sun, dawn, whiteness, flash.

string of lies

Page

46　　mass of illusions which surround us

　　　one of the announcers of truth

　　　I have been asleep. I can see more clearly than yesterday. I don't have this veil in front of me anymore; washed clean, simple, lucid [. . .] I could see everything clearly, without any distortion; I see everything how it seems, as it really is [. . .] I have no more illusions to twist things or hide them.

47　　such a magnificent display of heroism that we must not feel sorry about it.

　　　Alone on the fringe of the crowd, I sat down on a mile-stone. I grow cold hearing these words and orders which link the future to the past and one misfortune to another. I've already heard them for a long time. A lot of thoughts rumble inside me in a confused way. Suddenly I shouted 'No!'. An unshaped cry, a strangled protest of faith against the mistake which is overcoming us all. This first tentative cry I uttered almost like a man enlightened – but almost like a dumb person as well.

　　　I'm not the person to put words of enlightenment on the blank page.

　　　Humanity is the living name for truth.

　　　Truth is only revolutionary because of the confusion caused by mistakes. Revolution is order.

48　　I used to love you for myself. Now I love you for yourself.

　　　the individual is of less interest to me than the group. I am moving away from the particular to devote myself to the collective.

Chapter 3　Sentimentality and Resignation

51　　the only one of these writers who, born into the lower class of people, has not betrayed it in his writing.

　　　what seems to me to be important is that Philippe wanted to remain a man of the people.

　　　he didn't need to go to the ordinary people, he was one of them.

　　　that doesn't get me very excited, I follow the movement, but that's all. Perhaps that's not to my advantage, but I'd rather stay at home and think about what I want to write.

　　　when you see certain things at close quarters you feel sick with sadness. You want to weep. You feel angry with society and you develop into an anarchist.

51, 52　The artist shouldn't take part in a school Anyway, a school is a man who thinks arrogantly that he has made a real discovery and shouts it out everywhere. A few good souls who want to follow him lose their identity. The artist is a simple worker who listens to himself and, quietly and frankly, writes down what he hears.

52   I am happy and joyful, especially when I am sad.

He whom we hoped for came the following morning with a glass, a ruler and a few tools. He came as he should to work in his ordinary clothes and with his workman's face.

53, 54   But after twenty girls become bored because they are not intended to work aimlessly at dressmaking, because their bosoms should conceive and their hearts cherish. A little later there is a moment's relief in their lives which cry out for love. It's the last time that their strength stirs, the final attempt to clutch onto the piece of drift wood which can take them to the harbour. Marie was thrown up onto the shore by a tiny wave a long way from salvation.

Young girls, you who are sixteen, you turn into ridiculous, ugly old spinsters. From a flock of laughing creatures you turn into one of quiet old beasts joylessly eating grass in the fields awaiting violent death at the hands of the butcher.

And Marie was once twenty-five, twenty-six and now thirty. Every day she is bored as I have told you and every day passes by. Years, made up of great lumps of days pass by as well. Each one brings another wrinkle to the face and hardens the heart. [. . .] Marie understands life as she should [. . .] she is resigned to it but not without some bitterness. Is it possible not to complain about what is hurtful? Marie has said to herself: 'Life is made up of crude material things and crude people can take pleasure from them everywhere, but delicate people suffer a great deal.'

white, pink, fair, blue.

pure, humble, simple, smooth, quiet, delicate, gentle.

I'm interested in her suffering, I'd be pleased to bring her up in the way I enjoy bringing up children.

she already is to a certain extent.

55   When society corrupts certain souls you are witnessing a crime.

in which you would see a young working-class girl become a prostitute.

Marie [. . .] provides a wealth of documentation.

a poor pure creature chosen by fate to do evil. She is no longer herself but part of fate.

Bubu became a pimp because he lived in a society full of rich people who decide who does what. With their money they desire women. There must be pimps to supply them.

We are living in a world where the poor must suffer.

55 docile animals who are led to the local fields.

old women who walk heavily like cows and stand around at street corners.

tired like an animal which has given in.

a broken animal.

the swollen breasts of a worn out animal.

55, 56 He to whom it has been given to suffer more is worthy to suffer still more.

56 The electric lamps are surrounded as if by halos and light up the air between the houses, making a great stream of light which spills over the roofs and up into the sky. You bathe in this atmosphere as in a subtle fluid, a penetrating, electric bath. Then there are warm winds, the breath of a Parisian night like that of a howling beast with its sweat and staring eyes, breathing hard enough to pass out. One shout echoed another, a passer-by evoked desire, the street lamps burned him up like a wisp of straw, every being in the street swelled and cried out like a rutting animal appealing even to the most timid hearts.

Paris had taken them in her hand and had crushed all four of them.

powerful and [. . .] crush life out of them with their jaws.

57 He did exactly what he wanted to do. He knew how to pick a lock and could kill a man quite easily. Women showered him with signs of love just as birds sing their welcome to the sun and to new strength. He was one of those people whom no-one could subdue; his life, like theirs, involving danger was noble and fine.

dirty like their job.

For something to do they watched the passers-by and summed them up with a brief and often ironic remark. It recalled the day of the Creation when Adam, king of the world and sitting beneath an oak tree, inspected the animals, examined them and gave them names.

58 multiplicity of 'I'.

workers who are poor, workers who are comfortably off, republican bourgeois, reactionary bourgeois.

59 They ate quickly using cheap, iron knives which cut off large helpings of bread but small helpings of cheese.

When a member of the bourgeoisie went past he sensed it in advance by the lightness of his footsteps used to polished wooden floors.

59, 60 The other (Lartigaud) had eaten so much during the last year that the layers of fat were piling up and day by day you could count them. Like that he was pushed around the paths of his garden sitting in his little wheel-chair. He had become keen on flowers, and no-one would have guessed that he, a bourgeois, could have shown so much patience and care.

60   a rottenness inside him which came out in layers and increased in quantity just like bad luck which consumes poor people as it grows.

I needed to earn my living honestly.

61   She gave the appearance of being very modest, very honest and as though she was fully engrossed in her work. Sometimes she would put her hands together in a cross on her breast, would lean slightly to the right and silently flutter her eyelids.

a glorification of freedom.

63   an angel with outstretched wings.

the vermouth attacks your stomach and a bitterness develops which is really quite unpleasant. At this moment the blackcurrant arrives gentle, smooth and offers the words of Jesus: Happy are those who suffer for they will be comforted.

Angèle had grand ideas which she couldn't express.

64   a remedy for my weaknesses, a tonic which makes me feel very strong.

Part II

Introduction

67   all essential things in this world have been affected by the war, or more precisely, by the circumstances of the war.

the decadence of civilisation; the end of culture; the collapse of the world; the end of humanism.

68   a class of people who [. . .] exalt those values which go beyond merely temporal matters.

The mind is light. Our duty is to lift it above storms and to push aside the clouds which seek to blot it out.

first of all to remain intellectual, and to be part of the modern world; thereafter to resist various temptations which are on the look out for him.

When he feels too attracted by action a man who believes in intelligence must respond in the same way as the man who believes in moral standards when he sees himself becoming popular: he must be wary and be careful how he acts.

69   Everything is to be used, all means of destroying the notions of *family, fatherland* and *religion* are worth using.

69   In reality I tried my hardest to rediscover the simplicity of my working-class spirit. But for a long time it was in vain [. . .] You don't read books without being affected. [. . .] Sometimes culture has this effect of destroying our character.

70   There are not nor can there be working-class writers in a capitalist society; the training required to be a writer is incompatible with factory work – eight hours per day to get enough just to live.

Chapter 4   Proletarian and Populist Writing

72   Social art is art which can be justified as being useful. When it is addressed instead to the intellect art is superfluous.

which strictly speaking means 'having to do with society'.

72, 73   works having a clear moralising purpose and being capable of strengthening in their readers the will power to realise a new system in which we all believe and for which we are all struggling.

73   imbued with the active spirit of Communism.

Art, proletarian poetry, the novel, song, music, theatre, everything can serve as a means of magnificent propaganda. Art shapes feelings in the way that propaganda develops awareness and thinking strengthens the resolve to act.

Revolution is the action of the masses and the highest form of art will always be the expression of the spiritual life of people as a whole.

74   *Monde* does not depend financially or ideologically on any party, any political organisation. [. . .] *Monde* will not indulge in political polemics.

inspires and sustains at the same time as it expresses it, the great cry of the masses as they move towards freedom.

1. Do you believe artistic and literary production to be a purely individual phenomenon? Do you not think that it can or should reflect the major currents which determine the economic and social evolution of mankind?
2. Do you believe that literature and art which express the aspirations of the working class exist? What are, in your opinion, the main examples?

Proletarian literature today? Just another piece of opportunism.

74, 75   They can be of some use to the proletariat, they often do little more than introduce him to the ways in which the radical bourgeoisie feels and thinks. Sensitivy, thought, talent, modes of expression – intellectuals are formed by bourgeois culture.

75   make the very soul of the masses burst out.

75 Proletarian literature is the actual, living, precise form of popular literature heightened and imposed by historical evolution.

make them certain of their own strength.

Form must be organically linked with the subject in the way that the body is automatically and physiologically linked to life. [. . .] Writing has become a skin rather than a dress.

Without protesting we watch a general lowering of the ideological and artistic level of French literature which is ravished by the spirit of appeasement and satisfaction of post-war French bourgeois society.

a right-wing deviation.

76 in the ranks of revolutionary, proletarian literature.

nothing other than a weapon in the class struggle.

a man who is a practising revolutionary.

France is so far behind that it is impossible to say that at the present moment there is the slightest sign of revolutionary, proletarian literature.

the network of bourgeois illusions.

if political principles are introduced, the class struggle, allegiances fly out of the window and only a small minority remains.

77 it is saturated with marxism [. . .] with the deepest feeling of the unity of human struggle and of brotherly solidarity which are essential to the philosophy and psychology of the proletariat as an historically determined class.

In my view we should tell marxism to mind its own business, it has nothing to do with art.

77, 78 It is less a question of somewhere to go for entertainment however refined, than a meeting place. A unit will quickly be created in each locality, and gradually all those who have lost the taste for community life will find it again. It is a crystalisation in a class sense which directives about class struggle could never replace.

79 Almost always those who climb socially suffer because they are changed, they become half-castes, bastards, they lose the stamp of their class without assuming that of another. What is difficult is not to make the ascent but to do so and retain your integrity.

the bourgeois, the lazy and the rich.

If there is an art for the people it is a human art. It is the literature of the greatest writers, a great literature.

it both gathers together and offers comments and genuine experience.

79   it should set out the principal guide-lines for life's problems. In short, to be useful.

80   Proletarian literature [. . .] is the expression of a class, it is spontaneous [. . .]. It does not claim to be the aim of Art, but a means of combat.

      (Proletarian literature) speaks for a class and often expresses the hopes, the wishes of that class, for most of its manifestations are combative works. [. . .] It responds to the need of a class which is always uncertain as to where its daily bread is coming from.

      a perfectly gratuitous journey through the working class.

81   the need to earn a living by professional or practical means – in short just life.

      First of all we thought of 'humilism' but 'humilist' was uncomfortably close to 'humanist' and it was wrong according to Thérive to evoke the bleating, tearful books of Charles-Louis Philippe. Afterwards we considered 'demoticism' but the word seemed to me to be too learned and obscure for most people. Then the term 'populism' attracted us: it was clear and to the point.

      a literature full of anxiety and weakness, a style which typified the young bourgeois who tried to titillate their minds in order to give themselves a shock. [. . .] A reaction is starting. To get off the ground it must first modify the most popular of genres, the novel.

82   (Novels) about people, novels which people will read and which are not simple and artificial stories but great works of art.

      ordinary people who make up the mass of society. One of its aims is to bring the souls of ordinary people to life again.

      straightforward literary people who have nothing to do with politics. We do not think that we should, as is said, elevate people, educate the masses. We take ordinary people as they are and we describe them as they live. We like them in and for themselves.

      it must be secret not obvious.

      insignificant, ordinary people [. . .] whose lives also contain drama.

84   He came out of the station looking as he did when he went to mass, his nose pointing in one direction, his eyes in the other. No church bell was ringing for a service but he succumbed to the call of the brothel.

      A massive, silent building represented the injustice which they suffered through too much work and too little bread. This foreign god, hungry for their suffering, lived in their imaginations surrounded by mystery and shining with the reflection of gold.

      The memory of our suffering will give men the incentive to win at the next strike. Perhaps all we have lacked to prepare ourselves for victory are some dead people to avenge.

86   Politics faded before the pleasure of smoothing this rough plank until it was white.

the shell of an enormous sleeping head.

The hammer blows struck out their simple melody, the men called to one another. A young fellow busied himself winching up beams. He whistled like a chaffinch.

the fluttering game of ready-made expressions.

Those who are not with us are against us.

87   Mangeux knows all about the dumb suffering of kids. He knows how painful it is; he knows that it is never understood, ignored. And yet the child who seems to be carefree can be hiding a painful sore which will never heal. Already he knows hundreds of children whose souls have been ravaged by the war.

They tried to fix in their minds this tiny corner of the wood which was the centre of safety. How few of them would come back to it though.

Loulou couldn't understand this change which had suddenly come over him . . . Why was his father not working any more? He wasn't old enough to understand the link between his father's inactivity and the meagre amount of food they had to make do with every day.

Come on then! You won't feel so disgusted later. You'll hide behind these stiffs without being invited to do so . . .

None of them could give a damn. They didn't know why really . . . They simply couldn't care less. It's another way of being happy.

88   the internal and mystical life of humble people.

No-one could want to give orders less than he did. He didn't have enough energy to rebel.

the chromatic whine of a bullet which seemed to disappear into the ether.

they experienced an exquisite pride at being together, two of them like everyone else, like men and women who were not damned, like those who have agreed to help each other live.

89   the ideal illustration of what, at their worst, populist aims produce.

I do in fact wear gloves and a bowler hat [. . .] notorious signs of a bourgeois existence.

I wanted to be objective and truthful.

real buildings made out of vegetables.

89   Disturbing, odd faces; fat, red-faced, swollen peasant women, carters dressed in skins their whips hanging round their necks, young farmers' wives leaning against a wall of cabbages, their hair cut like a boy's, in silk stockings, hands on hips, a bag at their waist.

You drag monotony and boredom through the crowd which pays no attention. Fellow workers are few and so exhausted that they hardly talk. Their silence results more from old age and exploitation than hostility. You can get nothing out of these crumbling ruins.

90   Only having unfortunately a limited capacity I am obliged to cut short this kind of investigation which necessitates the ingurgitation of various liquids.

We're not men, we're animals.

I can sense a wave of anger against a society which abandons people to the point where they are obliged to steal in order to live.

Sitting close to the ground an impression of tiredness and extreme isolation evercomes you.

90,91   At least theoretically 'populism' is something which can not be realized. How can a proletarian literature exist when bourgeois culture, which would allow for its expression, is forbidden to those who really do know working people? And yet a 'populist prize' exists. In selecting Eugène Dabit's *Hôtel du Nord*, André Thérive and Léon Lemonnier, who launched the first manifesto encouraging the true depiction of humble people, awarded the prize to a masterpiece in a genre which ultimately would produce very little.

one of the finest, one of the most striking novels of proletarian literature.

clearly popular in inspiration.

since the author describes the customs of working people in it.

They want me to be a populist novelist! What is populism? They must always categorise you, put a label on your back.

I am quite incapable of obeying aesthetic demands.

simply with human considerations. This world which you devote yourself to is mine and I don't think I shall ever leave it. [. . .] And all the better if my work can be of some use.

92   For her (Louise) happiness was to live with those dearest to her without being ill or out of work.

I'm eighteen years old, I'm a worker like my parents, my life will be like theirs.

A hum of insects, the rustling of bushes, the caresses of the wind.

I reach out to catch hold of life and I only find its shadow.

93   My wish to be an individual fits badly with all these systems.

Is proletarian literature necessarily marxist, dogmatic and without freedom?

94   Broad shoulders, strong arms, a precise, supple way of walking, he was every bit a man. His blond crew-cut hair was silky above a broad smooth forehead.

A fine blue gaze, deep and gentle, full of smiles.

a story outside time.

95   'Right then François, what's going to happen?' 'What', said my father, 'I hope the revolution won't be long in coming now.'
She raised her arms heavenwards.
'Yes' he said, 'the Revolution'.
What was he talking about! Did people need revolution? It would only lead to misery. People were badly off already without that.

What was there to eat? Potatoes with pasta fried in water, a real feast? Sure, it's Sunday, God's day. To the glory of the Lord there'll be the thin end of a chop to gnaw with cabbage and plenty of gravy . . .

96   But for the moment [. . .] the proletariat is becoming aware of itself, it's coming out of the darkness and trying to organise itself, [. . .] Between them (the bourgeois) and us it's a fight to the death.

97   I'm the son of a worker and a worker of words. I'm completely at one with myself and I've remained what I always was.

the offspring of old people, the sad child of the last of the realists.

Chapter 5 The Beginnings of Socialist Realism

99   When we talk about socialist realism that does not mean that revolutionary romanticism is something different or in conflict with it. On the contrary we are living in an heroic period [. . .]. Heroism, brilliant achievements, selfless devotion to the revolution, the realisation of our realist dream – these are the essential characteristics of our period. [. . .] When we talk about socialist realism we have in mind that which in art represents the objective world, not only in its superficial or even essential details but in its fundamental circumstances and characteristics. We have in mind everything which represents life in all its truth with both its negative and positive aspects, with the victorious element of the forces of the socialist revolution. We have in mind the anti-capitalist nature of our works which nurture in our readers the will to struggle for a better future for mankind.

99, 100   First of all to encourage around us the growth of proletarian literature and art; to stress to people of the working class the need and the urgency for a proletarian literature and art in France; to denounce all the subterfuges and manoeuvres of the bourgeoisie in this respect.

100   We [the intellectuals] will persuade them that their interests are at one with those of the class of people who are oppressed and exploited like them, in different ways, to a greater degree, but for the same reasons by virtue of the same economic system.

it is clear that discussion must always remain brotherly; newcomers to the AEAR must have the impression that it is an organisation in which people can breathe and not feel that they are in the presence of some vain dogmatic attitude. But at no moment must discussion be weak.

the question of literary creation and of the forms it might take within the revolutionary movement.

101   Blow up the colonial volcano
Break open the French empire the ragged tricolour cracks
And the enormous body of the oppressed rises up and throws off
a stream of executioners and monsters
at the call of the Communist Party.

Up tormented souls of the world
to smash down the bourgeoisie
our blood flowers and the earth
belong to us   up   advance

They have all got thinner. But the boss's fortune, in spite of the crisis, swells like a belly.

I write because I felt the urgent need to make certain facts known and to disturb certain lies.

102   There are no fascist or communist novels only good or bad ones.

Apolitical works are works which militate for the preservation of the régime in power.

How should one write for the proletariat? The essential question about proletarian literature.

The hypocritical enslavement of neutrality in art and science.

art will not develop in a noble or splendid way until it is freed from the influence of money which is basic to our civilisation today.

102,3   Socialist realism is not a dogma, nor a collection of laws placing limits around artistic creation, reducing the wide variety of exploration and form to literary commands. On the contrary socialist realism is the natural expression of new socialist relationships and of a revolutionary conception of the world.

103   the true and historically accurate depiction of reality in its

revolutionary development (and) is able to show reality in historical movement, how the future is born out of the present.

a photographic technique stripped of social and didactic importance.

the very essence of the work incarnated in its imagery.

Socialist realism ensures that the artist has an exceptional possibility to display his creative initiative, to select genres, forms, different methods [. . .]. The aim of the Union of Soviet Writers is to create works of art which are worthy of the great period of Socialism.

105   I reckon that all literature is in danger once the writer sees that he is obliged to follow orders.

105,6   to speak a language which is accessible to their companions.

In nine out of ten cases, the revolutionary writer owes his formation to the humanities and to the teaching of the schools. His problem is how to break with the knowingly complicit systems, with its implied metaphors and allusions without falling into a disgusting affectation of 'popular' style.

106   Socialist realism presents for us, who are writers in a country where the revolution has still to be accomplished, particular problems since it requires the renewal both of the subject matter and of the form of novel, play and poem.

the re-education of men by men [. . .] the transformation of the social ape of our time into the socialist man of the future.

to overthrow this world which revolted us.

107   equal comrades [. . .] builders of socialism.

a language of the future, understandable to all without any loss of technical quality.

a critical realism which described reality with bitterness. But it could see no way out from this reality.

have the spirit of revolution pass into art without destroying it.

the relationship of the writer with the people with whom he feels at one.

108   not only a naturalist work but the expression of this socialist realism (to adopt the terminology of our soviet comrades) in which reality bears the stamp of a class, in which what is real is not an end in itself but an agent of change, its own change.

a novel which describes through individual people the classes to which they belong, through the action the struggle between these classes, and which by its depiction of past reality allows a glimpse of the socialist reality of tomorrow. [. . .] It is one of the first works to which the label socialist realism can be applied.

the workers were on the side of the women.

This impossibility really to state her position.

[which] simply refused to shut.

114   Money by post fell from the sky, came from afar, from the difficult M. Simonidzé who had oil wells.

She had not liberated herself from the things which her mother and father–the owner of the Bakou oil wells–loved. Sometimes she reproached herself for being there in a low-cut dress with this dinner-jacketed gangster in a box in Piccadilly. [. . .] But what could she do? She both loved and hated luxury at the same time. There were some evenings when she wanted to forget suffering. Her socialism had not yet got a very good colour.

115   She has stopped being a parasite and a prostitute. The world of work is opening its doors to her.

We are at the end of an era, on the threshold of a new world.

117   Revolutionary literature in the full, and not just in the formal sense of the word, will comprise all the dignifying pieces of writing which pave the way for the proletarian revolution drawing from it its themes and inspiration.

a particular class awareness. Proletarian literature will describe everything including bourgeois society and the natural world from a proletarian point of view.

this group of well-intentioned but impotent people.

make a certain number of vague and all-embracing protests against war and colonialism.

a very precise and very aware mass movement.

an organ of quite violent counter-attack.

117, 18   The writer is someone whose job it is to define for people and to make them aware of their highest values and greatest ambitions: he discovers the values implicit in their lives and justifies them in such a way that they can accept them because they are moving towards greatness and achievement.

118   Proof excludes art [. . .]. Proof belongs to the realm of science and is worked out by very precise techniques which are not those of art.

I didn't want to use my novel for political ends. But if there are political conclusions to be drawn from it, the subject compels that.

119, 20   That evening Antoine understood that he was a lonely man, a man without contacts with others. [. . .] He experienced difficult and cruel feelings. He shared the delight at having defeated the strikes, the delight of a strike-breaker. He was amazed at this. Then he hated the workers because in secret he envied them, because deep inside he knew that there was more truth in their defeat than in his bourgeois victory.

120   he begins to have dreams of greatness, to promise himself an important future [. . .]. Perhaps it will be difficult to achieve, but he knows himself how hard and tough he is, and he goes for a walk in the evening telling himself that he will make it . . .

he didn't realize that like many similar adolescents he was placing his stake in the huge game in which the principal bosses of the French bourgeoisie were beginning to be engaged.

during these pre-war years, French bourgeois society wallows in great calm and contentment, it has arrived, nothing untoward can happen to it, no catastrophes are suspended above its head, it enjoys a power which nothing seems to threaten.

121   whose jobs expire at nightfall.

all of them believed that world events, even the shifts of the planet didn't concern them. They felt definitively isolated, marvellously certain and protected; everything happened to entertain and distract them, pretexts for them in their games of observations and judgements. [. . .] They considered themselves to be wise, stable, happy. [. . .] And Antoine lived amongst them, he was one of them; month after month, he sank deeper and deeper into this sweet bed of habit, he went off to sleep. [. . .]

a member of the upper bourgeoisie who had family traditions.

M. Huet kissed the hands of provincial noble ladies in drawing rooms where the Bloyés never set foot. But Antoine's ambition had never aimed so high . . .

122   All men miss the pleasure to be had from collective activity.

They gave themselves over to pleasures which are forogotten today by those like them who finally come to know – like the workers whom they still despise – the anxiety of the weeks and months to come.

a way of making people aware [. . .] a means of carrying on a struggle against the bourgeoisie.

123   It was a town where everything was beginning: you would have thought you were back, a hundred years before, at the very beginning, at the first stirrings of the anger and power of the working class.

124   he closed his eyes, he only had to let himself be carried on by the mechanical movement of things; from this minute on he need take no more initiative.

124   Lange was dragged on by people's movement, he was alive, once again, like others, he was part of the machine, of conflict, he was no longer an observer, he knew what passion was. [. . .] his feeling of exultation was every bit as strong as sexual satisfaction.

125   They had just been shut up in the black well of the theatre: the room was dark and cold and the meeting at first had been like some descent into an underwater world with all these painted sirens who curled their tails under the sloping balcony, an underwater world above which a blue glass roof let in inadequate light like that of the moon under the sea.

like a swimmer who has come out of the water.

shell-fish or fish slowly moving in the water and seaweed of an aquarium.

wore basque hats, decorations and carried sticks.

126   After patience and hope violence will come.

They would gather the political meaning of the day later; first of all they thought about their numbers, their dignity and the end of their isolation. And perhaps the political meaning was simply that thousands of men had been capable of being angry after all.

127   They thought of time to come. This was how it was. [. . .] For years this irruption of history had seemed to be a dream and a fairy tale which had no more relevance for absent-minded, sleepy French provinces in a world of catastrophes than did the typhoons in the China sea. [. . .] A world was born. France took her place in the game played between nations; for her too the violence which reshapes history was beginning. No more plans or waiting in this unbelievable future in which victims would one day be counted in masses, in which individual deaths would not be particularly noticed: it would be like a natural cataclysm, a cyclone, a tidal wave.

The workers watched the guards form a thick black band across the opening to the boulevard where early in the afternoon the police had been in a thin line. They wondered about the day's meaning. We have stopped the fascists from marching, we have chased them off, it's a victory, but we have retreated in front of the guards and that perhaps is a defeat which cancels out the first victory. They wondered what they would do: disperse, go home? But they found it difficult to accept that the day had finished so badly after all. Anger was not appeased; anger nurtured over the years doesn't go away like hunger, anger is more demanding than thirst and hunger; it was not satisfied and kept them still up to the last moment in the hope of a second victory; anger had raised them up and was not going to let them fall again, it was not like the most profound law of their lives. They did not know then that they had so much anger in reserve.

132,33   I was one of those adolescents for whom becoming a Communist
          meant at the same time becoming a man. Joining the Party was all
          mixed up in me with initiation, the risk of death, of setting out on a
          real life.

133   *Les Lettres françaises* will be our weapon and by its publication we, as
          writers, mean to play our full part in the struggle to the death in which
          the French nation is engaged in order to be free from her oppressors.

          It is not just a question of being a patriot. Still more we have to act.

133,34   Works exalting patriotism and freedom, paying tribute to the
          'Francs-Tireurs et Partisans' who are bravely struggling to kick the
          hordes of Nazis and the collaborating servants out of France.

134   You don't write in a vacuum and for yourself; literature is an act of
          communication: the reader is just as vital as the author if a book is to
          be fully realized. Ultimately it is *for him* and *through him* that the book
          exists. [. . .] Literature is not an innocent and facile song which
          would fit in with any régime: but it does raise the essential political
          issue; to write is to claim freedom for everyone; if the work is not an
          act of freedom to be recognized by others then it is only an infamous
          piece of chit-chat.

          Today the *avant-garde* artist has the good fortune to be a sort of *public
          writer* – one who speaks for those who do not have the ability to write,
          who, like the magician of former times exorcises the crowd and like
          the psycho-analyst today aims to free people from evils they cannot
          precisely identify. The public writer is one who is both part of and in
          advance of an event, who describes it and comments upon it, works it
          out and illuminates it both socially and poetically.

135   Socialist realism is the æsthetic expression of this political force.

          Comrades the USSR is the only free way
          By which we shall go to find peace
          A peace which favours the gentle desire for life
          Night shrinks
          And the earth reflects a spotless future.

136   The time of artists is over. But we shouldn't be bitter. One of the
          temptations for the artist is to feel that he is at one with others and
          indeed people shout this to him gleefully. But that's not so at all. He is
          in the middle of everyone, neither higher nor lower than all those who
          work and struggle. His vocation when he is faced with oppression is to
          open prisons and to express the sorrow and happiness of everyone.
          [. . .] Without culture and the relative freedom which that implies,
          society, even a perfect one, is a jungle. That is why every authentic
          creative act is a gift for the future.

136   Every piece of writing has a meaning, even if this meaning is a long way from the one which the author had hoped to put in it. [. . .] The writer is essentially part of his period.

137   Literature, essentially, is the subjective expression of a society in a state of permanent revolution.

in turn the whole of art becomes a means, it becomes one of the links in the process, its ends and principles are external ones and it is controlled from the outside.

To have the unity of the world of the novel match that of the real world can only be done if there is an *a priori* judgement which eliminates from the latter anything which doesn't suit the doctrine. Realism called socialist realism is bound therefore by the logic of its nihilism to bring together the advantages of the didactic novel and of propaganda literature.

139   *La Nouvelle Critique* will unmask all lies, falsifications, ideological manoeuvres of those gravediggers of culture, of national independence and of progress.

The Stalin Prize for literature has been awarded to André Stil. For us, for our people that is like a brotherly and fighting greeting from the Soviet people in support of our struggle – evoked by the book – for peace and democracy, for freedom and independence.

The working class in France, our people, our Party see in this, we are sure, a further justification for our attachment and unshakeable love for the Soviet Union and for this mighty Stalin.

Yes, we love Stalin's country, and the reward granted to André Stil, who has known how to put his pen and his talent at the service of popular and national needs, goes straight to our heart. [. . .]

The award of the Stalin Prize to our comrade André Stil is further proof that the Soviet Union, the country of socialism, of true democracy of collaboration and peace, is not a 'foreign' country for working-class people.

140   The writer is not able to lag behind events, he must be part of the *avante-garde* and show people how they should evolve. Instructed by the method of socialist realism conscientiously and carefully studying the reality of our lives, forcing himself to fathom how our evolution is taking place, the writer's duty is to educate and to give ideological guidance to the people.

141   the most advanced literature in the world

at the height of its decadence and degradation.

a brilliant form with a profound content

Socialist realism is an interpretation of the world based on true historical development. First of all it is militant political action. The artist must play his part in man's fight to change the world, so that he can express the truth about the world.

141   The socialist writer must be aware of the way men develop, of their striving for better things, of their revolutionary development. Scrupulous as a historian he must also be a moralist.

142   Socialist realism takes its impetus from the new content of reality, the consequence of the victory of the socialist revolution. [. . .] It implies a new social role for the artist, his link with the revolutionary movement and his responsibility to it. In the strict sense of the word it is a way of understanding, of action and of work.

        To make this type of man and this class know and understand so that people will have a sense of the future and help in making it come about. Art can achieve this and do so for its own benefit.

142, 143 To be both heard and to serve it is necessary to speak.

143   A novel, a poem, everything written only has an existence once it has been publicly received.

        individual and collective adventures. [. . .] In this way two weaknesses are avoided: the schematization of the propaganda novel and the distortion of populism and of the proletarian novel.

144   We are not æsthetes and we know that form is all the more easy to find and to realize when we are quite certain about subject matter.

        a typical subject, expressed in a form which is not typical and therefore appropriate, would not be a typical subject matter.

        from an artistic point of view the most acute socialist awareness is not necessarily superior to bourgeois agonizing. There is no single rising and continuous line in art which goes from the least to the most refined moral and ideological perception.

        [which] aims less to denounce or exalt than to bother and disturb.

145   As yet we have neither understood nor explained the true secret of his art.

        to reduce the work of art to its ideological ingredients, is not only to lose sight of its specificity, but also not to take into account its relative autonomy and the unequal development of society and art.

        a multiplicity of styles, of schools [. . .]. Realism is therefore an attitude towards reality and not a method. Method at any time depends on the power of man over nature, on technical standards and social relationships, and it is the artist's, and only the artist's task to discover the style of expression be it in the plastic or written arts.

146   never accepts to be answerable to reason alone and even less to conform to its orders and to its limits.

        What is a creative person? Whether it concerns music, poetry, the novel, the theatre, cinema, architecture, painting or sculpture, the creator is not simply someone who puts together, who arranges various elements which have been given to him. In every work of art there is something which can not be accounted for merely in terms of ingredients and this something is man himself. Only a particular writer or artist was capable of producing the created work.

147 quality is not only a question of form, but primarily of content. [. . .] The quality of form itself is not only a matter of training and work but stems directly from the subject matter and the artist's response to it.

a form of art which takes its inspiration from the superior effectiveness of criticism and auto-criticism.

148 Under the influence of the work of a militant a new kind of work for the writer can, should and indeed does develop in which writing gets closer and closer to action. Between subject matter of this kind, these new ways of writing and the activities of the militant there is no longer any contradiction but interchange and mutual help. [. . .] Then these newly acquired methods are at odds with a life which no longer matches up to them and the writer experiences a contradiction between this life and the more advanced works which he would like to write.

complicity between the person who writes in this way and the public. [. . .] These conditions did exist for a few years. Then they deteriorated.

the demands of a 'realism' demanded by the public in the Soviet Union and popular democracies.

more than ever determined only to work with the people within the organisation of the C.P.

149 the initial situation in such a way that its latent contradictions are turned into clearly expressed conflicts.

An education based entirely on a study of classical tragedy led me quite naturally to consider history not simply as an accumulation of facts and as a continuous and random unravelling of events but as a development in which each of these events was, like a well-made tragedy, circumscribed by time, place and action. They were also linked in the way that one act is linked to another and one scene to the next.

Tragedy first showed me how to analyse reality. [. . .] a dramatic action, both uniform and multiple in its inherent conflicts which were always various and yet necessarily interconnected.

150 Why [not] write novels in which the act of reading moves forward like the action of a play and which provokes action? The usual readers of detective novels are easily tempted to play the part of policemen in real life, but a different kind of plot, constructed according to the same dramatic rules, could incite them to another kind of action.

Page

Chapter 7   André Stil, Roger Vailland, Pierre Courtade

151   an optimistic work thoroughly imbued with an indestructible faith in the victory of the French people.

a spokesman voicing truths already formulated . . . the purveyor of a cult.

152   a literature of the working class or a literature depicting the working class.

it seemed to me that to look at things as though from the outside was to be avoided from the beginning.

From the point of view of form in particular a great deal has yet to be explored. The voice of working-class people, their gestures, almost their breathing invite literary writing to be modified.

The preoccupation with reality pushes me, at first, to write what are almost pieces of literary or philosophical journalism [. . .] It is true that I did not try to conceal my preoccupation with struggle.

a real, spontaneous moment of inspiration. It must not be a response to some external order however informal.

153   Brought up in ignorance and to despise working-class people she had unthinkingly adopted ideas which he (her husband) put to her.

154   He feels bound to them by something stronger than ideas.

nouveau-riche style of living.

155   To say that politics didn't enter the class-room in such conditions is to talk nonsense. In real life children are up to their necks in politics. Those questions which their teacher won't answer they put to their parents. And it is sometimes an important experience for a child to see that the most lowly docker can explain things more thoroughly than the official purveyors of knowledge. That can go a long way, and not always in the right direction.

155,56   When you are enthusiastic in that way you remain alert all the time. Your head stays clear. How different at night. . . . Probably it is one of today's vices that in order to be sentimental about something you have to be behind this curtain of darkness and silence.

156   Freedom is simply the courage to act.

Dashed down in twenty four hours.

Tomorrow will arrive more quickly than people imagine and tomorrow, in our present world, is life, real life.

157   It's really in spite of everything that you find Léon, as a man, admirable, exceptional. He's about forty and has been a militant party member just about everywhere. He recalls in extraordinary detail and with amazing aptness all kinds of anecdotes. In this way he

gives the impression of carrying a bit of France around with him in the folds of his clothes. Sometimes it's said that a militant should give way before the Party. He remains what he is but his strength is at one with the Party's [. . .]. Because he is part of the Party, of its life, of its thinking, he knows how to express important, new things which nobody could see. Better still, by asking the right questions he prompts other people to say these things without showing that he knew them beforehand. [. . .]. In this you have the impression that in him you can see the reflection of Maurice.

Politics in the novel is like sugar in water. If the sugar has not melted in a glass of sugared water it means that it hasn't been properly prepared.

158   a peninsula of the town inside the factory.

The short story is like a spoonful of soluble reality to which the reader adds whatever amount of water he wishes.

But it's not a matter of this or that work. You can change your work ten times but you won't change life. It's something else that has to be changed.

159   as long as this war lasts we are all responsible.

War is rottenness and promiscuity. People become the opposite of what they are.

to practise the art of telling omission.

160   He was no longer the same [. . .] he wanted to redeem himself.

When they have returned the body, the question will be: will Party members and the younger people come to the funeral as they do for other soldiers? With their flags . . . that's the question which will be asked.

161   the indication to readers of how to act in the form of examples and positive heroes.

As a critic or a theoretician it is possible to take this formula as a guide. But at the moment of writing any formula has a restrictive rather than a liberating effect.

the specificity of novel writing.

162   My farewell to bourgeois culture.

He who isn't limited by profession or necessity.

other than in a completely communist perspective.

163   the militant communist, the bolchevik, an entirely new kind of man.

By bolchevik I don't mean anything to do with a nation. I'm making

a distinction between heroes and those who, while not being in themselves intrinsically less worthy, nonetheless recognise him (the
bolchevik) to be a model, a leader, and at a given time, a better
person.

164 Few novels are so free from schematization.

You can't imagine the extent to which my class has already decayed.

165 Who only thought of getting out of Clousot.

since you have been with Beau Masque comrades have had less
confidence in you [. . .] comrades in positions of responsibility must
have an irreproachable private life.

We have won. We are stronger.

166 Throughout the world and at the same time a new class of men was
beginning to become aware of its interests, of its potential strength
[. . .]. History was in the process of taking a decisive turn.

I'm setting out on a huge piece of fictional writing; central to it will be
a professional revolutionary figure – what I failed to achieve with
Pierrette Amable – the loneliness of the Communist when he is really
in the forefront of things.

167 I shan't write articles but a novel instead, it will have more impact.
It's too important.

168 peculiar singleness of style.

Affairs of the heart have nothing to do with the grandeur of the soul.

The best one of my novels, a real dream – or a dreamed reality – a
true story which can be completely interpreted by Freud, Marx and
plenty of others. It has all possible aspects of reality.

169 for a revolution, the date of which is always being put back.

170 'Between ourselves I wonder why books are forbidden. Do you know
anyone who has changed his mind because of a book? That's not what
makes people have new ideas.'

171 the very symbol of those contradictions which split many a
Communist of his generation who tried to remain true both to himself
and to the Party.

one of the men who incarnated the contradictions of our time most
poignantly.

171,72 I wonder if a Communist writer can produce novels about
Communism. That was probably the mistake I made. At best I could
only be a kind of Bernanos in my own church. That doesn't take us
very far . . . I can see that as a novelist I set off along a path which
didn't lead anywhere, and at the same time I can't escape, because

basically the only thing that interests me is politics and, in particular, Communism.

172   I was an actor, gentlemen, in a play which had to be played.

What with work and politics he burned himself out you see and what's more he had to live a pretty disordered life and eat any old how.

the qualities or blemishes, resources or weaknesses of a man on the point of balance between his private life and public commitment.

173   I was always told that a man could solve anything on his own.

He had hoped in vain to find that they shared his feelings. They hadn't followed the same path. They would never understand one another. But what is really important isn't just that.

The political habit of offering a confident smile to photographers which was intended to reassure the worthy inhabitants of Elseneur had caused his good humour to become a mask which formed part of his ceremonial dress, of the stake of honour and of the national anthem.

173,74   She didn't care about politics. In her family people had always voted republican and Jimmy, who came from the south was a democrat, but that wasn't important.

174   the-woman-who-helps-you-through-life-and-shares-your-worries-and-your-pleasures.

He [Jimmy] had lived surrounded by temptations, by publicised sexuality, which swamped the whole of life through newspapers, films and in the street. A fantastic mixture of thighs, breasts, smiles, underclothes and stockings. Nothing that was not directed towards sex.

a person who is looking for something.

175   He knew that a completely different life was beginning for him, that from now on he would be a fundamentally different man, that neither happiness nor daily life would seem the same.

He didn't yet know the extent to which he would be expected and how difficult it would be for him to keep the small flame which he had lit burning during the storm.

176   The soldiers are too *interesting* from a literary point of view, that is to say they are complex, full of contradictions, too human.

177   But the young people of today standing by the counter in 'L'Avenir' were continuing the Potemkin's journey.

178   I'm talking to you about things I've felt . . . sort of . . . in human terms, and you answer in abstractions.

178   I'd rather be a good sympathiser than a mediocre communist.

petit bourgeois outlook which because of my background I've had
difficulty in getting rid of.

179   We are building the twenty-first century in a nineteenth-century setting.
. . . While you . . . you have a nineteenth-century society in a twentieth-
century setting.

179,80   Simon was sure that a change in him which had been coming for years
had now occurred. There was something light about it and which he
intended from now on to direct not just on himself but towards other
people and things too. [. . .] 'to know how to recognize what is
essential'. Cazaux didn't know what he was doing. He thought he was a
communist, he behaved like one even over details, but what really
mattered was missing: he didn't believe in the historical necessity of
Communism.

The dramatic movement from one situation to another which is radically
and qualitatively new.

Conclusion

182   We were still talking theology.

creative freedom for the artist.

the specificity of artistic creation.

compatible with the general policy of the Party.

realism without limits

183   He, for example, who would write a book and assume, because I am a
Communist, that the difficulty is already accounted for or who would
think that the book would solve it . . . I mean someone who would create
in his book a Communist world which aroused no objections, who would
write a novel illustrating what I already believed in for those people who
are already convinced – such a person, I must say, would be for me quite
simply totally unreadable.

There is no light without shade. A book without shadowy areas is a
nonsense and doesn't deserve to be opened.

an art which continually goes beyond itself. Nothing is more foreign to it
than formula, recipe, repetition. And whether it is a question of painting
or writing, what is always being questioned is experience, movement,
development.

183   The novel is, in my view, a way of speaking which goes beyond what is actually being said. It is this extra dimension which I value.

184   as far as any text expands into extra-textual material, it has prepared the way for a study of this historical material.

       an emphasis on the signifying agent.

186   The finest book will not prevent a child from suffering; you don't prevent evil, you fight it.

Page		*Notes*

230   (3)   old formulas to this extent and to embark in new directions.

       (11)   Given our shyness, our unease in working class surroundings, our dread of the rabble, it will never be known how much this ugly, wretched document cost us. This job of being the conscientious detective agent for the popular novel is by far the worst job for a man with aristocratic feelings.

231   (16)   In Balzac's world the bourgeoisie and the aristocracy are both represented. The common people, the worker is never there. But in the distance the voice of the absent masses is heard, the silent movement of the people who are going to burst into political life, to sovereignty . . .

232   (12)   It turned out that the Académie Goncourt awarded the prize to *Le Feu*. The censors, embarassed by the whole affair, were afraid of scandal and preferred to keep quiet.

233   (3)   the old hulk of society in which we live.

       (4)   I don't think it is vital for a writer to be cultured. I see him like a savage, a barbarian.

       (8)   If I start to feel sad again I read one of Dostoievsky's thoughts which I have stuck up on my wall.

       (10)   As for 'Bubu' you didn't have the impression that all my sympathy went to Bubu, that I had him win because he was the strong, active character and that I condemned his opponent.

       small but solid.

       a good booze-up.

234   (8)   The intellect serves nothing. We are servants of the intellect. There is no other master. We are there to bear it and to defend it and to gather all those who have gone wrong back to it.

235   (8)   Weakened from the beginning by an absence both of ideological foundations and of consequent aims proletarian literature could

never formulate a clear programme, organise itself into a coherent movement.

236   (3)   I now understand that the reality which had to be expressed lay not in the appearance of the subject but at a depth where this appearance had little importance [. . .] A few people wanted the novel to be a sort of filmed sequence of events. This was an absurd idea. Nothing is further from what we have seen in reality than such a filmed record.

(5)   If 'writers are the engineers of the soul' do not forget that the highest task of an engineer is to invent. Art is not submission, it is a conquest.

(11)   the almost total lack of what is called image.

237   (15)   Really, all my life [. . .] I have much preferred what I might call my way of making things known: to write in order to understand and then transmit what I have learned to other people.

238   (7)   The novel can only be justified if it communicates in a way which is not open to any other genre.

239   (18)   Anything cooked up before being written down will seem cold to the reader [. . .] anything fixed like this must be avoided [. . .]. To demand the reader's attention, to waken him up and surprise him is what, if possible, is necessary.

(21)   the simple indication that the Party is there.

(25)   neighbours talked about the first resistance workers. He listened to BBC broadcasts in French. He wasn't very interested.

(30)   He loved Stalin, not as a god but rather as the symbol of a man to whom everything was possible. Logical and clear sighted, open and opposed to abstraction he was the complete opposite of the petit bourgeois.

240   (49)   The solution you suggest – the *Elseneur* solution – seems to me to be an escape.

(3)   the great art of our new epoch.

Notes

FOREWORD

1. *The Collected Essays, Journalism and Letters of George Orwell,* (4 vols) Penguin Books, Harmondsworth, 1970. See vol. II, 'My Country Right or Left 1940–1943', pp. 334–7.
2. For a full discussion of this phenomenon see in particular D. Caute, *The Fellow Travellers,* Weidenfeld & Nicolson, London, 1973.
3. J. A. Morris, *Writers and Politics in Modern Britain (1880–1850),* Hodder & Stoughton, London, 1977.
4. *La Littérature internationale,* no. 5–6, 1934.
5. Op. cit., Gallimard, Paris, (Collection Idées) 1964, pp. 17–27. First published 1948.
6. This point is well made and illustrated by Ian Higgins in his Introduction to *An Anthology of French Poetry of the Second World War,* Methuen, London, 1982.
7. The Surrealists' involvement with the Communist Party which falls outside the scope of this book has been the subject of a number of studies. See in particular: R. S. Short, 'The Politics of Surrealism, 1920–36' *Journal of Contemporary History,* vol. II, 1966, pp. 3–25 and J. H. Matthews, 'Surrealism, Politics and Poetry' in K. McRobbie (ed.) *Chaos and Form,* University of Manitoba Press, Winnipeg, 1972, pp. 171–81. For an excellent account of Aragon's moment of crisis in particular see C. G. Geohegan, 'Surrealism and Communism: The Hesitations of Aragon from Kharkov to the "Affaire Front Rouge"', *Journal of European Studies,* vol. VIII, no. 1, March 1978, pp. 12–33.
8. 'Le Théâtre du peuple', *Cahiers de la Quinzaine,* Série V, Cahier 4, Paris 1903.
9. A team of researchers at the Ecole Normale Supérieure in Paris under the direction of Roger Fayolle is currently working on 'La littérature socialiste en France 1880–1914'. Particular emphasis is being given to the theatre.
10. André Deütsch, London, 1964 and Presses Universitaires de Grenoble, 1972.
11. The fullest historical accounts of such a tradition are to be found in the various surveys by Michel Ragon. Of these *Histoire de la littérature prolétarienne en France,* Albin Michel, Paris, 1974 is the most informative to date.
12. Much of Vallès' writing was prompted by events of the Commune. Literary and artistic reflections of the Commune have been widely studied. A useful

229

recent work offering some indication of the richness of the subject is J. A. Leith (ed.), *Images of the Commune*, McGill-Queen's University Press, Montreal and London, 1978.

PART I
INTRODUCTION

1. Albin Michel, Paris, 1974. See also *Les Ecrivains du Peuple*, Vigneau, Paris, 1947 and *Histoire de la littérature ouvrière*, Les Editions Ouvrières, Paris, 1953.
2. Editions J'ai Lu, Paris, 1964. See also Bénigno Cacérès, *Les Autodidactes*, Seuil, Paris, 1967.
3. Fourastié, p. 8.
4. Ragon, p. 15.
5. I am grateful to my colleague John Fox for drawing my attention to this poem.
6. *Oeuvres Complètes*, Treuttel and Würtz, Paris, 1820, vol. IV, p. 55.
7. Quoted in Jules Huret, *Enquête sur l'évolution littéraire*, Charpentier, Paris, 1891, p. 436.

CHAPTER 1: 'UN ROMAN QUI AURA POUR CADRE LE MONDE OUVRIER'

1. References are to the Flammarion–Fasquelle edition, Paris 1930.
2. A reply to an article signed 'Ferragus' (Louis Ulbach), 'La littérature putride' (*Le Figaro*, 23 January 1868) in which both *Germinie Lacerteux* and *Thérèse Raquin* are attacked for their bad taste and corrupting influence.
3. Sainte-Beuve praised the Goncourts for having succeeded in leaving 'à ce point des vieilles données, et d'entrer dans des sillons si neufs'.
4. In *Emile Zola: Les Rougon-Macquart*, ed. H. Mitterand, vol. II, Bibliothèque de la Pléiade, Paris, 1961, p. 374. (References to this edition will hereafter be designated *Zola* (Pléiade) vol. I etc.)
5. Letter to Lacroix quoted from Zola's manuscripts, ibid., pp. 1539, 40.
6. Préface (1877), ibid., pp. 373, 4.
7. Ibid., p. 374.
8. Quoted ibid., p. 1539.
9. Quoted in *Zola* (Pléiade), vol. III, 1964, p. 1822.
10. 'Notes sur la marche générale de l'œuvre' (i.e. Les Rougon-Macquart) and Les Romanciers naturalistes, quoted in F. W. J. Hemmings, *Emile Zola*, Clarendon Press, Oxford, 1966 p. 73 and p. 35.
11. *Journal*, 22 August 1875 'On ne saura jamais, avec notre timidité naturelle, notre malaise au milieu de la plèbe, notre horreur de la canaille, combien le vilain et laid document, avec lequel nous avons construit nos livres, nous a coûté. Ce métier d'agent de police consciencieux du roman populaire est bien le plus abominable métier que puisse faire un homme d'essence aristocratique'.
12. E. Caramaschi, *Réalisme et impressionisme dans l'œuvre des Frères Goncourt*, Goliardica and Nizet, Pisa and Paris, [no date], p. 271.

13. Caramachi suggests (pp. 268, 9) that these scenes are worthy of Balzac; he also claims that they are evidence of the essential viciousness of the common people and an indictment of them.
14. *Journal*, 24 October 1864.
15. Ricatte, p. 261.
16. 'Dans ce monde (de Balzac), la bourgeoisie et l'aristocratie sont représentées. Le peuple, l'ouvrier, n'apparaît jamais. Mais comme on entend au loin la voix du grand absent, sous toutes les ruines amassées, la sourde poussée du peuple qui va jaillir à la vie politique, à la souveraineté . . .'. Article in *Le Rappel* (13 May 1870) quoted in *Zola*, (Pléiade), vol. III, p. 1814.
17. Quoted from the 'ébauche' for *L'Assommoir* in *Zola* (pléiade), vol. II, p. 1543.
18. See J. Dubois, *L'Assommoir de Zola*, Librairie Larousse, Paris, 1973, pp. 116–19, for an indication of the growing concern for alcoholism during the second half of the nineteenth century.
19. Dubois, ibid., p. 87.
20. *Zola* (Pléiade) vol. II, p. 1545.
21. References to the novel contained in *Zola* (Pléiade), vol. II are given in the text after quotations.
22. *Zola*, Gallimard, Paris, 1932, p. 114. And for contemporary reactions see F. J. W. Hemmings, *Emile Zola*, OUP, London, 1953 (2nd edn. 1966) p. 123.
23. *Zola*, (Pléiade) vol. III, p. 1815.
24. Quoted ibid., p. 1816.
25. *Journal*, 16 January 1884.
26. Droz, Geneva, 1972. See also I.-M. Frandon, *Autour de 'Germinal', la mine et les mineurs*, Droz, Geneva, 1955; E. M. Grant, *Zola's 'Germinal'; A Critical and Historical Study*, Leicester University Press, 1962 and 1970. For a different, very partial view see P. Lejeune, *Germinal. Un roman antipeuple*, Nizet, Paris, 1978.
27. Quoted by Zakarian, pp. 129, 30.
28. Quoted ibid., p. 159.
29. *Le Figaro*, 18 September 1884. Quoted in Grant, pp. 10, 11.
30. *La Nation*, 8 March 1885. Quoted in Zakarian, p. 164.
31. Quoted from the *ébauche* of the novel by C. Smethurst, *Zola: 'Germinal'*, Arnold, London, 1974.
32. References to the novel contained in *Zola* (Pléiade), vol. III, are given in the text after quotations.
33. Compare with descriptions in Barbusse's *Le Feu* and indeed in many novels of the First World War.
34. The opening (p. 1141) and closing (p. 1591) references to the mine are almost identical and form a kind of parenthesis around the novel sealing off the action from the rest of existence.
35. Henri Mitterand, *Discours du roman*, PUF, Paris, 1980.

CHAPTER 2: HENRI BARBUSSE AND MILITANCY

1. Quoted in J. Duclos and J. Fréville, *Henri Barbusse*, Editions Sociales, Paris, 1946, p. 23.

2. 31 August 1935. Quoted in *Henri Barbusse Ecrivain et Révolutionnaire*, Editions sociales internationales, Paris, 1935, p. 36.
3. *Henri Barbusse*, p. 42.
4. *Une heure avec Frédéric Lefèvre*, (vol. III), NRF, Paris, 1925, p. 172.
5. Quoted in A. Vidal, *Henri Barbusse, soldat de la paix*, Editions Français, réunis, Paris, 1953, p. 167.
6. Quoted ibid., p. 168.
7. Quoted in V. Brett, *Henri Barbusse: sa marche vers la clarté, son mouvement Clarté*, Editions de l'Académie Tchécoslovaque des Sciences, Prague, 1963, p. 222.
8. *Three French Writers and the Great War. Barbusse, Drieu la Rochelle, Bernanos*, CUP, Cambridge, 1975, p. 32.
9. Barbusse's *carnet* is contained in the 1965 edition of *Le Feu*.
10. *Carnet*, p. 295.
11. Ibid., p. 292 and p. 300.
12. According to Romain Rolland, after its serialization in *L'Oeuvre*, Barbusse had several hundred copies of the book printed without cuts and allowed it to be presented for the Prix Goncourt. 'Il se trouva que l'Académie Goncourt couronna *Le Feu*. La censure, très embarrassée, craignit le scandale et préféra se taire'. R. Rolland, *Journal 1914–19*, Albin Michel, Paris, 1952, p. 1127. And see the articles by J. Meyer, '"Le Feu" d'Henri Barbusse', *Europe*, January 1969, pp. 16–67, and 'Publication et retentissement du "Feu"', *Europe*, September 1974. This special issue carries the transactions of the international Barbusse *colloque* held in May 1973.
13. For some illustrations see the articles by Meyer.
14. D. Caute, *Communism and the French Intellectuals*, p. 319; J. King 'Henri Barbusse: *Le Feu* and the Crisis of Social Realism', *The First World War in Fiction*, (ed.) H. M. Klein, Macmillan, London, 1976, pp. 43–52.
15. References are to the Flammarion edition, 1916.
16. 'Against Nature: Jean Giono and *Le Grand Troupeau*,' in Klein, pp. 73–83.
17. 'Guerre et roman dans l'entre-deux-guerres', *Revue des Sciences Humaines*, Fasc. 109, 1963, pp. 77–95.
18. D. Bonnaud-Lamotte has argued that though Barbusse's vocabulary is largely authentic his syntax is not. 'Les Ecrivains français du XXe siècle en URSS: la réception du *Feu* d'Henri Barbusse', *Oeuvres et Critiques*, vol. II, 1977, pp. 59–74.
19. Quoted in Vidal, p. 86.
20. References are made to the Flammarion edition, 1919.
21. *Communism and the French Intellectuals*, p. 320.
22. Les Ecrivains réunis, Paris, 1927.

CHAPTER 3: SENTIMENTALITY AND RESIGNATION

1. For an account of his early years in particular see M. Ray, 'L'Enfance et la jeunesse de Charles-Louis Philippe', *Nouvelle Revue Française*, no. 14, March 1910, pp. 169–94. This memorial issue of the *NRF* together with that of *Europe* (September 1960) contain a number of informative articles, and extracts from diaries and correspondence. Further useful information is

contained in F. W. J. Hemmings, *The Russian Novel in France*, OUP, 1950, ch. 10.

2. *Lettres de jeunesse, à Henri Vandeputte*, NRF, Paris, 1911. References to Philippe's correspondence with Vandeputte are hereafter given in the text.

3. During the time he was close to the group of writers centred on *L'Enclos* we also find him writing to Marcel Ray of the need for an art which would challenge the values of 'la vieille baraque sociale où nous sommes'.

4. He is also quoted as expressing some distrust of culture in general: 'Je ne crois pas qu'il soit nécessaire à un écrivain d'avoir une culture. Je le vois comme un sauvage, comme un barbare. Il faut qu'il ait le goût du sauvage.' Michel Arnauld, 'L'Œuvre de Charles-Louis Philippe', *NRF* (March 1910) p. 160.

5. References are to the NRF edition (1916).

6. References are to the Garnier/Flammarion edition by Bruno Vercier in 1978. The novel was first published by the Editions de la Revue Blanche (1901).

7. Vercier makes the interesting point that the opening of *Babu* can be read as a 'réécriture' of that of Zola's *Nana*. Vercier, pp. 19, 20, n3.

8. See Hemmings, p. 157. And the letter to Vandeputte, 27 November 1899: 'Si les chagrins reviennent, je relis une pensée de Dostoievsky que j'ai inscrite sur mon mur.'

9. 'Charles-Louis Philippe, le populisme et la littérature prolétarienne', *Les Cahiers Bleus*, no. 55, March, 1930.

10. In 1902 Philippe wrote to André Ruyters: 'Pour "Bubu", tu n'as donc pas senti que toute ma sympathie allait à Bubu, que je lui donnais la victoire parce qu'il était le personnage actif et fort, que je condamnais son antagoniste', *NRF*, (March 1910), p. 250. Philippe frequently, it appears, would make claims for his own physical robustness: 'petit mais costaud' is a remark regularly attributed to him by those who have written about him since his death. In view of his history of ill health, his relatively unspectacular career, his readiness to spend publishers' advances on 'une bonne cuite' (see his letters to Vandeputte), and his attempts to make an impression on others, it does not seem unreasonable to suggest that he suffered from a considerable inferiority complex. This would also explain his 'discovery' of Nietzsche and, in terms of his novels, invite a rewarding investigation of his portrayal not only of weak male characters, but of women.

11. Vercier, 'Introduction' pp. 24–34.

12. Fasquelle, Paris, 1902 and 1906.

13. Vercier, p. 32.

PART II
INTRODUCTION

1. *Variété, I*, Note 1, *Œuvres*, Vol. I (Pléiade), Gallimard, Paris, 1957, p. 1000.

2. O. Spengler's *Der Untergang des Abendlandes* (Beck, Munich, 1923) was translated into French and published 1931–33 by M. Tazerout.

3. In *Essais et nouveaux essais critiques*, Gallimard, Paris, 1952, pp. 7–24. First

published in *La Nouvelle Revue Française*, vol. XXI, no. 125, February, 1924, pp. 149–58.
4. 'Pour une littérature responsable', *Vendredi*, 8 November 1935. See J.-J. Brochier (ed.), *Paul Nizan: Intellectuel Communiste*, Maspero, Paris, 1960, pp. 138–40.
5. For a discussion of the currency of 'intellectual', see in particular W. M. Johnston, 'The origin of the Term "Intellectuals" in French Novels and Essays of the 1890s', *Journal of European Studies*, vol. IV, no. 1, March 1974, pp. 43–56.
6. Pauvert, Paris, 1965. First published by Grasset, Paris, 1927.
7. Ibid., p. 118.
8. Op. cit., Ollendorff, Paris, 1915, p. 37. On 26 June 1919 Rolland also published in *L'Humanité* an article 'Déclaration d'Indpéndance de l'Espirt': 'L'Esprit n'est le serviteur de rien. C'est nous qui sommes les serviteurs de l'Esprit. Nous n'avons pas d'autre maître. Nous sommes faits pour porter, pour défendre sa lumière, pour rallier autour d'elle tous les hommes égarés.' Rolland also projected this claim for independence into his novel *Clérambault* (1920) in which the chief character is finally assassinated (on Good Friday), a martyr for his cause.
9. 'Nouvelle Lettre à Ramon Fernandez sur l'idée de Révolution', *Les Derniers Jours*, no. 6, 15 May 1927, pp. 1–4.
10. *Service Inutile*, Grasset, Paris, 1935, p. 161.
11. *Manifestes du Surréalisme*, Pauvert, Paris, 1972, p. 138.
12. *Caliban parle*, Grasset, Paris, 1928, p. 35. For a more recent and interesting treatment of this problem in fiction see P. Lainé, *L'Irrévolution*, Gallimard, Paris, 1971.

CHAPTER 4: PROLETARIAN AND POPULIST WRITING

1. Bernard, p. 53.
2. Barbusse was aware that *Monde* would be attacked. Despite the fact that the review had been founded with RAPP support, Barbusse never fully accepted that the policy of proletarian writing in the Soviet Union could be directly transferred to France. For him the writer remained a separate, gifted being. The responsibility for the investigation and 'reorganization' of *Monde* was given to Nizan by Thorez. The exchange of letters (11–17 March 1931) between him and Barbusse, is marked by the latter's openness and refusal to take offence. See A. Cohen-Solal and H. Nizan, *Paul Nizan, communiste impossible*, Grasset, Paris, 1980, pp. 275–82 and C. G. Geohegan, 'Surrealism and Communism: The Hesitations of Aragon from Kharkov to the "Affaire Front Rouge"', *Journal of European Studies*, vol. VIII, no. 1.
3. Published 1931–32 under this title and 1933–1939 as *La Littérature internationale*. It was printed in Moscow in four languages: Russian, English, French, German. The French representatives on the editorial committee were Barbusse, Rolland and Vaillant-Couturier.
4. He expressed the same view in *Monde*, December 1931.
5. For an account of the various developments centred on Poulaille see P.-A.

Loffler, *Chronique de la littérature prolétarienne française de 1930 à 1939*, Subervié, Rodez, 1967.

6. Compare this with Martinet's description of 'une petite chambre avec une grande table dedans, des planches sur trétaux, et une douzaine d'escabeaux' etc. in 'Nécessités contradictoires: grande conception, petit début', *Culture prolétarienne*, p. 88. Throughout this article Martinet employs a language in which words like *famille, foyer, organisme, prolongement naturel* occur regularly.

7. See René Bonnet, 'Le Musée du Soir', *Entretiens; Henry Poulaille*, Subervié, Rodez, 1974, pp. 127–33.

8. A detailed account of Poulaille's activities during these years has yet to be written. In *L'Humanité*, 20 November 1937 he rather grudgingly acknowledged that he may have been too idealistic: 'frappée d'impuissance à ses débuts par une absence de bases idéologiques et de buts conséquents, la littérature prolétarienne ne put jamais formuler un programme clair, s'organiser en un mouvement cohérent.'

9. Éditions Valois, Paris, 1930. References are to this edition.

10. *Populisme*, La Renaissance du livre, Paris, 1931, p. 108. In addition to the article in *L'Œuvre* Lemonnier produced four others all of which are contained in this volume: 'Du Naturalisme au Populisme', *La Revue mondiale*, 1 October 1929; 'Populistes d'hier et demain', *L'Œuvre*, 15 October 1929; 'Le Roman populiste', *Mercure de France*, 15 November 1929; 'Populisme', *Les Nouvelles Littéraires*, 18 January 1930. References are to this collection. The only extensive study of populism to date is the unpublished doctoral thesis: E. Einhorn, *The Populist Movement in French Literature*, (University of Cape Town, 1952). A copy is deposited in the Bibliothèque Nationale.

11. In *Populisme*, pp. 112–28.

12. N. Racine-Furland nicely defines Lemonnier's view of the working class as 'pointilliste, individualiste'. 'Les Mouvements en faveur de la littérature prolétarienne en France (1928–1934)', *Entretiens: Henry Poulaille*, pp. 77–98.

13. Gallimard.

14. Ragon, for example, in *Histoire de la littérature prolétarienne en France*, p. 160.

15. *Nouvel Age Littéraire*, p. 147.

16. References are to the Grasset editions with the exception of *Le Pain Quotidien*, Ferenczi et fils, Paris, 1939.

17. Grasset and Plon.

18. *Populisme*, p. 187.

19. *Nouvel Age Littéraire*, p. 25.

20. References are to the following editions, *Petit Louis*, Gallimard (1930); *L'Hôtel du Nord*, Denoël (1977); *La Maison du peuple*, Grasset (1953); *Angélina*, Grasset (1934).

21. In M. Dubourg, *Eugène Dabit et André Gide*, Pernette, Paris, 1953.

22. *Nouvel Age Littéraire*, p. 380.

23. *Populisme*, p. 115.

24. In Dubourg, p. 7.

25. Quoted in Ragon, p. 168.

26. *Journal Intime*, Galliard, Paris, 1939, p. 171.

27. Quoted by Einhorn, p. 77.

28. *Journal Intime*, p. 25.

29. 'Louis Guilloux's working class novels: some problems of Social Realism', *Modern Language Review*, vol. 68, 1973, p. 76.
30. See King ibid., and Camus, 'Avant-propos', in *La Maison du peuple*, Grasset, Paris, 1953, p. 15.
31. King, p. 73.
32. *La Littérature internationale*, no. 2, 1934, p. 159.
33. Vol. 1, no. 1, p. 4.

CHAPTER 5: THE BEGINNINGS OF SOCIALIST REALISM

1. For a discussion of reactions in the Soviet Union see G. Struve, *Twenty-five years of Soviet Russian Literature (1914–1943)*, Routledge and Sons Ltd., London, 1946.
2. 'La littérature soviétique au XVIe anniversaire de la Révolution d'octobre', *La Littérature internationale*, no. 1, 1933, pp. 120–8.
3. Compare such a view with one of that most 'bourgeois' of writers Marcel Proust: 'La réalité à exprimer résidait, je le comprenais maintenant, non dans l'apparence du sujet, mais à une profondeur où cette apparence importait peu [. . .] Quelques-uns voulaient que le roman fût une sorte de défilé cinématographique des choses. Cette conception était absurde. Rien ne s'éloigne plus ce que nous avons perçu en réalité qu'une telle vue cinématographique', 'Le Temps retrouvé', *A la recherche du temps perdu*, Pléiade, Gallimard, 1954, vol. III, pp. 882, 83.
4. The principal speeches are contained in *Soviet Writers' Congress 1934*, Lawrence and Wishart, London, 1977. First published as *Problems of Soviet Literature* (ed. H. G. Scott), Martin Lawrence Ltd., London, 1935. Quotations are from the 1977 edition.
5. Malraux had also observed: 'Si "les écrivains sont les ingénieurs des âmes" n'oubliez pas que la plus haute fonction d'un ingénieur, c'est d'inventer. L'art n'est pas une soumission, c'est une conquête.' Quoted by J.-L. Houdebine, 'Jdanov ou Joyce', *Tel Quel*, Spring 1977, no. 69, p. 38.
6. Denoël et Steele, Paris, 1935. The talks were 'D'Alfred de Vigny à Avdéenko' (Paris, 14 April 1935); 'John Heartfield et la beauté révolutionnaire' (Paris, 12 May 1935); 'Message au Congrès des John Reed Clubs' (New York, late April 1935); 'Hugo réaliste' (Paris, 5 June 1935); 'Le Retour à la réalité' (Paris, 25 June 1935).
7. *L'Humanité*, 12 August 1935.
8. *L'Humanité*, 7 August 1937. The review was also of Drieu la Rochelle's two recent books *Rêveuse bourgeoisie* and *Avec Doriot*.
9. All references are to the *livre de poche* edition of the novel published in 1954.
10. R. Garaudy, *L'Itinéraire d'Aragon*, Gallimard, Paris, 1961, p. 317.
11. In a further review which appeared in *La Littérature internationale* in December 1935, Mirski, having praised the novel's simplicity and Aragon's use of spoken language, registers his approval – somewhat extraordinarily – for 'l'absence presque totale de ce qu'on appelle image'!
12. Not by chance has she chosen Nietzsche's *Thus spoke Zarathoustra* for her bedside reading.
13. Quoted by various critics: M. Raimond, *Le Signe des temps*, SEDES, Paris,

1976, p. 236; P. Daix, *Une Vie à changer*, Seuil, Paris, 1975, pp. 271, 2; D. Arban, *Aragon parle avec Dominique Arban*, Seghers, Paris, 1968, p. 109.

14. *Pour un réalisme socialiste*, p. 8.
15. 'En réalité, toute la vie, [. . .] j'ai de beaucoup préféré ce que vous me permettrez d'appeler ma méthode de connaissance: écrire pour connaître, et par là communiquer à autrui ce que j'ai appris.' *Entretiens avec Francis Crémieux*, Gallimard, Paris, 1964, p. 15.
16. First published respectively in *La Revue des vivants*, September–October 1932; *Europe*, July, 1935; *Regards*, no. 61, March, 1935; *Vendredi*, no. 1, November, 1935.
    Selections of Nizan's most important literary articles are to be found in Brochier, *Paul Nizan: Intellectuel communiste* and S. Suleiman, *Pour une nouvelle culture*, Grasset, Paris, 1971.
17. See J. Leiner, *Le Destin littéraire de Paul Nizan et ses étapes successives*, Klincksieck, Paris, 1970, p. 266.
18. 'La Littérature révolutionnaire en France'. Quoted in Leiner, p. 124.
19. Ibid.
20. Review of *Tu seras ouvrier* by G. Guéguen-Dreyfus, *Monde*, 15 March 1935.
21. Letter to J.-R. Bloch (24 June 1933) quoted by Leiner, p. 162.
22. Ibid.
23. 'Sur l'humanisme', *Europe*, July 1935.
24. 'Pour une poétique du roman à thèse: l'exemple de Nizan', *Critique*, November 1974, vol. XXX, no. 330, pp. 995–1021. Youssef Ishaghpour considers it to be too pessimistic to qualify as a work of socialist realism. *Paul Nizan. Une figure mythique de son temps*, Le Sycamore, Paris, 1980, p. 84.
25. References are to the 1933 edition published by Grasset.
26. A. King, *Paul Nizan, Ecrivain*, Didier, Paris, 1976, p. 95.
27. Nizan had been invited to spend a year in the Soviet Union from January 1934. For his reactions see S. de Beauvoir, *La Force de l'âge*, Gallimard, Paris, 1960, p. 213 and Leiner, pp. 195, 6.
28. In Brochier, vol. I, pp. 141–94.
29. Paul Nizan. Committed Literature in a Conspiratorial World, Princeton University Press, Princeton, 1972, p. 125.
30. Leiner makes this point well. In particular she draws attention to the dinner-party conversation in ch. V.
31. References are to the 1968 Gallimard edition.
32. Is this an allusion to Nizan's own brief fliration with Valois' neo-fascist *ligue Le Faisceau?*
33. A. King, p. 122.

PART III
CHAPTER 6: THE NEW LEFT

1. See in particular J. Fauvet, *Histoire du Parti Communiste français*, Fayard, Paris 1964, 1965 (new edition 1977); R. Tiersky, *Le Mouvement communiste en France*, Fayard, Paris, 1973; A. Rossi, *Les Communistes Français pendant la Drôle de Guerre*, Iles d'Or, Paris, 1951 and *La Guerre des papillons 1940–1944*, Iles d'Or, Paris, 1954.

2. Op. cit., vol. I, Gallimard, Paris, 1946, p. 32, n1.
3. Op. cit., Seuil, Paris, 1970, p. 51.
4. *Communism and the French Intellectuals*, p. 154.
5. 'L'Artiste et son temps', *Essais*, ed. R. Quilliot, Bibliothèque de la Pléiade, Paris, 1965, p. 804.
6. References are to the 'Idées' edition, Gallimard, Paris, 1964.
7. *Essais*, p. 673. Cf. Simone de Beauvoir: 'Le roman ne se justifie que s'il est un mode de communication irréductible à tout autre'. 'Littérature et Métaphysique', *Les Temps Modernes*, April 1946, p. 1154.
8. A. Zdhanov, *Sur la littérature, la philosophie et la musique*, (Introduction by J. Duclos), Editions de la Nouvelle Critique, Paris, 1948.
9. Cf. Daix, 'Les jeunes gens de Stendhal et les nécessités du réalisme socialiste', *Les Lettres françaises*, 25 August 1949.
10. A neat summary of the aims of the Batailles du Livre are provided by Elsa Triolet's 'Prospectus' for the Bibliothèque de la Bataille du Livre in *Pensée*, no. 37, 1951, p. 37.
11. Prévost has emerged as one of the more flexible and perceptive left-wing critics of recent years. See the collection of articles republished in *Littérature, Politique, Idéologie*, Editions Sociales, Paris, 1973.
12. The text 'Résolution sur les problèmes idéologiques et culturels' of the Conference is in 'Les Intellectuels et le parti communiste français. L'alliance dans l'histoire', *Cahiers d'histoire de l'Institut Maurice Thorez*, no. 15, 1976, pp. 149–60.
13. Editions de la Nouvelle Critique, Paris, 1952.
14. Bouchet-Chastel, Paris, 1953. References are to the text in vol. V of the *Oeuvres complètes de Roger Vailland*, (ed. J. Recanati), Editions Rencontre, Lausanne, 1967 (12 vols).
15. *Le Pays des Mines*, Editions Cercle d'Art, Paris, 1951. Stil later acknowledged that his praise of Fougeron had been excessive.
16. *L'Optimisme librement consenti*, Stock, Paris, 1979, p. 105.
17. Vailland had already hinted at this attitude in his essay 'De l'Amateur', *Le Regard froid*, *OC*, vol. VIII, p. 119.
18. *Ecrits Intimes*, Gallimard, Paris, 1968, p. 203.
19. Ibid., pp. 442–52.

CHAPTER 7: ANDRE STIL, ROGER VAILLAND, PIERRE COURTADE

1. *La Nouvelle Critique*, no. XXXI, December 1951.
2. No. XXXV, April 1952.
3. Ibid., no. LXI, January 1955, p. 102.
4. Op. cit., No. 79, p. 2099.
5. *L'Optimisme*, p. 93.
6. Ibid., p. 96.
7. Ibid., p. 97.
8. This is taken to the point where Stil actually invents words: e.g. *foudroyage*.
9. *L'Optimisme*, p. 103.
10. Ibid., p. 105.

11. References are to the three volumes published by les Editeurs Français Réunis, *Au Château d'eau* (1951); *Le Coup de canon* (1952); *Paris avec nous* (1953).
12. This is especially true of *Les Lettres françaises* which continued well into the 1950s to publish anti-German material – stories, articles and cartoons.
13. The only substantial recapitulations of time are found in vol. II, chs. VII–IX and X–XIII, and vol. III, ch. XX.
14. *L'Optimisme*, p. 111.
15. Ibid., p. 111 and p. 113.
16. References are to the editions published by Les Editeurs Français Réunis.
17. Ibid., p. 133.
18. *L'Optimisme*, p. 108. Stil also believed that the reader should be jolted into a reaction: 'Ce qui est tout cuit, déjà avant l'écriture, apparaîtra refroidi au lecteur [. . .] il faut éviter le tout cuit [. . .] Exiger, réveiller, étonner, à chaque instant si possible, l'attention du lecteur' (ibid., p. 147).
19. This efficiency is also reflected in the simple fact that the stories become more compact.
20. *Le Foudroyage* was banned immediately after its appearance.
21. Charlemagne in *Le Blé égyptien*, for example, is '(le) simple signe de l'existence du parti', *L'Optimisme*, p. 132.
22. *L'Optimisme*, p. 271.
23. Ibid.
24. Ibid., p. 281.
25. *Ecrits Intimes*, p. 73. And Duc in *La Fête*: 'Les voisins parlaient des premiers maquis, il écoutait chez eux les émissions en français de la B.B.C. Cela ne le concernait pas' (*OC*, XII, p. 187).
26. Ibid., p. 194.
27. *OC*, vol. VIII, p. 21.
28. *Ecrits Intimes*, p. 271. Courtade's reply is to be found pp. 287–9.
29. *OC*, II, pp. 211, 12.
30. Elizabeth Vailland: 'Il aimait Staline, non comme un Dieu mais, au contraire, comme le symbole de l'Homme, celui qui peut tout, lucide et logique, libre et anti-métaphysique, le contraire en somme du petit bourgeois' (*L'Express*, July–August 1972). And see *Ecrits Intimes*, pp. 484–90.
31. *Ecrits Intimes*, pp. 448, 9.
32. References are to the texts in *OC*, vols. VII and III.
33. *Ecrits Intimes*, p. 475.
34. Quoted in 'Vailland, militant communiste: témoignages de militants de l'Ain', *Entretiens: Roger Vailland*, Subervié, Rodez, 1970, p. 92.
35. For a discussion of this aspect of the book see the studies by Brochier, Flower and Recanati.
36. *Ecrits Intimes*, p. 712.
37. *325,000 francs*, (ed.) D. O. Nott, English Universities Press, London, 1975, p. lxxii.
38. From an unpublished interview recorded shortly before Vailland's death. A recording was generously lent to me by Elizabeth Vailland.
39. References are to the 10/18 edition, 1970. Of Malraux's projected book only *Les Noyers d'Altenburg* was published.

40. J. Recanati, *Un gentil stalinien*, Mazarine, Paris, 1980, p. 140.
41. *L'Express*, 16 May 1963.
42. *Ecrits Intimes*, pp. 723, 4.
43. *Autocritique*, pp. 129, 30.
44. *Ecrites Intimes*, pp. 679, 80.
45. References are to the Bibliothèque Française edition, 1949.
46. This theme is also central to an unfinished novel *Le Jeu de Paume* a few extracts of which are reproduced in *Chorus*, no. 6, Autumn 1965, pp. 43–8.
47. 'Pierre Courtade, un intellectuel communiste', *La Nouvelle Critique*, no. 147, June, 1963, p. 21.
48. *Littérature dégagée*, Gallimard, Paris, 1955, pp. 86, 7.
49. References are to the Julliard, edition, 1956. In his letter to Vailland (11 April 1962) Courtade interestingly rejects the allegorical method which he employs in *Elseneur*: 'La solution que tu me proposes (la solution *Elseneur*) m'apparaît comme une manière de fuite'. *Ecrits Intimes*, p. 680. Courtade's use of allegory in this novel relates, however, not so much to the tradition of that style of writing during the Resistance, but, allegedly, to what were 'des raisons de parti'.
50. References are to the editions published by Editeurs Français Réunis.
51. *Communism and the French Intellectuals*, p. 331.
52. See for example his attack on the formalist interpretation of the film, p. 44 and p. 50.
53. *Expérience du drame*, p. 134.

CONCLUSION

1. 'Direction Argenteuil. Quelques jalons sur un chemin', *La Nouvelle Critique*, Deuxième série, No. XCI, February, 1976, p. 48.
2. 'Les Intellectuels et le Parti Communiste Français', p. 146 and p. 142.
3. None the less in his speech on receiving the Lenin Peace Prize in 1958 Aragon adopted a very orthodox position and approved socialist realism which 'he claimed was 'le grand art des temps nouveaux'. Quoted in *La Nouvelle Critique*, CXXVIII, November 1979, p. 31.
4. *Œuvres romanesques croisées*, Vol. XXVI, Laffont, Paris, 1967. 'La Fin du "Monde réel"', *Postface*, p. 314.
5. Ibid., p. 297.
6. *Littérature, Politique, Idéologie*, p. 149. Articles originally published in *La Nouvelle Critique*, nos. XXXIX, XL, XLI (December 1970, January and February 1971).
7. *Les Ecrits de Sartre*, (ed.) M. Contat and M. Rybalka, Gallimard, Paris, 1970, p. 671.
8. Abroad. *British Literary Traveling between the Wars*, OUP, New York and Oxford, 1980.

Select Bibliography

A bibliography containing all the works consulted for this book would be excessively long. This one, therefore, is confined to those critical, historical and theoretical works which have been of particular value. Details of novels discussed in the text are to be found in the footnotes; those of many specific articles which have appeared in the journals listed below are given either in the text itself or in the footnotes.

The principal newspapers and journals consulted are: *Bulletin Communiste, Cahiers du Bolchevisme, Cahiers du Communisme, Clarté, Commune, Esprit, Europe, France Nouvelle, L'Humanité, Les Lettres françaises, Littérature de la Révolution, La Littérature internationale mondiale, Monde, La Nouvelle Critique, Pensée, Regards, Les Temps modernes, Vendredi.*

Adereth, M., *Commitment in Modern French Literature: a Brief Study of 'Littérature Engagée' in the Works of Péguy, Aragon and Sartre*, Gollancz, London, 1967.

Andreu, Pierre, 'Les idées politiques de la jeunesse intellectuelle de 1927 à la guerre', *Revue des Travaux de l'Académie des Sciences morales et politiques*, Second Semester, 1957.

Andreu, Pierre and Grover, Frédéric, *Drieu la Rochelle*, Hachette, Paris, 1979.

Anissimov, I., 'Le Réalisme socialiste dans la littérature mondiale', *La Nouvelle Critique*, January 1955.

Aragon, Louis, *Pour un réalisme socialiste*, Denoël & Steele, Paris, 1935.

—— *L'Homme communiste*, 2 vols, Gallimard, Paris, 1946 and 1953.

—— *La Culture et les Hommes*, Editions Sociales, Paris, 1947.

—— *Littératures soviétiques*, Editions Denöel, Paris, 1955.

Aragon, L. and Triolet, E., *Œuvres romanesques croisées*, Laffont, Paris, 1964.

Aron, Robert, *Histoire de Vichy, 1940–44*, Fayard, Paris, 1954.

Bachelin, Henri, *Charles-Louis Philippe: son œuvre*, Editions de la Nouvelle Critique, Paris, 1929.

Barbusse, Henri, *Lueur dans l'abîme*, Editions Clarté, Paris, 1920.

—— *Lettre aux Intellectuels*, Ressegna Internazionale, Rome, 1921.

—— *Manifeste aux intellectuels*, Les Ecrivains réunis, Paris, 1927.

—— *Russie*, Flammarion, Paris, 1930.

—— *J'Accuse*, Paris, 1932.

—— *Zola*, Gallimard, Paris, 1932.

—— *Lettres de Henri Barbusse à sa femme*, Flammarion, Paris, 1937.

—— *Paroles d'un combattant*, (Articles et Discours, 1917–1920), Flammarion, Paris [no date].

241

Bardel, Pierre, 'Henry Poulaille et la littérature prolétarienne', *Europe*, March–April 1977.

Henri Barbusse, écrivain et révolutionnaire, Editions sociales internationales, Paris, 1935.

Barthes, Roland, *Le Degré Zéro de l'écriture*, Seuil, Paris, 1953.

Beauvoir, Simone de, *Mémoires d'une jeune fille rangée*, Gallimard, Paris, 1958.

Benda, Julien, *La Trahison des clercs*, Pauvert, Paris, 1965.

Berl, Emmanuel, *Mort de la morale bourgeoise*, Gallimard, Paris, 1929.

—— *Mort de la pensée bourgeoise*, Grasset, Paris, 1929.

—— *Lignes de chance*, Gallimard, Paris, 1934.

—— *Présence des Morts*, Gallimard, Paris, 1956.

Bernard, Jean-Pierre, 'Le Parti Communiste Français et les problèmes littéraires (1920–39)', *Revue française de science politique*, vol. XVII, no. 3, June 1967.

—— *Le Parti Communiste Français et la question littéraire, 1921–1939*, Presses universitaires de Grenoble, Grenoble, 1972.

Bloch, Jean-Richard, *Carnaval est mort: Premiers essais pour mieux comprendre mon temps*, Editions de la NRF, Paris, 1920.

—— *Destin du siècle: Seconds essais pour mieux comprendre mon temps*, Rieder, Paris, 1931.

—— *Offrande à la politique*, Rieder, Paris, 1933.

—— *Naissance d'une culture*, Rieder, Paris, 1936.

Boak, Denis, *Jules Romains*, Twayne Publishers Inc., New York, 1974.

Bodin, Louis, *Les Intellectuels*, PUF, Paris, 1962.

Bonnaud-Lamotte, Danielle, 'Le langage d'une revue "prolétarienne" étudié à l'aide de l'informatique', *Europe*, March–April 1977.

Bouvier, Emile, *Initiation à la littérature d'aujourd'hui*, La Renaissance du Livre, Paris, 1928.

Brett, Vladimir, *Henri Barbusse: sa marche vers la clarté, son mouvement Clarté*, Editions de l'Académie Tchécoslovaque des Sciences, Prague, 1963.

Brombert, Victor, *The Intellectual Hero*, Faber, London, 1962.

Cadwallader, Barrie, *Crisis of the European Mind: a Study of André Malraux and Drieu la Rochelle*, University of Wales Press, Cardiff, 1981.

Calder-Marshall, Arthur, 'Fiction', *Fact*, July 1937.

Camus, Albert, *Essais*, Gallimard (Bibliothèque de la Pléiade), Paris, 1977.

Carr, Reg, *Anarchism in France: the Case of Octave Mirbeau*, Manchester University Press, Manchester, 1977.

Casanova, Laurent, *Le Communisme, la Pensée et l'Art*, Editions du PCF, Paris, 1947.

—— *Le Parti communiste, les intellectuels et la nation*, Editions de la Nouvelle Critique, Paris, 1949.

—— *Responsabilités de l'Intellectuel Communiste*, Editions de la Nouvelle Critique, Paris, 1949.

Caute, David, *Communism and the French Intellectuals*, André Deutsch, London, 1964.

—— *The Illusion*, André Deutsch, London, 1971.

—— *The Fellow Travellers*, Weidenfeld & Nicolson, London, 1973.

Cogniot, Georges, *Les Intellectuels et la Renaissance Française*, Editions du PCF, Paris, 1945.

Cohen-Solal, Annie and Nizan, Henriette, *Paul Nizan, communiste impossible*, Grasset, Paris, 1980.

Craig, David, (ed.), *Marxists on Literature: an Anthology*, Penguin Books, Harmondsworth, 1975.

Dabit, Eugène, *Journal Intime (1928–1936)*, Gallimard, Paris, 1939.

Daix, Pierre, *Sept siècles du roman*, Editeurs Français Réunis, Paris, 1955.

—— *Aragon, une vie à changer*, Seuil, Paris, 1975.

Debray, Régis, *Les Rendez-vous manqués*, Seuil, Paris, 1975.

Domenach, Jean-Marie, 'Le P.C.F. et les intellectuels', *Esprit*, May 1949.

Douglas, Kenneth, 'The French Intellectuals: Situation and Outlook', *Modern France* (ed. E. M. Earle), Princeton University Press, Princteon, 1951.

Dubourg, Maurice, *Eugène Dabit et André Gide*, Pernette, Paris, 1953.

Duclos, Jacques and Fréville, Jean, *Henri Barbusse*, Editions Sociales, Paris, 1946.

Escarpit, Robert, *Sociologie de la littérature*, PUF, Paris, 1958.

Etiemble, *Hygiène des Lettres II, Littérature dégagée (1942–1953)*, Gallimard, Paris, 1955.

Fauvet, Jacques, *Histoire du Parti Communiste Français*, 2 vols, Fayard, Paris, 1964 and 1965. (Revised in one volume 1977.)

Field, Frank, *Three French Writers and the Great War: Barbusse, Drieu la Rochelle, Bernanos*, Cambridge University Press, 1975.

Fisher, David James, 'The Rolland-Barbusse Debate', *Survey: a Journal of East a n d West Studies*, vol. 20, no. 2/3, Spring–Summer 1974.

Flower, J. E., *Roger Vailland: the Man and His Masks*, Hodder & Stoughton, London, 1975.

—— *Writers and Politics in Modern France (1909–1961)*, Hodder & Stoughton, London, 1977.

Fournier, Albert, 'Charles-Louis Philippe', *Europe*, September 1960.

Fréville, J. (ed.), *Les Grands textes du Marxisme sur la littérature et l'art*, Editions Sociales internationales, Paris, 1936.

Fussell, Paul, *The Great War and Modern Memory*, OUP, New York and London, 1975.

—— *Abroad, British Literary Traveling Between the Wars*, OUP, New York and Oxford, 1980.

Garaudy, Roger, *Literature of the Graveyard*, International Publishers, New York, 1948.

—— *L'Eglise, le Communisme et les Chrétiens*, Editions Sociales, Paris, 1949.

—— *L'Itinéraire d'Aragon*, Gallimard, Paris, 1961.

—— *D'un réalisme sans rivages*, Plon, Paris, 1963.

Geoghegan, C. G., 'Surrealism and Communism: The Hesitations of Aragon from Kharkov to the "Affaire Front Rouge"', *Journal of European Studies*, vol. VIII, no. 1, March 1978.

Gide, André, *Retour de l'URSS*, Gallimard, Paris, 1936.

—— *Retouches à mon Retour de l'URSS*, Gallimard, Paris, 1937.

Ginsburg, Shaul, *Raymond Lefebvre et les origines du communisme français*, Editions Tête de Feuilles, Paris, 1975.

Girard, M., 'La littérature peut-elle s'accorder avec la vérité sociale?', *Informations Sociales*, January 1957.

Goldman, Lucien, *Pour une sociologie du roman*, Gallimard, Paris, 1964.

Green, Mary J. M., *Louis Guilloux: an Artisan of Language*, French Literature Publications Company, York, South Carolina, 1979.

Grousset, René, *Le Réveil de l'Asie*, Plon, Paris, 1933.

Grover, Frédéric J., *Drieu la Rochelle and the Fiction of Testimony*, University of California Press, Berkeley and Los Angeles, 1958.

Guéhenno, Jean, *Caliban parle*, Grasset, Paris, 1928.

Hamilton, Alistair, *The Appeal of Fascism*, Blond, London, 1971.

Hemmings, F. W. J., *The Russian Novel in France, 1884–1914*, OUP, London, 1950.

—— *Emile Zola*, (2nd edn) Clarendon Press, Oxford, 1966.

Herbert, Eugenia W., *The Artist and Social Reform: France and Belgium 1885–1898*, Books for Libraries Press, Free post, New York, 1971.

Hertz, Henri, *Henri Barbusse: son œuvre*, Editions du Carnet-Critique, Paris, 1920.

Hommage à Eugène Dabit, NRF, Paris, 1939.

Houdebine, Jean-Louis, 'Jdanov ou Joyce', *Tel Quel*, no. 69, Spring 1977.

—— 'L'Impasse du langage dans le Marxisme', *Tel Quel*, no. 69, Spring 1977.

Howe, Irving, *Politics and the Novel*, New Left Books, Stevens & Sons Ltd, London, 1961.

Huret, Jules, *Enquête sur l'évolution littéraire*, Charpentier, Paris, 1891.

Information Sociales, ('Littérature et grand public') January 1957.

Les Intellectuels et le P.C.F. L'Alliance dans l'histoire, Cahiers d'histoire de l'Institut Maurice Thorez (no. 15), Paris, 1976.

Irvine, W. D., 'French Conservatives and the "New Right" during the 1930s', *French Historical Studies*, vol. VIII, no. 4, Fall 1974.

Ishaghpour, Youssef, *Paul Nizan. Une figure mythique et son temps*, Le Sycamore, Paris, 1980.

Jameson, F., *Marxism and Form: Twentieth Century Dialectical Theories of Literature*, Princeton University Press, 1971.

Jameson, Storm, 'Documents', *Fact*, July 1937.

Jefferson, Carter, *Anatole France: the Politics of Skepticism*, Rutgers University Press, New Jersey, 1965.

Johnson, Roy, 'The Proletarian Novel', *Literature and History*, October 1975.

Kadish, Doris, 'L'ironie et le roman engagé: "Les Beaux Quartiers" de Louis Aragon', *French Review*, no. XLV, February 1972.

Kanapa, Jean, *Situation de l'intellectuel (Critique de la Culture*, vol. I), Editions Sociales, Paris, 1957.

—— *Socialisme et Culture (Critique de la Culture*, vol. II), Editions Sociales, Paris, 1957.

King, Adèle, *Paul Nizan, Ecrivain*, Didier, Paris, 1976.

King, J. H., 'Philosophy and Experience: French intellectuals and the Second World War', *Journal of European Studies*, vol. I, no. 3, September 1971.

—— 'Louis Guilloux's ambiguous epic: *Le Sang noir'*, *Forum for Modern Language Studies*, vol. VIII, no. 1, January 1972.

—— 'Louis Guilloux's working class novels: some problems of Social Realism', *Modern Language Review*, vol. LXVIII, 1973.

Klein, H. M. (ed.), *The First World War in fiction*, MacMillan, London, 1976.

Klein, Wolfgang, 'Barbusse et le mouvement littéraire communiste autour de la conférence de Kharkov', *Europe*, March–April 1977.

Kunnas, Tarmo, *Drieu la Rochelle, Céline, Brasillach et la tentation fasciste*, Les Sept Couleurs, Paris, 1972.

Laquer, Walter, 'Literature and the Historian', *Journal of Contemporary History*, vol. II, no. 2, April 1967.

Larnac, Jean, *La littérature française d'aujourd'hui*, Editions Sociales, Paris, 1948.

Lazare, B., *L'Ecrivain et l'art social*, Bibliothèque de l'art social, Paris [1896].

Le Cardonnel, Georges et Vellay, Charles, *La Littérature contemporaine (1905)*, Mercure de France, Paris, 1905.

Lecherbonnier, Bernard, *Aragon*, Bordas, Paris, 1971.

Lehmann, A. G., 'The Writer as Canary', *Journal of Contemporary History*, vol. II, no. 2, April 1967.

Leiner, Jacqueline, *Le Destin littéraire de Paul Nizan et ses étapes successives*, Klincksieck, Paris, 1970.

Lemonnier, Léon, *Manifeste du roman populiste*, J. Bernard, Paris, 1930.

—— *Populisme*, La Renaissance du livre, Paris, 1931.

Leroy, Maxime, 'Le Prolétariat vu par Zola dans *L'Assommoir*', *Preuves*, October 1952.

Lewis, Wyndham, *The Writer and the Absolute*, Methuen, London, 1952.

Loffler, Paul A., *Chronique de la littérature prolétarienne française de 1930 à 1939*, Editions Subervié, Rodez, 1967.

—— *Chronique de l'Association des Ecrivains et des Artistes révolutionnaires* (Le Mouvement littéraire progressiste en France) 1930–1939, Editions Subervié, Rodez, 1971.

Loubet del Bayle, Jean-Louis, *Les Non-conformistes des années 30*, Seuil, Paris, 1969.

Lukács, G., 'Narrate or describe', *Writer and Critic, and Other Essays* (ed. A. Khan), Merlin Press, London, 1970.

Macherey, Pierre, *Pour une théorie de la production littéraire*, Maspero, Paris, 1974.

Malraux, André, *La Tentation de l'Occident*, Grasset, Paris, 1926.

—— *Le Temps du mépris*, Gallimard, Paris, 1935.

Mander, John, *The Writer and Commitment*, Secker & Warburg, London, 1961.

Martinet, Marcel, *Culture prolétarienne*, Librairie du Travail, Paris, 1935.

Massis, Henri, *La Guerre de trente ans: Destin d'un âge 1909–1939*, Plon, Paris, 1940.

Michel, Henri and Mirkine-Guetzevitch, Boris, *Les idées politiques et sociales de la Résistance (Documents clandestins – 1940–1944)*, PUF, Paris, 1954.

Mitterand, Henri, *Le Discours du roman*, PUF, Paris, 1980.

Moranski, Stefan, 'Vicissitudes in the Theory of Socialist Realism', *Diogenes*, no. 36, Winter 1961.

Morel, Jean-Pierre, 'Littérature prolétarienne et transformations du genre romanesque', *Europe*, March–April 1977.

Morin, Edgar, *Autocritique*, Julliard, Paris, 1959.

Muir, Edwin, *Essays on Literature and Society*, Hogarth Press, London, 1965.

Nadeau, Maurice, *Histoire du Surréalisme*, Seuil, Paris, 1947.

—— *Documents surréalistes*, Seuil, Paris, 1948.

Naville, Pierre, *La Révolution et les intellectuels*, Gallimard, Paris, 1975.

Necker de Saussure, Mme. (Mme. de Staël), *Oeuvres complètes*, vol. IV, Treuttel et Würtz, Paris, 1820.

Nelson, Brian, 'Lukács, Zola and the Aesthetics of Realism', *Studi Francesi*, no. 71, May–August, 1980.

Nizan, Paul, *Aden-Arabie*, Maspero, Paris, 1971.

—— *Les Chiens de garde*, Maspero, Paris, 1971.

Normand, Guessler, Henri Barbusse and his *Monde* (1928–35), *Journal of Contemporary History*, vol. XI, nos. 2, 3, 1976.

Norrish, P. J., *Drama of the Group: a Study of Unanimism in the plays of Jules Romains*, Cambridge University Press, 1958.

O'Connell, David, 'Eugène Dabit: A French Working-Class Novelist', *Research Studies*, vol. 41, no. 4, December 1973.

Orwell, George, *The Collected Essays*, Journalism and Letters of George Orwell, 4 vols, (ed. Sonia Orwell and Ian Angus) Penguin Books, London, 1970.

Ory, Pascal, *Nizan. Destin d'un révolté. 1905–1940*, Editions Ramsey, Paris, 1980.

Panichas, G. A. (ed.), *The Politics of Twentieth Century Novelists*, Hawthorn Books Inc., New York, 1971.

Perus, Jean, 'De l'usage du mot "prolétariat" en littérature', *Europe*, March–April 1977.

Philippe, Charles-Louis, *Lettres de jeunesse à Henri Vandeputte*, Gallimard, Paris, 1911.

Plumyène, Jean and Lasierra, Raymond, *Les Fascismes français*, Seuil, Paris, 1963.

Politzer, Georges, *La fin d'une parade philosophique: le bergsonisme*, Pauvert, Paris, 1968.

—— *La Philosophie et les mythes*, Editions Sociales, Paris, 1969.

Poulaille, Henry, 'Charles-Louis Philippe, le populisme et la littérature prolétarienne', *Cahiers Bleus*, Editions Valois, Paris, 1930.

—— *Nouvel Age Littéraire*, Valois, Paris, 1930.

—— *La Littérature et le peuple*, Les Humbles, Paris, 1937.

Prévost, Claude, *Littérature, Politique, Idéologie*, Editions Sociales, Paris, 1973.

Prigent, Edouard, *Louis Guilloux*, Presses universitaires de Bretagne, Saint-Brieuc, 1971.

Racine, Nicole, 'Une revue d'intellectuels communistes dans les années vingt: *Clarté* (1921–1928)', *Revue française de science politique*, vol. XVII, no. 3, June 1967.

Ragon, Michel, *Les écrivains du peuple*, J. Vigneau, Paris, 1947.

—— *Histoire de la littérature ouvrière*, Les Editions ouvrières, Paris, 1953.

—— 'Dans quelle mesure les classes populaires participent-elles à la vie littéraire contemporaine?', *Informations Sociales*, January 1957.

—— *Histoire de la littérature prolétarienne en France*, Albin Michel, Paris, 1974.

Rahv, Philip, *Literature and the Sixth Sense*, Faber & Faber, London, 1970.

Random, Michel, *Le Grand Jeu*, (2 vols), Denoël, Paris, 1970.

'Le réalisme socialiste', *Esprit*, February 1959.

Reck, Rima Drell, *Literature and Responsibility*, Louisiana State University Press, Boston Rouge, 1969.

Redfern, W. D., 'Political Novel and Art of Simplicity: Louis Guilloux', *Journal of European Studies*, vol. I, no. 2, June 1971.

—— *Paul Nizan. Committed Literature in a Conspiratorial World*, Princeton University Press, 1972.

Relinger, Jean, 'Les conceptions de Barbusse sur la littérature prolétarienne', *Europe*, March–April 1977.

Rémond, René, 'Les intellectuels et la politique', *Revue Française de Science Politique*, vol. IX, no. 4, December 1959.

Revai, Joseph, *La Littérature et la Démocratie populaire*, Editions de la Nouvelle Critique, Paris, 1950.

Rolland, Romain, *Au-dessus de la mêlée*, Ollendorff, Paris, 1915.

—— *Journal 1914–1919*, Albin Michel, Paris, 1952.

Romain, Claude, *Nouvel Age Littéraire*, Victorion Frères et Cie., Paris [no date].

Roman et Société, Colloque 6 November 1971 (Publications de L'histoire littéraire de la France), Colin, Paris, 1973.

Rühle, Jurgend, *Literature and Revolution*, Pall Mall, London, 1969.

Sabatier, Pierre, *Germinie Lacerteux des Goncourt*, Sfelt, Paris, 1948.

Sartre, Jean-Paul, 'La Nationalisation de la littérature', *Situations, II*, Paris, 1948.

—— 'Présentation des *Temps Modernes*', *Situations*, II, Paris, 1948.

—— *Qu'est-ce que la littérature?*, Gallimard, Paris, 1948.

—— *Plaidoyer pour les intellectuels*, Gallimard, Paris, 1972.

—— *Politics and Literature* (Translated by J. A. Underwood and John Calder), Calder and Boyars, London, 1973.

—— *Un théâtre de situations* (Textes choisis et présentés par Michel Contat et Michel Rybalka), Gallimard, Paris, 1973.

Schalk, David L., *Roger Martin du Gard: The Novelist and History*, Cornell University Press, Ithaca, New York, 1967.

—— *The Spectrum of Political Engagement* (Mounier, Benda, Nizan, Brasillach, Sartre), Princeton University Press, Princeton and Guildford, 1979.

Sérant, Paul, *Le Romantisme fasciste*, Fasquelle, Paris, 1959.

Serge, Victor, *Mémoires d'un révolutionnaire, 1901–1941*, Seuil, Paris, 1951.

Short, R. S., 'The Politics of Surrealism, 1920–1936', *Journal of Contemporary History*, vol. II, no. 2, 1966.

Siegel, Paul (ed.), *Leon Trotsky on Literature and Art*, Pathfinder Press, New York, 1970.

Skreb, Zdenko, 'Littérature engagée', *Literary Criticism and Sociology* (Yearbook of Comparative Criticism, vol. V, ed. J. P. Strelka) The Pennsylvania State University Press, University Park and London, 1973.

Sorel, Georges, *La valeur de l'art social*, G. Jacques, Paris, 1901.

—— 'D'un écrivain prolétaire', *Essais divers* in *Matériaux d'une théorie du prolétariat*, Rivière, Paris, 1929.

—— *Réflexions sur la violence*, Rivière, Paris, 1936.

Soucy, R., 'French Fascist intellectuals in the 1930s: an old New Left', *French Historical Studies*, Spring 1974.

Soviet Writers' Congress 1934, The Debate on Socialist Realism and Modernism in the Soviet Union, Lawrence and Wishart, London, 1977. (First published as *Problems of Soviet Literature*, ed. H. G. Scott, Martin Lawrence Ltd, London, 1935).

Stil, André, *Vers le réalisme socialiste*, Editions de la Nouvelle Critique, Paris, 1952.

Strickland, G. R., 'The Novels of Louis Guilloux: a Recommendation', *The Cambridge Quarterly*, vol. 5, no. 2, Autumn 1970.

Struve, Gleb, *Twenty-five years of Soviet Russian Literature (1918–1943)*, Routledge & Sons Ltd., London, 1946.

Suleiman, Susan, *Paul Nizan: Pour une nouvelle culture*, Grasset, Paris, 1971.

—— 'Pour une poétique du roman à thèse: l'exemple de Nizan', *Critique*, vol. XXX, no. 330, November 1974.

Swingewood, A., 'Literature and Praxis: a Sociological Commentary', *New Literary History*, vol. V, no. 1, Autumn 1973.

Thoorens, Léon, 'Approche de Louis Guilloux', *Revue Nouvelle*, vol. 19, 1954.

Touchard, Jean, 'Le Parti Communiste Français et les intellectuels', *Revue française de science politique*, vol. XVII, no. 3, June 1967.

Touchard, Jean and Winock, Michel, *La Gauche en France depuis 1900*, Seuil, Paris, 1977.

Triolet, Elsa, *L'Ecrivain et le livre*, Editions Sociales, Paris, 1948.

Trotsky, Léon, *Literature and Revolution*, University of Michigan Press, Ann Arbor, 1960.

Vailland, Roger, *Expérience du drame*, Corrêa, Paris, 1953.

Valéry, Paul, *Oeuvres*, vol. I, Gallimard (Bibliothèque de la Pléiade), Paris, 1957.

Vandromme, Pol, *La Droite buissonnière*, Editions des Sept Couleurs, Paris, 1960.

Vidal, A., *Henri Barbusse, soldat de la paix*, Editions Français réunis, Paris, 1953.

Virtanen, Reino, *Anatole France*, Twayne Publishers Inc., New York, 1968.

Weber, E., 'Revolution, counter-revolution; what Revolution?', *Journal of Contemporary History*, vol. IX, no. 2, 1974.

Wohl, R., *The Generation of 1914*, Harvard University Press, New York, 1979.

Zdhanov, A., *Sur la littérature, la philosophie et la musique*, (Introduction by J. Duclos) Editions de la Nouvelle Critique, Paris, 1948.

Zeldin, Theodore, *France 1848–1945*, vol. I, *Ambition, Love and Politics*, OUP, London, 1973; vol. II, *Intellect, Taste and Anxiety*, OUP, London, 1977.

Zevaès, A., 'Jules Vallès et le Naturalisme', *Commune*, no. 37, September 1936.

Index